# Understanding Theology
# and Popular Culture

To Robert Beckford,
for all the help, support, and encouragement


and to Stephen Philp,
for all the quality pop culture moments

# Understanding Theology and Popular Culture

Gordon Lynch

**Blackwell**
Publishing

BLACKWELL PUBLISHING
350 Main Street, Malden, MA 02148-5020, USA
108 Cowley Road, Oxford OX4 1JF, UK
550 Swanston Street, Carlton, Victoria 3053, Australia

First published 2005 by Blackwell Publishing Ltd

5    2008

*Library of Congress Cataloging-in-Publication Data*

Lynch, Gordon, 1968–
  Understanding theology and popular culture / Gordon Lynch.
      p.  cm.
  Includes bibliographical references and index.
  ISBN 978-1-405-11747-0 (alk. paper) – ISBN 978-1-405-11748-7 (pbk. : alk. paper)   1.
Christianity and culture.   2. Theology.   I. Title.
  BR115.C8L96 2004
  261–dc22
                                        2004009788

A catalogue record for this title is available from the British Library.

Set in 10 on 13 pt Electra
by SNP Best-set Typesetter Ltd., Hong Kong
Printed and bound in Singapore
by Ho Printing Singapore Pte Ltd

The publisher's policy is to use permanent paper from mills that operate a sustainable forestry policy, and which has been manufactured from pulp processed using acid-free and elementary chlorine-free practices. Furthermore, the publisher ensures that the text paper and cover board used have met acceptable environmental accreditation standards.

For further information on
Blackwell Publishing, visit our website:
www.blackwellpublishing.com

# contents

# figures and tables

## figures

## tables

# acknowledgments

The author and publisher gratefully acknowledge the permission granted to reproduce the copyright material in this book:

Nick Danziger for the photographs of the House of Lords library and women playing bingo in Glasgow, taken from Nick Danziger, *The British*, Harper-Collins, 2001.

Enesco Corporation for the images of figurines from the Precious Moments Chapel Exclusive range.

Corbis picture library for the photographs of the production line of Ford Model T cars, the interior of the Galeries Lafayette, Marilyn Manson, and Eminem.

Diesel Ltd for the image of the "Fun is now sponsored by Diesel" poster advert.

Harley Davidson for the image of the 2002 Road King Classic advert.

Every effort has been made to trace copyright holders and to obtain their permission for the use of copyright material. The publisher apologizes for any errors or omissions in the above list and would be grateful if notified of any corrections that should be incorporated in future reprints or editions of this book.

# preface

The study of theology, religion, and popular culture is a growth area. Every year there are increasing numbers of modules and courses exploring this subject, more papers are presented on it at academic conferences, and more and more journals and books are getting published in this area. Despite, or perhaps because of, this growth, it is also a very difficult area on which to get a clear overview. "Popular culture" may appear with increasing regularity in books and courses in theology and religious studies, but the reasons that lead scholars to explore this subject can be as wide ranging as their methods. One of the unfortunate characteristics of this subject area, in which most of the best literature still comes in the form of book chapters and journal articles, is that authors rarely have time to explain their aims or methods before launching into the discussion of their particular topic. Similarly authors rarely explain how their particular work relates to other studies conducted in this area. For someone who is new to this subject, then, the literature can appear to be as fragmented as pieces of patchwork waiting to be sewn into a quilt and it can be difficult to perceive any order or coherence to it.

One of the primary aims of this book is to provide more clarity to our understanding of aims and methods in the study of theology, religion and popular culture. Later in the book, I explore a range of reasons why theologians and scholars of religion are interested in studying popular culture and consider how each of these different approaches can be helpful in answering questions relating to the nature of contemporary religious beliefs, values, and practices, as well as more normative questions about which beliefs, values, and practices might be better than others. I also go on to look in more detail about particular methods that can be used in this kind of study. At this level, I hope that the book will be useful for teachers, students, and researchers in terms of giving a clearer overview of this subject area and the kind of work that is being conducted within it.

This book is not simply a summary of existing approaches to this area, however. In the chapters to come, I make my own pitch for what I see as the particular contribution that the discipline of theology can make to the academic study of popular culture. Central to my argument is the notion that the study of popular culture should appropriately involve an element of *evaluation*. In everyday life, we continually make evaluative judgments about what kinds of popular cultural resources and practices are worthwhile, healthy, useful, or pleasurable. Yet, as Simon Frith (1998) observes, some more recent academic studies of popular culture have developed sophisticated analyses of social and cultural processes, but shied away from the question of whether some forms of popular culture are actually *better* in some sense than others. This has led to a certain style of popular culture studies which can be seen as indiscriminately celebratory of all forms of popular culture or which is simply banal. I would argue that a full academic engagement with popular culture requires that we engage in a rigorous analysis of the truthfulness, meaningfulness, goodness, justice, and beauty of popular cultural texts and practices. Furthermore I would suggest that theological traditions and methods have a distinctive role to play in this process of evaluation. Towards the end of this book, I describe this academic project in terms of developing a theological aesthetics of popular culture, a process which involves learning to develop a critical dialogue between theological norms and specific examples of popular culture.

In making the case for developing theological evaluations of popular culture, I am also conscious that I am wanting to distance my approach from certain forms of religious critique of popular culture that periodically break into wider public consciousness. It is not too hard, for example, to think of Christian responses to films such as *The Last Temptation of Christ* or *Dogma*, or to, say, the *Harry Potter* novels, which are very high on criticism and very low on thoughtful analysis. This is unfortunate as faith communities – even in the more ostensibly secularized parts of Western society – still have considerable potential to constructively as cultural agents, both by offering critiques of contemporary culture and through developing their own forms of cultural and artistic practice.

Part of the discipline of learning to develop constructive theological evaluations of popular culture involves cultivating what Michael Dyson (2001) has referred to as "ethical patience," the ability to hear and understand popular culture on its own terms before seeking to critique it. Now to talk in terms of interpreting a particular form of popular culture "on its own terms" may imply too strongly that popular cultural texts and practices convey a single clear voice or message that can be understood to all-comers. I recognize that is unlikely to be the case as the way in which we make sense of particular forms of popular culture will always be shaped by the assumptions that we bring from our particular background and context. Nevertheless I think that the notion of hearing popular culture "on its own terms" is nevertheless a helpful reminder that it is possible to make better or worse interpretations of popular culture. Judging popular culture on the basis of our own preformed religious and cultural assumptions, without allowing the possibility for these to be challenged or changed in some way by our study of popular culture, will not help us to become better cultural critics or more thoughtful theologians.

So whilst I want to make a case for the importance of theological evaluation of popular culture, I also want to avoid forms of critique that are hasty, ill-informed, or lacking appropriate evidence. To improve our practice of the theological evaluation of popular culture requires us to be clear about what methods and approaches can helpfully guide our work. Partly this involves being clear on how we go about undertaking theological reflection in relation to popular culture. Partly it is also about understanding a range of methods used more generally in cultural studies and textual criticism that help us to interpret and make sense of popular culture before we bring any theological norms or judgments to bear on it. A major part of this book is therefore concerned with clarifying methodological issues in the theological evaluation of popular culture, and I hope this will prove to be a useful resource to students and researchers who are interested in developing work in this field.

From my comments so far, it will have become clear that I am particularly interested in this book in exploring how theology as an academic discipline can contribute to the critical evaluation of popular culture. I believe, though, that there is also a significant amount of material to help those who identify themselves more with "religious studies." The early part of the book is concerned with thinking about the nature of popular culture and some of the particular distinguishing features of contemporary Western popular culture. This material will be particularly useful for those interested in studying the relationship, say, between religious groups and the media or consumer culture, as well as those interested in studying the religious functions of popular culture. The more detailed methods of cultural analysis explored later in the book will also be as relevant for work in the field of religious studies as in theology. To see theology as a fundamentally normative discipline, and religious studies as fundamentally descriptive or analytical, is a false distinction to my mind. In the study of religion and popular culture, there are already helpful examples of scholars working in the field of religious studies who adopt a critical approach to their subject matter (see, e.g., Lelwica, 2000; Rycenga, 2001). Whilst those working in the discipline of religious studies will generally not base their critiques of contemporary culture on the norms of particular religious traditions (unlike most theologians), it is still appropriate for scholars of religion to ask critical questions about what promotes or hinders well-being within a given cultural context. I hope that this book will encourage both those working in theology and religious studies to continue to develop critical approaches to the study of popular culture.

Before moving on to give a brief overview of the content of the book, I would like to add a further quick comment. In writing this book as an academic based at the University of Birmingham I am deeply conscious of, and deeply indebted to, the tradition of cultural studies that was developed here within the Centre for Contemporary Cultural Studies (CCCS). The closure of the CCCS was a tragic loss for our university and for the wider academic community. I will not dwell here on the circumstances of its closure, but hope that my work preserves and maintains something of the CCCS's concerns and commitments.

The Birmingham tradition of cultural studies was always about a concrete commitment to social and cultural transformation. Sometimes I fear that this emphasis is lost in some of the literature on theology, religion, and popular culture. Indeed I hope that one of the effects of this book will be to encourage more interest amongst theologians and religious scholars in not only the ideas and commitments of the CCCS but also of the Frankfurt School, in particular Theodore Adorno. Evaluating popular culture certainly involves thinking critically about the values and beliefs that are represented or acted out within it. But such a critical evaluation also involves asking questions about the social and political processes of the production and consumption of popular culture, and sooner or later leads us to ask critical questions of the wider global capitalist structure which popular culture now inhabits.

Having offered some broad introductory remarks about my aims in writing this book, I will now say something briefly about its structure and content. The book essentially comes in three parts. In the first part (chapters 1–4) I introduce a range of concepts, theories, and debates that form the basis for the academic study of contemporary Western popular culture and explain why those working in the disciplines of theology and religious studies have a useful contribution to make to this field of study.

One of the striking features of much of the literature on theology, religion and popular culture is that "popular culture" is rarely defined. Yet far from being a simple or uncontested term, the nature of "popular culture" has been the focus of fierce academic and cultural debate. Chapter 1 therefore explores the ways in which different writers have sought to define "popular culture" and shows how these definitions reflect a fundamental concern with evaluative questions such as what forms of culture are humane and healthy and what it means to build constructive individual and communal lives. I also introduce the broad definition of popular culture as the environment, practices, and resources of everyday life that is used as the basis for discussion in the rest of the book. In chapter 2, I go on to look more specifically at why those involved in the disciplines of theology and religious studies have been interested in the study of popular culture. I suggest that the main questions that have driven this field of study concern the relationship between religious communities and traditions and the resources and practices of everyday life, the possibility that popular culture serves religious functions in contemporary society, the nature of an appropriate missiology for Western culture, and the potential for using popular culture as a medium for theological reflection. This chapter therefore seeks to clarify some of the key questions and aims that guide the study of theology, religion, and popular culture in order to provide a clearer agenda for work in this field in the future.

In chapters 3 and 4, the discussion returns to wider concepts and debates that form an important framework for the study of popular culture in theology and religious studies. Chapter 3 examines some distinctive features of contemporary Western popular culture. Noting the influence of industrialization on Western society, the chapter goes on to explore in more detail the specific roles that electronic media and consumer culture play in the contemporary construction of meaning and identity. The relationship between media, consumer culture, and global capitalism is then discussed towards the end of the chapter. Chapter 4 considers a range of debates about the potential harmful effects of popular culture. Attention here is given particularly to Adorno's critique of the role of the "culture industry" in perpetuating an oppressive capitalist social structure, critiques of the effects of contemporary forms of media (drawing on the work of Neil Postman and Pierre Bourdieu), and critiques of the effects of media content. This latter issue leads both into a discussion of issues of media representation as well as debates around "media effects" theories.

In chapters 1–4, then, my primary concern is to introduce readers to a core set of issues that arise in relation to the academic study of contemporary Western popular culture, and to provide a clearer outline of the main forms of the study of popular culture within theology and religious studies. Without an understanding of such concepts and debates, and without a clear sense of the specific nature and aims of their work, theologians and scholars of religion cannot expect their studies of popular culture to carry much weight in the wider academic community.

In the second part of the book (chapters 5–8), the focus shifts much more to exploring methodological frameworks and approaches that theologians and religious scholars might use in the study of popular culture. Chapter 5 explores what it means to develop a specifically theological critique of popular culture. The chapter examines the nature of theology as a discipline, and uses H. Richard Niebuhr's work to demonstrate how the theological study of popular culture will be influenced by certain core theological assumptions about the nature of culture. Drawing on models of contextual and practical theology, the chapter goes on to present a theological methodology for the study of popular culture based on the revised critical correlational approach developed by David Tracy and Don Browning. This method is subsequently used as a basis for the specific studies of theology and popular culture in the next three chapters.

In chapters 6–8, attention turns to a series of case studies of theological evaluations of specific examples of popular culture. Each of these case studies serves to demonstrate how a particular method of cultural analysis can be used to clarify the meaning and significance of the particular form of popular culture that we are studying. Thus in chapter 6, after an initial broad overview of different approaches to popular cultural analysis, an author-focused (or "auteur criticism") approach is used to develop a discussion of whether or not the treatment of violence in the music of Eminem can be seen as redemptive. Chapter 7 uses text-based approaches, namely semiotics, narrative analysis, and discourse analysis, to examine how a particular episode of *The Simpsons*, "Homer the Heretic," reproduces a particular cultural discourse of American civil religion. This is then explored in relation to a critical discussion of Stanley Hauerwas' rejection of the notion that religion exists to support the practices and institutions of liberal democracy. Chapter 8 then explores how ethnographic methods can make an important contribution to the theological study of the meanings and uses of popular culture in "real world" settings. This chapter is particularly important given the tendency amongst some theologians to make broad generalizations about the lived significance of popular culture based on anecdotal or purely theoretical evidence. The focus for this chapter is a discussion of an ethnographic study that I have been involved in which studied the religious functions of club culture, and which raises theological questions about the adequacy of clubbers" discourses for making sense of "oceanic" or "mystical" experiences encountered on the dance-floor.

Given the constraints of any single book, it is inevitable that there are significant parts of contemporary popular culture that are not covered by these case studies. I have chosen these individual case studies because I think they provide helpful and illuminating examples for the particular method that I am seeking to use for each case. My intention in this book is not to provide a comprehensive critique of contemporary popular culture. At present I am unconvinced that there is a sufficient depth of understanding of popular culture within theology and religious studies to attempt successfully such a broad overview of contemporary culture.[1] Rather, for the time being, I think we need to proceed on the basis of more detailed case studies that will help us to understand more clearly the conceptual and methodological issues at stake in this kind of study. At the same time I am conscious that there are major areas of popular culture which have still not received detailed attention within theology and religious studies. Amongst these still neglected areas, I would include fashion, advertising, interior and home design, and video games. My hope is that the discussion offered in this book will encourage researchers in the future to look at a wide range of forms of popular culture (including these neglected areas of study) and to continue to develop greater methodological and critical rigor in their work.

In the concluding part of the book (chapter 9) I draw the threads of my discussion together to argue for the need to develop a theological aesthetics of popular culture. This chapter explores what "aesthetics" means in this context, why academics have been slow to develop an aesthetics of popular culture and what the key elements of a theological aesthetics of popular culture might be.

Developing this book has been an interesting and demanding process, and I am grateful to a number of people without whom it would not have been completed. My thanks go to everyone at Blackwell publishers for all their support in the production of this text, especially to Rebecca Harkin for her supportive and constructive editorial comments. I have been fortunate to have had opportunities to share this material with a range of people and to get their valuable feedback on it. A version of chapters 2 and 5 was presented as a paper at the contextual theology seminar of the Department of Religions and Theology at the University of Manchester. The analysis of Eminem's music in chapter 6 was presented as a research paper at the Queen's College research seminar in Birmingham. Versions of chapter 8 have also been presented at departmental research seminars in the Department of Religious Studies at Lancaster University and the Department of Theology and Religious Studies at Cardiff University. A version of this chapter was also presented at the Religion and Popular Culture seminar at the annual meeting of the American Academy of Religion in Atlanta in 2003. The material used in this book has also been formed and reworked through the process of teaching undergraduate modules in theology and popular culture in the Department of Theology at Birmingham University, as well as supervising undergraduate and research students in this area. I am very grateful to everyone who has helped and challenged me with this material. My conversations and contact with both Robert Beckford and Duncan Flatman has been invaluable in shaping the ideas presented here, and I must also give particular mention and thanks to Emily Badger, Giles Beck, Donna-Louise Bryan, Francesca Carnevali, Elaine Graham, Paul Heelas, Matthew Hilton, Jeff Keuss, Demi Kranikoglou, Geoff Lanham, Ollie Leggett, Alison Marsh, Hugh McLeod, Rob Miller, Stephen Pattison, Jo Pearson, Martyn Percy, Anthony Pinn, Alliya Stennett, Martin Stringer, John Swinton, Frankie Ward, Pete Ward, Heather Widdows, Isabel Wollaston, Toni Woodward, and Linda Woodhead. Whilst the final responsibility for the content of what follows is mine alone, I am once again struck by how the process of writing a book like this is dependent on a range of good friendships and collegial relationships. I hope this book proves to be a good way of sharing what I have learnt from each of these people.

Gordon Lynch
University of Birmingham
April 2004

# Chapter 1

# what is "popular culture"?

I have almost as many problems with "popular" as I have with "culture." When you put the two terms together the difficulties can be pretty horrendous.

(Hall, 1981)

## introduction

Academic disciplines and debates have their trends and fashions – rather like high street clothing stores, only academic fashions tend to last longer than the latest skirt length or color. In many universities in the 1980s and early 1990s, it was hard to attend a seminar in the humanities and social sciences without the notion of "postmodernism" cropping up at some point. More recently debates concerning "globalization" seem to be taking over as a major new focus for academic concern across a range of disciplines.[1] Another major trend in Western academic work which has been growing steadily since the early 1960s has been an interest in the study of "popular culture." Books, articles, and research theses that explore popular culture are now being produced by scholars working in anthropology, art and design history, cultural and communication studies, the study of literature, geography, history, philosophy, and increasingly within theology and religious studies.

Texts on popular culture in relation to theology and religious studies began to be published in the early 1970s, with one of the initial interests in this area being the relationship between theology and film (see, e.g., Cooper and Skrade, 1970; Hurley, 1970). Since then, film has continued to be a major focus of theological studies of popular culture, but books and articles have also been published which explore the theological or religious significance of TV shows, sports, pop music, consumer culture, and the mass media (see Forbes and Mahan, 2000, for a useful annotated bibliography of this literature). The creation of the "Religion and Popular Culture" study group within the American Academy of Religion, and the development of specialist journals such as the Journal of Religion and Film and the Journal of Religion and Popular Culture, further indicates that this is a growing area of interest amongst theologians and scholars of religion.

The primary aim of this book is to provide an overview of key debates and methods for those working in theology and religious studies who want to engage in the critical study of popular culture. In the first part of the book, we will explore a range of concepts and debates that are central to popular culture studies, as well as thinking about what particular areas of interest theologians and scholars of religion have within this field. A key starting point – and one often neglected in the literature on popular culture in theology and religious studies – is to think about what is really meant by the term "popular culture." Exploring this issue will be the central topic for this opening chapter.

## defining "popular culture"

So what exactly is "popular culture"? One of the striking features of many recent publications on popular culture in theology and religious studies is that it is relatively rare for writers to define precisely what they mean by this term. Now to worry about such issues of definition may just seem rather pedantic on my part, but as a starting point for this book, I'd like to suggest that when we begin to explore how to define "popular culture" we start making some interesting discoveries.

When I began doing the research for this book, I asked a colleague who is a specialist in the study of popular culture in his particular discipline if he could tell me what popular culture was and why he thought people studied it. "Well," he replied, "I can certainly tell you why people have written about popular culture in my subject, but I'm not sure I can tell you exactly what it is." Now his difficulty in defining popular culture is not a consequence of lack of study or academic effort on his part. Indeed the disarming honesty of my colleague illustrates a point that I want to go on and explore in greater depth in this chapter. This is that "popular culture" is not a concept whose meaning is agreed upon by everyone who claims to study it, nor is it in fact an object that simply exists "out there" in the real world waiting for us to come and do research on it. Rather "popular culture" is a term that has been used in quite different ways by different writers depending on the particular academic project that they are committed to (see also Strinati, 1995, pp.xviiff; Storey, 2003).

Whilst the idea that "popular culture" has no universally agreed definition may be somewhat disconcerting at this point in our discussion, this is in reality no different to many other terms that we commonly use in theology and religious studies. Concepts such as "spirituality," or indeed "religion" itself, do not have commonly agreed definitions (see, e.g., King, 1999). Indeed the value of these terms is not as labels that correspond to realities in the external world (even if words could function in this way in this first place).[2] Rather terms like "religion" or "popular culture" are useful in so far as they make certain kinds of activity possible, such as academic research and debate, by helping us to think about the world in certain kinds of ways.

One of the reasons why the term "popular culture" has so many different meanings amongst academic writers is that it is rarely defined in its own right. Indeed it is more commonly defined in relation to other forms of culture. As John Storey (2001) puts it:

> Part of the difficulty stems from the implied *otherness* which is always absent/present when we use the term "popular culture" . . . [P]opular culture is always defined, implicitly or explicitly, in contrast to other conceptual categories: folk culture, mass culture, dominant culture, working-class culture, etc . . . Moreover . . . whichever conceptual category is deployed as popular culture's absent/present *other*, it will always powerfully affect the connotations brought into play when we use the term "popular culture." (Storey, 2001, p.1)

There are three key ways in which "popular culture" has been defined in relation to a cultural "other" or "others":[3]

1  popular culture as an opposing cultural form to *high culture* or *the avant-garde*;
2  popular culture as a category that is defined in relation to both *high culture* and *folk culture*, or which is seen as displacing *folk culture*;
3  popular culture as a form of social and cultural resistance against *dominant culture* or *mass culture*.

We will now consider each of these distinctions in turn.

## popular culture, high culture, and the avant-garde

One of the key ways in which a number of writers have understood popular culture is to distinguish it from another opposing form of culture, such as high culture or the avant-garde. Usually this distinction has been made in order to emphasize the inferior and debased quality of popular culture. Indeed, the writers who have been most important in introducing debates about popular culture into academic and artistic contexts have often been those who were most implacably opposed to its apparent power and influence. Important figures in this regard have been the British writers Matthew Arnold and F.R. Leavis, as well as American critics such as Clement Greenberg and Dwight McDonald.

In his book *Culture and Anarchy*, first published in 1869, Matthew Arnold argued that culture should be thought of as "the best that has been thought and known in the world" (Arnold, 1889, p.31), and that maintaining and developing such culture represented the only secure basis for a civilized society. Arnold can therefore be seen as an advocate of *high culture*, a form of culture which is often understood in terms of a classical tradition of literature, philosophy, and the arts.

Arnold did not suggest that this culture was necessarily simply the preserve of the aristocratic or upper classes. Indeed he argued that across all social classes there were some people with a "humane spirit," and that exposure to the civilizing effects of culture would encourage this humanity and desire for social perfection amongst those capable of feeling it. Nevertheless, it is clear that Arnold perceived a clear distinction between the civilized culture that he valued and the culture of the working-class masses, which he saw as hedonistic, immature, and anarchistic. Writing in a period of growing political organization in the British working-classes, Arnold argued that political institutions should act to maintain a social framework in which civilized culture could be preserved, and that the authority of these institutions should be respected, even if the working-classes found them repressive.

The elitist tone of Arnold's writing is maintained in the subsequent work of F.R. Leavis, whose writing was most influential from the early 1930s to the late 1950s. Like Arnold, Leavis claimed that true cultural judgment and taste was the preserve of a limited social group. As a literary critic, Leavis saw this group as comprising those who had the ability to appreciate the classic texts of Western literature and the classic products of Western art. The existence of such a cultural elite was essential though, in his view, to the well-being of society:

> Upon this minority depends our power of profiting by the finest human experience of the past; they keep alive the subtlest and most perishable parts of tradition. Upon them depend the implicit standards that order the finer living of an age, the sense that this is worth more than that, this rather than that is the direction to go, that the center is here rather than there. In their keeping . . . is

Figure 1.1   These photographs by Nick Danziger illustrate the difference between notions of "high" and "popular" culture. In the (upper) picture of the House of Lords library in London, the environment emphasizes elite knowledge and aesthetics. In the (lower) picture of women playing bingo in Glasgow, we see an example of mass-produced entertainment. (© Nick Danziger)

the language, the changing idiom, upon which fine living depends, and without which distinction of spirit is thwarted and incoherent. (Leavis, 1930, p.4).

Like Arnold, then, Leavis also saw those with proper cultural taste and judgment as the guardians of civilized society. For it is only through the cultural wisdom and sensitivity that this elite has refined through their engagement with the classic canon of Western art and literature that society can hope to maintain any sense of moral and aesthetic judgment. Leavis saw the growing forms of popular entertainment (particularly Hollywood film) and the popular press as a dangerous threat to such cultural discrimination. These forms of popular distraction were designed merely as commercial enterprises and had no fundamental commitment to the cultural education of the general public. In the context of a rapidly changing social and cultural environment, then, Leavis argued for the need for an educated minority to maintain its cultural taste and judgment in the threat of commercially compromised forms of mass culture.

A related argument about the debased nature of mass or popular culture was advanced from the 1930s onwards by the leading American art critic, Clement Greenberg. Unlike Arnold and Leavis, though, who contrasted popular culture with the high culture of classic literature, art, and philosophy, Greenberg sought to contrast mass culture with new and progressive forms of culture, the *avant-garde*. As an art critic, Greenberg argued that the most important and progressive movement in twentieth-century art was the trend towards abstraction and away from figurative art in which the artist seeks to reproduce a recognizable image of the real world (see Greenberg, 1940). "Pure art," in Greenberg's terms, could therefore be found in the work of an abstract painter such as Piet Mondrian, whose later work consisted of geometrical shapes and a limited range of colors, as well as the work of the later American abstract expressionist painters, such as Jackson Pollock, Mark Rothko, and Barnett Newman. This movement to abstraction in art was, argued Greenberg, part of a wider trend in the arts to clarify the essence of each discipline (whether music, art, sculpture, or literature) and to express this essence rather than attempt to mimic other forms of artistic production.

Whilst Greenberg saw this progressive avant-garde movement in the arts as a positive sign of cultural development, he also detected an opposing, more insidious, cultural trend in popular culture or "kitsch" (Greenberg, 1939). According to Greenberg, the kitsch of pulp fiction, popular music, magazines, and Hollywood movies is a product of industrialized societies in which the working and lower-middle classes gained sufficient income to require some form of cultural entertainment, but insufficient education or leisure-time to appreciate more demanding forms of art and culture. As a consequence, mass-produced, "ersatz culture" began to be sold to the lower classes in various forms which offered "pre-digested" forms of entertainment that offered easy pleasures to its audience without requiring much intellectual or analytical effort on their part. Where as avant-garde art is serious and demanding, kitsch is accessible, commercial, and undemanding. Thus, again, for Greenberg, popular or mass culture can be seen as an insidious alternative to genuine artistic and cultural development.

Whilst there is a degree of contrast between the support of Arnold and Leavis for a classic canon of Western art and literature, and Greenberg's enthusiastic reception of progressive developments in the arts, there is evidently a common ground in their assessment of popular culture. For all of them, popular culture is debased, detached from true sources of cultural inspiration, and threatens to overwhelm the great achievements of human culture in a mass of mediocrity and banality. As Dwight McDonald (1957, p.62) observed "mass Culture is very, very democratic: it absolutely refuses to discriminate against, or between, anything or anybody. All is grist to its mill, and all comes out finely ground indeed."

For contemporary readers, reared on the populism of late modern liberal democracies (see, e.g., Chaney, 2002), the social and cultural elitism of writers such as Arnold, Leavis, and Greenberg can seem unintelligible at best, and deeply distasteful at worst. In their defense one might wonder whether the undiscriminating populism of our age is in serious danger of reducing culture to the level of the mediocre and the banal. Furthermore, when Leavis and Greenberg were writing in the 1930s, it is understandable that they should be suspicious of mass culture, when popular forms of art and entertainment had a significant role in the management of the populations within totalitarian regimes in the Soviet Union, Nazi Germany, and Fascist Italy.

Nevertheless, there are grounds for challenging any simplistic division between high culture/the avant-garde and popular culture, particularly when this division is also made between upper/bourgeois and working-class cultures. Firstly, the idea of a canon of classic literature, art and music is not a stable phenomenon – indeed what is perceived as classic literature and arts can change significantly within a matter of decades (see, e.g., Levine, 1996, pp.91ff.). The idea of *high culture* should therefore be seen as the creation of certain writers working at certain historical contexts, rather than something that is a universal and timeless cultural category (DiMaggio, 1998).[4] Furthermore, distinguishing between high and popular cultures fails to acknowledge the complexity of the cultural life of the majority of the population. Thus, for example, in his article "Culture is ordinary," Raymond Williams (2001) reminds us that working-class culture has its own integrity, and would, for some people, include an appreciation of classical music and poetry that would seem incompatible with other forms of popular cultural entertainment. With reference to Clement Greenberg, we might also add the question, "which avant-garde?" For it is clear that other twentieth-century artists whose work can be considered avant-garde, particularly those associated with Dadaism and surrealism, were strongly committed to using images and objects from everyday popular culture as part of their radical artistic practice (see Motherwell, 1989; Kuenzli, 1996; Highmore, 2002). Whilst we might question the detailed arguments of Arnold, Leavis, and Greenberg, their work has been highly significant in shaping debates concerning popular culture. Indeed, their enduring influence can be seen in the skepticism that many people in the academic community continue to hold towards the notion of the study of popular culture as a serious academic pursuit (for more detailed analysis of this skepticism see, e.g., Levine, 1996, pp.3ff.).

## popular culture and folk culture

If one way of defining popular culture is to contrast it with an opposing other, such as high culture or the avant-garde, then a second approach is to contrast it with two other cultural forms, namely high culture and folk culture. This is the approach taken by the editors of a recent major collection of essays on religion and popular culture, Bruce Forbes and Jeffrey Mahan (2000, pp.2f.), who distinguish between these cultural categories in the following way:

> To employ suggestive examples from the realm of food: high culture is a gourmet meal, folk culture is grandma's casserole, and popular culture is a McDonald's hamburger. All three are forms of "culture," which is intended here as a neutral term that includes the whole range of human products and thoughts that surround our lives, providing the context in which we live . . . The distinctions between the three classifications of culture (high, folk, and popular) have to do especially with the size of their audiences, and perhaps also the means by which they are transmitted. High or elite culture, often transmitted in a written form (a literary magazine, the score of an opera, a gourmet cookbook), has a limited audience by its very intention, and is addressed to persons who are perceived to have superior backgrounds or more sophisticated taste. Folk culture, often transmitted orally (family recipes, local legends, regional marriage customs), also has a limited audience, because oral communication is roughly limited to the more immediate family, community, or other local or regional group. Popular culture might be communicated in many ways, but it

most often becomes widespread, and thus popular, though mass media . . . As
its very name implies, popular culture is marked by its larger audience. (Forbes
and Mahan, 2000, pp.2–3)

This triangular distinction between high, folk and popular culture can be
presented in a purely descriptive way as it is here, in which these three different categories appear as different but equal forms of culture.

For other writers, though, the contrast between folk and popular culture
serves as a critical tool for identifying fundamental problems with popular
culture. In this more critical account, the emergence of industrialized
societies focused around mass production and consumption generated a
commercialized popular culture that displaced more authentic, traditional
folk cultures. Dwight McDonald articulated this critique neatly when he
commented:

> It is also true that Mass Culture is to some extent a continuation of the old Folk
> Art which until the Industrial Revolution was the culture of the common
> people, but here, too, the differences are more striking than the similarities.
> Folk Art grew from below. It was a spontaneous, autochthonous expression of
> the people, shaped by themselves, pretty much without the benefit of High
> Culture, to suit their own needs. Mass Culture is imposed from above. It is
> fabricated by technicians hired by businessmen; its audiences are passive
> consumers, their participation limited to the choice between buying and
> not buying. (McDonald, 1957, p.60)

This critique of commercialized forms of mass culture displacing the traditional culture of the common people was also a central theme in Richard
Hoggart's (1957) seminal book, *The Uses of Literacy*. Here Hoggart argued
that traditional forms of English working-class culture were under threat from
new, less communally-rooted entertainments such as American film and
popular music.[5] Whilst offering a powerfully-worded critique of emerging
forms of popular culture, Hoggart's book also had the effect of validating the
academic study of working-class culture. When he subsequently founded the
Centre for Contemporary Cultural Studies at Birmingham University, UK, in
1961, this became a leading research center which, as we shall see shortly, in
time generated some quite different understandings of popular culture to
those initially suggested by Hoggart (see Turner, 2003).

The relationship between high, folk, and popular culture has therefore
been characterized in two different ways. Forbes and Mahan set out a relationship in which all three of these cultural categories remain meaningful in

contemporary society, and in which each are presented as equally valid forms of culture. Writers such as Dwight McDonald and Richard Hoggart (as well as Leavis and Greenberg), however, suggest that folk culture is something that is now largely threatened or indeed displaced by commercialized forms of popular culture. Furthermore, they argue that popular culture has the effect of weakening community and ensuring social and political compliance. It is culture provided *for* the people, rather than being the authentic culture *of* the people.

Whilst these distinctions between high, folk, and popular culture are indeed informative and provide another perspective on how we might understand popular culture, there are again significant problems. Firstly, it is unclear how useful or meaningful the distinction is between folk and popular culture in contemporary society. Truett Anderson (1996, p.1), for example, reports the attempt by some young people in Lapland to mix traditional yodeling with techno music (a blend they refer to as "techno-yoik"). Is this music an example of folk culture or popular culture? Similarly another recent major anthology of essays on religion and popular culture contains an essay by Wade Clark Roof (2001) on the religious significance of barbecues in the American South. Roof's discussion of the significance of the practices of preparing, cooking and eating the barbecue clearly explores a widespread cultural practice in parts of America. But is this folk culture or popular culture? In my home city in Britain, a popular form of entertainment at the moment are salsa dancing nights in which people learn and dance salsa routines. Now salsa dance is folk culture, but it is a traditional folk culture in Cuba and other parts of Latin America. When people learn salsa dancing in Britain now, is this folk culture or popular culture? The idea that people in contemporary Western societies construct their lives from a range of different cultural resources, traditions, and practices – a practice referred to as bricolage – suggests that making clear distinctions between folk culture and popular culture may not be particularly easy or meaningful in our contemporary contexts.

There is also a danger amongst writers such as McDonald and Leavis that an overly romanticized contrast is drawn between "authentic," preindustrial folk culture and debased, commercialized mass culture. For example, the increasing rates of literacy and availability of cheap song lyric sheets meant that as early as the seventeenth-century, British "folk" music began to develop standardized conventions about correct lyrics for particular songs (see Easton et al., 1988, p.44). Folk culture was therefore liable to certain forms of standardization well before the onset of the Industrial Revolution. Furthermore, forms of preindustrial folk culture such as the carnival, or the original British version of football,[6] were arguably tolerated by the ruling classes precisely because they provided an outlet for social frustration other than organized political protest. To imagine that folk culture was simply the culture *of* the people, and that it served no hegemonic function in maintaining their social compliance may well then be somewhat naïve (see Reay, 1985; Easton et al., 1988). Indeed any theory of popular culture that involves some kind of narrative of a "cultural fall" from some glorious past of high or folk culture requires a critical scrutiny of its historical accuracy and adequacy.

## popular culture and dominant/mass culture

A third way in which popular culture has been defined is to suggest that it has a far more positive social function than that attributed to it by many of the writers whom we have considered so far. This third approach is to see popular culture as a potential or actual form of cultural resistance to the dominant culture within a given society. One of the leading writers to have made a case for this approach is Stuart Hall, who like Hoggart was a leading figure in the Centre for Contemporary Cultural Studies at Birmingham University. Hall (1981) has argued that we can best understand "popular" culture not as that which is simply "popular" with the masses or with a particular list of popular entertainments and practices, but as the opposing dialectical force to the dominant or elite culture within a given society. Popular culture, in this sense, is therefore whatever is excluded from the elite or dominant culture in a given society. Moreover "popular" culture is also the focus of attempts by that social or cultural elite to shape or control the culture of the mass classes, and is where those mass classes both concede to and resist those forms of social control. Hall's understanding of popular culture is therefore based in an understanding of social and cultural struggle in which dominant social groups seek to maintain their power and shape the wider population according to their view of the world, and in which the mass population partly accepts and partly resists this cultural influence.

Hall's understanding of popular culture reflects the notion of subculture that emerged out of the Birmingham Centre for Contemporary Cultural Studies (see, e.g., Hall and Jefferson, 1976; Hebdige, 1979). Hebdige describes subcultures as attempts by those outside the dominant group in a given society to take existing items, images or practices in that culture and to give them new meanings that resist dominant ideas and values. At the heart of subculture, suggests Hebdige, is a "refusal" – a refusal to be defined and limited by the identities of the "normal," dominant social order. Hebdige's own classic study of a subcultural form explored how the punk movement assimilated a wide range of cultural products, from safety-pins, tartan kilts, and reggae music, to attempt to set out a new identity for disillusioned white youth who did not wish to be incorporated into dominant notions of white racism and nationalism.

A similar understanding of popular culture has also been proposed by John Fiske (Fiske, 1989). Up until now in this chapter, I have been using the terms "mass" and "popular" culture interchangeably, but Fiske contrasts the two. Mass culture, he argues, is the cultural system of commercially produced and marketed entertainments and commodities that are offered to the mass population. Popular culture, by contrast, is what people actually do with these entertainments and commodities in their real lives, which may have little to do with the meanings or uses that their commercial producers intended for them. Fiske's work is strongly influenced by the work of the French social theorist, Michel de Certeau (see de Certeau, 1984; Buchanan, 2000). De Certeau suggested that the majority of people have little control of the cultural products and entertainments out of which they shape their lives. We have little direct control, for example, over the content of TV schedules or Hollywood films. Yet this does not mean that we are merely passive consumers, rather we maintain our freedom in the way in which we consume and make use of these cultural products. We may not have designed the territory in which we live our day-to-day lives, but we still retain some freedom in choosing how to act within that territory.

The work of Hall, Hebdige, Fiske, and others, therefore offers a different understanding of popular culture to those critics who simply define it as the debased shadow of high culture or the avant-garde, or as the commercially compromised usurper of authentic folk culture. In their work, popular culture becomes a set of cultural practices in which people can attempt to resist dominant cultural ideas that are oppressive, out-dated, or out of touch with their experience or aspirations. There are some differences in the degree of optimism that these writers have for the possibility of genuine cultural resistance. Hall sees this as an on-going cultural battle in which neither the dominant nor the masses win any final victories, and Hebdige (1979, p.3) speculates on whether subcultural refusal ends up being any more significant than "graffiti on the prison wall." Fiske, by contrast, is more genuinely optimistic of people's ability to resist manipulation and coercion by dominant cultural elites. Each of these writers, though, see more potential for the exercise of human agency, imagination, and creativity through popular culture than many of the writers we have discussed so far in this chapter.

Again, there are problems with this approach, though. We might question, for example, how adequate it is to characterize society in terms of a dominant social elite and the wider population who are excluded from this elite. Indeed in late modern, multicultural societies we are increasingly aware that there is more than one form of social and cultural domination, and more than one kind of dominating group. For example, white feminist writers have clearly articulated the social and cultural domination that men exert over women, but these feminists have in turn been subject to critique by black womanist writers for failing to take sufficient account of social and cultural domination on grounds of color and ethnicity (see, e.g., hooks, 1981). Furthermore it is evident that people who take part in what may look like subcultural groups or practices may not attribute subcultural meanings to them at all or intend this to be any kind of resistance against a perceived social order. Rather wearing elements of punk clothing might be an expression of a person's personal taste or their desire to associate themselves with a particular current trend (see Muggleton, 2001).

From our discussion so far, it is clear that there is no academic consensus on what the term "popular culture" means. The way in which a particular writer defines "popular culture" is clearly shaped by the wider academic and cultural project with which they are concerned, and the definitions that we have noted here are clearly conflicting and contradictory. In attempting to give a definition of popular culture, one option open to us is simply to align ourselves with one of the approaches that we have just described, and for example, to adopt the understanding of popular culture offered by Greenberg, McDonald, Hall, or Fiske. Another option, and one that I would like to explore now, is to attempt to find some common assumptions about popular culture that underlie each of these definitions which might give us a broader starting point for thinking about this subject.

## popular culture and everyday life

In a historical study of British popular culture between the mid-sixteenth and mid-eighteenth centuries, Barry Reay (1998, p.1) suggests that popular culture "refers to widely held and commonly expressed thoughts and actions." This is clearly a very broad definition, but I would suggest it is helpful in that it makes a basic connection between popular culture and the shared context, practices and resources of "everyday life." Indeed if we think back over the definitions of popular culture that we explored earlier in the chapter, it is possible to suggest that each of these writers assumed that popular or mass culture related to the everyday lives of the wider population of the particular society that they were writing about. These writers might not have always approved of what made up the everyday lives of these people; Arnold's complaints about uncouth working-class behavior are perhaps particularly noteworthy in this regard. But nevertheless, whether regarded as a source of concern or celebration, popular culture was assumed by each of these writers to be bound up with what it meant to live an ordinary day-to-day life in a particular social and cultural context.

It might be tempting at this point to suggest that popular culture is therefore the shared environment, practices, and resources of everyday life for *ordinary* people within a particular society. This again would be too simplistic, however (see, e.g., Highmore, 2002, pp.1ff.). Who do we consider ordinary? To what extent is the day-to-day life of a young black man in the south side of Chicago comparable to the day-to-day life of a white young woman in a small town in Ohio? Or to what extent is there any similarity between the day-to-day life of a female Bangladeshi immigrant living in the East-end of London and the day-to-day life of a retired man living in an affluent village in Sussex? Are all of these people ordinary, and if so is there any continuity or common ground to ordinary life in contemporary society? The day-to-day lives of these people are likely to be very different to each other in terms of what these people may be able to do, buy, what they will be interested in, who they will talk to and interact with, what they will talk to other people about and what they will seek out as entertainment. To use the term "ordinary" people (or indeed the term "popular") can create the image for us of a homogenous population who all do the same kinds of things, engage with the same kinds of people, have the same kinds of opportunities and ability to consume, and who are amused by broadly the same kinds of things. As David Chaney reminds us, though:

> The popular is not a natural, transparent, term of description; it is a weapon in a variety of struggles to cope with the crippling unease of a recognition that there are limitations to *any and all* way(s) of talking about ourselves. The history of collective life is not a continuous landscape under the harmonious sun of a universal language. (Chaney, 1993, p.193)

Terms like "popular," "ordinary," or even "everyday life" can therefore function in ways that may offer reassurance that we know what we are talking about, but in reality act in ways that obscure the genuine complexities of social and cultural life. If we try to bear these complexities in mind, however, I would suggest that there may still be some value in thinking about popular culture as the shared environment, practices, and resources of everyday life in a given society. The fact that everyday life can be constituted in such different ways for members of a different society might incline us to think more in terms of popular *cultures* (an option preferred by Barry Reay). The popular cultural world of the Bangladeshi immigrant in London is likely to be significantly different to that of the retired white man living in an affluent area, for example, particularly if the Bangladeshi woman does not speak English. Nevertheless, if we remain aware these complexities, associating popular culture with everyday life can have certain benefits for our academic work in this area.

There are three particular benefits that I would like to suggest. Firstly, if we think about popular culture as the shared environment, practices, and resources of everyday life then this offers us a broader understanding of popular culture than is sometimes evident in studies undertaken by academics in theology and religious studies. Academic training for theologians and religious scholars often focuses around the study of texts, whether sacred texts such as the Torah, Qu'ran, or the Bible, or other historical texts such as the writings of leading historical theologians or other religious figures. Given this focus on texts within the discipline, it is perhaps unsurprising that when people trained in theology and religious studies have come to study popular culture they have focused on popular cultural texts such as TV shows, music videos, films, pop songs, or pop literature (see, e.g., Beaudoin, 1998). Whilst these studies can generate some interesting insights on these particular popular cultural "texts," to focus simply on these can produce a skewed perspective on the wider patterns and practices of everyday life (on this issue, see also Storey, 1999; Chaney, 2002). Engaging with mass-produced forms of entertainment is an important element of everyday life for many people in contemporary Western society. But reading, watching, and listening to these popular "texts" is only one part of everyday life, in which other parts may consist of cooking and eating, caring for children or other dependents, spending time at work or with friends, having sex, tidying, mending or improving our homes, washing, dressing or daydreaming. To think of popular culture as the environment, practices, and resources of everyday life reminds us that popular culture may be as much to with these other activities as with interacting with specific popular "texts" such as films or TV programs.

What I am suggesting here is that theologians and religious scholars have tended to adopt what Raymond Williams has referred to as a "documentary" approach to the study of culture, which focuses on the significance of artifacts and texts produced by a particular society. What I would like to advocate as a complementary alternative is the culturalist approach proposed by Williams that studies (popular) culture more as a "way of life" for particular people in particular contexts, rather than simply as a collection of texts and other cultural products. This broader approach involves looking at the wider structures, relationships, patterns and meanings of everyday life within which popular cultural texts are produced and "consumed." As we shall see in the coming chapters (especially chapters 6–8), both the documentary and culturalist approaches have particular uses for those working in theology and religious studies who wish to engage with popular culture, and both of these approaches require us to develop use different skills and methods in our academic work. It is important, however, for theologians and scholars of religion not to become trapped in "textual" approaches to the study of popular culture, and to miss out on some of the questions that are raised by a wider culturalist method. Whilst this might seem a rather abstract claim at the outset of the book, the importance of this issue will become clearer as our discussion develops in the coming pages.

A second benefit from thinking about popular culture as the environment, practices, and resources of everyday life is that it helps us to locate the study of popular culture as part of a longer project of academic enquiry (see Highmore, 2002). At the start of the chapter, I noted that academic interest in popular culture had been steadily growing since the early 1960s. In fact, the volume of academic books and articles on this subject has risen dramatically in just the past twenty years.[7] Given the ebb and flow of trends in academic work, it is quite conceivable that the study of "popular culture" may have become unfashionable in twenty years time, or more likely, that we will have conceived a new conceptual approach to studying this subject that may have dispensed with the term "popular culture" altogether. If this is the case it may be useful to see current interest in "popular culture" not merely as a twentieth-century fin-de-siècle fad, but as part of a longer academic project of engaging analytically and critically with the practices and resources of everyday life.

The study of "everyday life" has not always been perceived to be an appropriate focus for academic or artistic activity. Indeed it was only in the later nineteenth century, with the development of the discipline of sociology and the sustained images of everyday life in the work of French Impressionist painters, that the everyday began to subjected to sustained critical and artistic attention. The twentieth century, however, has seen a growing commitment in academic contexts to treat the everyday as a serious focus for study. The work of Freud, at the turn of the twentieth century, attributed fundamental significance to apparently trivial everyday phenomena such as dreams, jokes, mistakes, and slips of the tongue, and his work in turn influenced artistic movements such as Dadaism and surrealism. The writing of social and cultural theorists such as George Simmel and Walter Benjamin in the early decades of the twentieth century gave a critical approach to questions concerning the social function of money and shopping arcade culture. The emerging discipline of anthropology began to shift in the early part of the twentieth century from a focus purely on "primitive" cultures to a growing interest in the ethnography of Western cultures. The study of the Middletown project was thus undertaken in the United States in the 1920s and the Mass Observation project set up in Britain in the following decade. By the time that explicit academic studies of popular culture began to be undertaken in the 1960s, and the Pop Art movement exemplified by Andy Warhol was ostensibly celebrating the images and products of consumer culture, there had already been a long history of the academic and artistic study of everyday life. It is helpful, then, not to perceive the study of popular culture as a wholly new academic venture, but as part of a longer tradition in which the environment, practices, and resources of everyday life have been considered to be suitable subjects for critical academic study.

Finally, I would suggest that there is a third significant benefit to thinking about popular culture in terms of the environment, practices, and resources of everyday life. This is that it offers a more open definition of popular culture than many of the definitions that we considered in the first part of this chapter. By not attaching itself to any prior position on cultural values or cultural politics, the view of popular culture that I am suggesting here has the potential to allow a greater consensus about the nature of the subject that we are studying. Again, it is important to reiterate that what I am suggesting is not *the* definition of "popular culture," that establishes once and for all what popular culture is out there in the "real world." Rather I would claim that thinking about popular culture as the shared environment, practices, and resources of everyday life is a useful way of approaching this subject because it both helps us to maintain a open mind to studying whatever may be significant in everyday life in a particular social context.

## but why study everyday life?

One of the dangers of the study of everyday life is that it risks descending into the trivial and the banal. In its worst forms, the study of popular culture can appear to be an academic holiday, in which scholars have a break from their more normal weightier interests, and write texts on forms of popular culture that particularly interest or amuse them. Alternatively, it can be a kind of academic tourism in which a researcher engages with some exotic form of popular culture, and returns with some anecdotal souvenirs but makes no significant contribution to critical debate on that issue.

Ultimately, academics need to be accountable in explaining why the study of popular culture is a significant and appropriate focus for their work. The issue of why theologians and scholars of religion should study popular culture is something that we will return to in more depth in the next chapter. For now though, we can observe that the longer academic project of the study of everyday life has been undertaken for two particular reasons.[8]

Firstly, some writers have engaged in this kind of study because they believe that the analysis of everyday resources or practices has an important *explanatory* significance in helping us to understand more about the nature of human existence or the nature of human society. These explanations may well take us beyond the "common-sense" interpretations of everyday life. As Hegel said, "the familiar is not necessarily the known" (Gardiner, 2000, p.1). Freud's belief that phenomena such as dreams revealed key insights into the structure and content of the human psyche is a good example of an explanation of human existence that arises out of everyday life and which helps us to see everyday things in a new light.

Secondly, other writers have emphasized the important of the study of the everyday because of their commitment to particular cultural and political projects. For such writers, the study of the everyday has an important *critical*, *liberatory*, or *ideological* function in raising our awareness of oppressive structures and concepts within our own cultural context (see, e.g., Giroux, 1994; hooks, 1996). Thus, by raising awareness of oppressive social and political ideas that may lay hidden within seemingly innocuous forms of popular culture, it becomes possible for us to resist these, and to think and act in less dehumanizing ways.

This distinction between explanatory and liberatory/critical approaches to the study of popular culture is also a useful one when we come to think about how we study popular culture within theology and religious studies. Indeed, as we shall explore more in the next chapter, some scholars in these disciplines are primarily interested in studying popular culture because they hope to offer clearer explanations of religious experiences, trends, and processes in the contemporary world. By contrast other theologians and scholars of religion are more interested in a liberatory/critical engagement with popular culture in an attempt to identify the ways in which it is both constructive and destructive.

## conclusion

This chapter has aimed to introduce some of the key issues in approaching the study of popular culture, initially by considering the different ways in which writers have defined what "popular culture" is. We have seen that popular culture has often been defined in relation to a cultural "other" or "others," and explored a range of ways in which this relationship has been thought about (e.g., in relation to concepts such as high, folk, or mass culture). We have noted the problem of reaching an agreed definition of popular culture, and discussed the idea that it would be a mistake to assume that popular culture is a straightforward object waiting to be studied "out there" in the "real world." Whilst acknowledging that terms such as "popular" and "everyday" can obscure the complexities of social life, I have suggested that it may be most constructive to see the term "popular culture" as a term that points us towards the study of the environment, practices, and resources of everyday life. Such an understanding of popular culture might allow us to keep a more open mind about what might usefully be studied in this subject area, as well as helping us to understand our work as part of a larger tradition of academic study.

By examining these various definitions of popular culture, it is clear that this field of study inevitably raises questions about cultural values and cultural politics. Some of the central questions are:

1  how can we map what is happening within our contemporary culture?
2  what cultural images, texts, ideas and values can help us to build a humane and civilized society (cf. Arnold, Leavis)?
3  where are the progressive forces in contemporary culture, and what is threatening these or holding them back (cf. Greenberg)?
4  what forms of culture foster healthy, discriminating, and responsible human communities (cf. McDonald, Hoggart)?
5  in what ways can people resist the dominant ideologies of their society or find opportunities for authentic self-expression (cf. Hall, Hebdige, Fiske)?

Underlying these attempts to define popular culture are therefore, not simply a concern for how we might describe the structures and practices of contemporary society, but far-reaching questions about cultural values and cultural politics. We may not agree with the answers that specific writers have proposed to some of these questions. But nevertheless, these questions – about what resources can help us to live good and meaningful lives, about the nature of healthy human community and the nature of human liberation – are all issues that are deeply significant for human society.

Studying popular culture can therefore involve both the analysis and critique of contemporary society. In the next chapter, we will look in more detail at what kinds of interests and concerns have led people working in theology and religious studies to examine popular culture, and to think about how these disciplines can make a useful contribution to the field of popular culture studies.

# Chapter 2

# why should theologians and scholars of religion study popular culture?

## introduction

In the introduction to her book *Outlaw Culture*, bell hooks (1994, p.2ff.) comments that the study of popular culture has become increasingly "cool" in academic circles. This would certainly seem to be the case in the context of theology and religious studies. Since the publication of early studies in theology and film (see, e.g., Cooper and Skrade, 1970; Hurley, 1970), there has been a growing number of books, articles, and conferences exploring theological and religious aspects of popular culture. Major academic publishers in theology and religious studies are commissioning and producing increasing numbers of titles in this area, and even books with little direct relevance to popular culture are often packaged in ways that hint at pop culture connections (e.g., through using stills from Hollywood films for book covers).

It is possible that this development partly reflects an attempt on the part of theology and religious studies to be "trendy." The public perception of theology and religious studies as academic disciplines has tended to suffer as the influence of religious institutions has declined in Western society. By focusing on issues of popular culture rather than metaphysical debates in which the public has, by and large, little interest, these disciplines could therefore be seen as trying to "rebrand" themselves in a more attractive way for a contemporary market. Certainly the pressures for these disciplines to think in this way should not be underestimated in the context of an academic market-place in which competition to attract students is increasingly fierce.

Whilst the desire to make theology and religious studies more appealing to a contemporary public is understandable, there are also certain dangers in this impetus. As hooks comments, if people study popular culture primarily because it is "cool" then they risk missing the point that the study of popular culture is important because it can be a personally, culturally and socially transformative activity.

As we saw in the previous chapter, the academic study of popular culture raises a number of important questions. How can we understand the nature of contemporary society? What cultural resources can help us to live good, truthful, and meaningful lives? And what forms of popular culture can help to shape healthy forms of society and encourage humane relationships between its members? People involved in the disciplines of theology and religious studies have an important role to play in the academic study of popular culture precisely because they have distinctive and valuable contributions to make in answering these questions.

The aim of this chapter is to map out the different broad approaches that those working in theology and religious studies have taken to attempt to answer these larger questions. I want to suggest here that there are four main approaches that have emerged so far, and that each of these is potentially valuable in exploring serious issues about how we understand and critique contemporary culture.[1] These approaches are:

1  *the study of religion in relation to the environment, resources and practices of everyday life* (in particular asking about how popular culture shapes religious belief and activities or is appropriated by religious groups, how religion is represented in popular culture, and how religious groups interact with popular culture);
2  *the study of the ways in which popular culture may serve religious functions in contemporary society*;
3  *a missiological response to popular culture*;
4  *the use of popular cultural texts and practices as a medium for theological reflection.*[2]

Understanding these broad approaches to the theological and religious study of popular culture is important for clarifying how these disciplines might contribute to wider debates in cultural studies – something which has not yet happened to any significant degree.[3] But understanding these approaches can also provide us with a map that can help us, on a more basic level, to identify what particular theologians or religious scholars are trying to do when they write about popular culture. One of the confusing aspects of the rapid growth of literature in this field is that there are several different interests and concerns that are being explored within it, and individual writers do not always clarify how their work fits within this greater whole.

This map of the field will therefore help us to understand the major ways in which people working in theology and religious studies have tended to write about popular culture, as well as highlighting the distinctive contribution that these disciplines can make to serious questions of cultural analysis and criticism. The rest of the chapter will now take each of these four approaches in turn and explain them in more depth.[4]

## studying religion in relation to everyday life

In recent years, religious studies as a discipline has tended to shift its focus away from examining religions as abstract systems of ritual and belief, or from studying the practices of religious elites, towards exploring how religions function in everyday contexts. If we think of popular culture in terms of the environment, resources, and practices of everyday life, then it is unsurprising that this trend has led those studying contemporary religion to engage with popular culture.

Studying contemporary religion in relation to popular culture has tended to take three different forms.

Firstly, there is the study of the ways in which popular cultural texts and practices have shaped the beliefs, structures or practices of religious groups. Forbes (2000, p.12) refers to this as the study of "popular culture *in* religion." One example of this kind of study is William Romanowski's (2000) article on the development of the Christian Gospel music scene in America from the 1970s onwards, which sought to combine overtly Christian lyrics with contemporary styles of popular music. Romanowski traces how what was intended to be a form of evangelistic outreach based on popular music instead became a structured, commercialized music scene geared to an Evangelical subculture. The commercialization of this music scene came to be seen as a problem by some who were committed to a "purer" understanding of this form of musical ministry. Such tensions were further highlighted when those Christian gospel artists, such as Amy Grant, who managed to achieve crossover success into the mainstream pop market did so by dropping all overt religious references from their lyrics. Romanowki's study thus identifies some of the complex issues that arise when a religious group (in this case, Evangelical Christianity) seeks to appropriate forms and practices current in wider popular culture.[5]

Another example of such a study is David Morgan's (2003) analysis of the role of mass print media in nineteenth-century American Protestantism. Although Catholicism has historically been more clearly associated with the use of visual media for communicating theology, Morgan argues that mass-produced printed tracts played an important role as a medium of religious experience both for committed Protestants and their potential converts. These tracts were influential – not simply for the basic biblical and theological texts that they included – but also through the sketches that illustrated the vices of drinking alcohol or failing to observe the Sabbath, as well as the blessings of the Christian life. Morgan provides a range of accounts of converts describing these tracts as a medium through which they experienced a sense of divine challenge about how they were conducting their lives and were prompted to repent from their former ways. The appropriation of a particular cutting-edge popular cultural form, print media, thus influenced Protestant approaches to mission as well as the kinds of religious experience that believers and converts reported.[6]

A number of other examples of this kind of study can be given. Writers such as Laurence Moore (1994), Stewart Hoover (2000), and David Lyon (2000) have written on the way in which religious groups have sought to adapt and communicate their beliefs in the context of consumer culture. Pete Ward (1996, 1999) has done interesting work on the implications of the appropriation of popular musical forms in the context of Christian worship. Similarly John Ferré (2003) has written about the appropriation of narrative fiction as an evangelistic tool amongst some nineteenth-century Protestants.

The value of this kind of study is that it can help to clarify how contemporary religion is shaped by engaging with, or appropriating, practices, texts, and resources that are used in wider contemporary culture. These studies show both how religious groups can benefit from cultural appropriation (as in the case of Morgan's study), as well as some of the complex issues raised by the interaction between religious motivations and practices and more general cultural forms (as with Romanowski).

A second type of study of the relationship between religion and popular culture is to consider how religion is represented in wider forms of popular culture. This is, as Forbes (2000, p.10) puts it, the study of "religion *in* popular culture." One of the most common forms of this type of study is the extensive literature on the representation of Christ in film (see, e.g., Baugh, 1997; Tatum, 1997; Stern et al., 1999). Other writers have, however, looked at the representation of more generic religious figures, such as the wise Oriental monk (Iwamura, 2000), or at the way in which a range of religious believers and institutions are represented in TV programmes such as *The Simpsons* (Dalton et al., 2001).

Studying the way in which religions or religious figures are represented in the media can have an important critical element. Such studies can make us more aware of cultural biases in the way in which we perceive particular individuals or groups. This can be particularly significant when those biases are acted out in individual behavior or (even more damagingly) in national foreign policy. An important current debate of this kind concerns the representation of Islam in Western media. Rubina Ramji (2003) argues that Western popular entertainment typically portrays Islam in negative terms, e.g., as repressive, backward, and intolerant. The notion of the "Islamic terrorist" has become an increasingly common one in Western film since the collapse of communism in Eastern Europe, yet the connection between an entire faith and violent activity is never made outside the context of Islam. Films never refer, for example, to "Christian terrorists." Indeed when Islamic figures are represented positively in Western films it is usually only if they have been Westernized or "made civilized" by exposure to a Western character. Ramji argues that these persistently negative representations of Islam become particularly dangerous when they limit citizens' ability to think critically about Western foreign policies that damage Islamic countries or groups. Another perspective on this debate is provided by Mark Silk (2003), who notes that after 9/11, the American media consistently emphasized images of American Muslims expressing their horror at this terrorist attack. These "positive" images of Muslims expressing their peacefulness and patriotism to the U.S. were intended to minimize the threat of a violent backlash against the American Muslim community. Whilst Ramji is undoubtedly correct about the perpetuation of certain negative stereotypes of Muslims in contemporary Western film, Silk's observations indicate that media representations of Islam may at times be more complex than Ramji suggests.

Analyzing how religion is represented in contemporary media is not therefore simply a case of describing these representations. Rather it involves asking what these representations may tell us about wider biases, values, and concerns in contemporary society, what interests these representations might serve, and how these representations may be helpful or damaging to particular groups or individuals. This kind of study is often referred to as *ideological critique* (see Lyden, 2003, pp.27ff.) and fits within the broader concern with issues of representation in cultural criticism that we will look at in some more detail in chapter 4.

A third kind of study of the relationship between religion and popular culture concerns the way in which religious groups interact with wider popular culture. This approach is not concerned with how religious groups appropriate particular forms of popular culture, but with how religious groups relate to popular cultural texts and practices that they perceive to be part of contemporary culture beyond the normal boundaries of that group.

Religious groups have often been at the forefront of responses to new developments in popular culture (see, e.g., the role of the Catholic Church in setting out principles for the censorship of Hollywood films in the middle part of the twentieth century, Lyden, 2003, p.129). It is not uncommon for religious groups to react negatively to current forms of popular culture: as one Methodist writer commented in 1843, "nothing can be more killing to [religious] devotion than the perusal of a book of fiction" (Ferré, 2003, p.83). It is also possible to see more positive examples, however, such as the award of Catholic prizes for outstanding films at public film festivals (Ortiz, 2003). Examining the ways in which religious groups interact with popular culture is thus another useful approach to studying the interaction between religion and the environment, resources and practices of everyday life.

One example of this is Wagner's (2002) study of the varied responses of Christian groups to the Harry Potter books and films. Wagner describes how Christian responses to Harry Potter have taken widely different forms, even within the confines of conservative Evangelicalism. She notes objections that the Harry Potter stories encourage children to participate in occult activities and encourage disregard for established rules and proper authority. By contrast, she notes other Christian writers who have suggested that the Harry Potter books represent a fantasy understanding of magic that is quite separate to contemporary Wicca and that the moral framework of the books encourages virtues such as loyalty, love, and self-sacrifice. This debate has found a particularly heated focus as teaching materials based on Harry Potter are increasingly used in American public schools, and some conservative Christian groups have moved to try to ban them. Wagner comments that this raises basic questions about the nature of the relationship between Church and State in America, and of what criteria can be used to judge which religious materials can and cannot be taught in American classrooms.

This type of study by Wagner helps to highlight some of the assumptions that can guide religious responses to popular culture, namely that if children read about witchcraft then they are more likely to practice it.[7] It also identifies some of the wider issues that emerge out of religious debates on these issues (e.g., what are healthy and harmful forms of popular culture? And how do we judge what is healthy or not?). Studying religious responses to popular culture can therefore make us more aware of the guiding assumptions and methods that religious groups use to engage with popular culture, as well as issues of the nature and effects of popular culture that may be of more general concern within wider society.

In this part of the chapter, then, we have identified three different types of study that examine the relationship between contemporary religion and the

Figure 2.1   "He is the Bright Morning Star" and "There is a Christian Welcome Here." These porcelain figurines manufactured and sold by Precious Moments illustrate how religious piety and capitalist consumer culture can become deeply intertwined.

environment, resources, and practices of everyday life. One assumption that can often underpin these kinds of study is that it is possible to make clear distinctions between what is "religion" and what is "popular culture." As we saw back in chapter 1, however, terms like "religion" and "popular culture" do not refer to neat, independent realities that exist "out there" in the real world, but are concepts that help us to think about the world in particular ways. Whilst these concepts may indeed be helpful for our ability to analyze and think critically about our societies, there will also be points at which clear distinctions between "religion" and "popular culture" begin to break down.

Rycenga (2001), for example, examines the significance of the "Precious Moments" chapel, the flagship store for one of the world's most popular brand of collectible porcelain figures. These figures, which often depict sentimentalized religious figures and bear religious mottos, blur the boundaries of religion and popular culture. For in one sense they are religious artifacts, in that they offer particular representations of religious figures, yet in another sense they are part of popular culture as they function as consumer commodities. As Rycenga (2001, p.141) comments, the "Precious Moments" chapel provides a clear illustration of "the collapsed logics of religious sentiment and capitalism."

Studying the relationship between "religion" and "popular culture" can be very useful in clarifying our understanding of how religious groups function, of the implications of contemporary representations of religion, and of the issues raised by religious responses to popular culture. Such academic work needs to be conducted, however, with a sense that the terms "religion" and "popular culture" are conceptual tools rather than neatly defined entities, and that cultural forms and practices may at times defy being categorized in this way. Indeed if popular culture serves religious functions within contemporary society, then popular culture itself may be seen to have a "religious dimension" (Lyden, 2003, p.108). It is to this possibility that we shall now turn.

## studying the religious functions of popular culture

Attempts to define what "religion" is have proven to be as complex as attempts to define the term "popular culture" (see, e.g., Hamilton, 1995; Klass, 1995). Two contrasting definitions that have emerged out of debates amongst sociologists of religion are *substantive* and *functionalist* views of religion.

A *substantive* definition understands religion as characterized by certain core elements, e.g., belief in a deity/deities or other supernatural force, people who have special religious roles such as priest or shaman, sacred scriptures or tradition, rituals, and sacred space. Depending on which of these elements one considers to be an essential aspect of "religion," a social movement can be defined as religious or not depending on the extent to which it has these core elements. According to this approach, Christianity would, for example, clearly count as an example of a religion. Christianity involves belief in a transcendent God, specialized figures such as priest, ministers, monks, and nuns, sacred scriptures in the form of the Bible, rituals such as baptism and the Eucharist, and sacred spaces in the form of churches, monasteries, cathedrals, and other sacred sites. Using this substantive approach it is much more tenuous to describe supporting a soccer team as a religion, for this does not require belief in supernatural forces or have an established set of sacred scriptures. To think about the soccer match as a religious ritual, or stadiums representing sacred spaces to fans, is likely to look like rather forced analogies from this substantive perspective.

There are significant problems with substantive definitions of religion, however. It is unclear, for example, how we should judge what the "core elements" of religion are. Indeed it can be difficult to establish a common set of core elements that are universally present in what we traditionally think of as major world religions. Theravada Buddhism, for example, is often thought of as a religion yet it does not involve belief in a deity or supernatural force. Furthermore, attempts by Western scholars to define the substantive elements of religion tend to emphasize precisely those elements that are prevalent in Western religion. Even concepts such as "supernatural beings" that appear to be simply descriptive terms, contain basic cultural assumptions about what, for example, constitutes a "supernatural being." Thus, from a Western perspective, the belief that ancestors continue to exert an influence on the world of the living and should be paid due reverence can look like a belief in supernatural beings as there is no observable, empirical evidence of the on-going presence of these ancestors. Yet in cultures in which regard for ancestors plays a central role, ancestors may be experienced as everyday figures as much as any other living, breathing person (see, e.g., Klass, 1995, pp.25ff.). Whilst it may appear straightforward, from a "common-sense" perspective, to be able to give a universal definition of religion, based on its core elements, in practice such definitions tend to collapse under the weight of their cultural assumptions and their inability to capture the complexities of different societies.

The *functionalist* approach to defining religion does not assume that religion is characterized by certain core elements, but by its ability to perform certain functions for individuals or wider society. Those working broadly within this approach have identified three different functions that religions potentially serve:

1   a *social* function: religion provides people with an experience of community and binds people into a social order of shared beliefs and values that provides a structure for their everyday lives (see, e.g., Durkheim, 1915);
2   an *existential/hermeneutical* function: religion provides people with a set of resources (e.g., myths, rituals, symbols, beliefs, values, narratives) that may help people to live with a sense of identity, meaning and purpose (see, e.g., Geertz, 1973);
3   a *transcendent* function: religion provides a medium through which people are able to experience "God," the numinous or the transcendent (see, e.g., Hick, 1990, pp.161ff.).[8]

Whilst it may be helpful to keep these three functions of religion in mind whilst studying popular culture, it is worth noting that scholars who adopt a functionalist approach to religion do not necessarily consider each of these three functions to be equally important. Clifford Geertz (1973, p.90) has, for example, defined religion as "a system of symbols which acts to establish powerful, pervasive, and long-lasting moods and motivations in men [sic] by formulating general conceptions of a general order of existence and clothing these conceptions with such an aura of factuality that the moods and motivations seem uniquely realistic." This represents a classic statement of the notion that religion primarily serves existential and hermeneutical functions. Thus religions provide resources that establish a framework through which we "naturally" make sense of the world and think about how to live our lives. This definition, however, contains no sense that God, supernatural beings, or the "transcendent" have to play a role in this framework. Indeed nihilist forms of existentialism (see, e.g., Sartre, 1948), could be seen as performing this religious function if they provide people with a framework for understanding the world and how to live one's life. Geertz's definition of religion therefore does not include any sense that religion should provide a medium for encountering transcendence or the divine.

It would obviously be too strong to say that the three functions of religion that we have just noted are mutually exclusive. But at the same time, within a functionalist approach, it would be a mistake to assume that a particular cultural phenomenon has to demonstrate all three functions in order to be fully "religious." Clearly our view on this will be influenced by our understanding of what represents the core functions of religion, which may be just as arbitrary and culturally influenced as substantive views of religion.

Whilst functionalist definitions of religion cannot escape problems of arbitrariness and cultural bias that effect all attempts to define religion, a number of scholars have suggested that a functionalist approach offers a promising way for thinking about the religious dimension of popular culture (see, e.g., Nelson, 1976; Beaudoin, 1998; Mazur and McCarthy, 2001; Lyden, 2003).

Interest in studying the religious dimension of culture was originally given a significant impetus in the twentieth century through the work of the theologian Paul Tillich. Tillich suggested that religion could be understood as "ultimate concern," that is our fundamental guiding beliefs and values about what is most important in life. Thus, in Tillich's view, any form of belief that genuinely provides the basis for a person's or community's life could be understood as "religious." Tillich went to argue that if religion is the search for and expression of "ultimate concern," then culture is itself a manifestation of this fundamental religious orientation. In other words, the various forms that culture takes arise out of the fundamental beliefs and values of that culture (i.e., that culture's "religion" or "ultimate concern"). Or as Tillich (1959, p.42) put it, "religion as ultimate concern is the meaning-giving substance of culture, and culture is the totality of forms in which the basic concern of religion expresses itself."

Tillich's understanding of the religious basis of culture has prompted a number of theologians and religious scholars to think in more depth about the religious significance of contemporary culture beyond the boundaries of the Church or other religious institutions.[9] In recent years there has been a particular growth in interest in using functionalist understandings of religion to explore whether popular culture serves religious functions in contemporary society. The motivation for this kind of study is somewhat different in North America compared to Europe. In North America, religious observance remains at relatively high levels, despite some evidence of younger adults having declining involvement in religious institutions (see, e.g., Davie, 2002). Studying the religious functions of popular culture in North America can thus also involve thinking about how popular culture supplements and interacts with more traditional forms of religious belief and observance. In Western Europe, however, the rapidly declining rates of church attendance means that there is a reasonable case for examining whether popular culture is now replacing more traditional forms of religion as a source of community and meaning and a medium for encountering transcendence. In this context, studying the religious functions of popular culture is more akin to studying the forms, beliefs, and practices of a new mass religious movement. This distinction can be over-stated – many people in America may well turn to popular culture rather than traditional forms of religion in today's "spiritual marketplace" (Roof, 1999). Nevertheless, concerns about the rapid decline of institutional Christianity in Western Europe does lend a particular edge to debates about the religious significance of popular culture.

Theologians and scholars of religion in both North America and Europe have suggested a number of ways in which contemporary popular culture can be understood to fulfill religious functions:[10]

1    The *social* function of popular culture. A growing number of books and articles have, for example, suggested that sport performs a comparable social and communal function to traditional forms of religion (see, e.g., Hoffman, 1992, pp.6ff.). When sports fans watch their team playing, they are being bound into a community organized around certain beliefs and values, such as a particular notion of masculinity or a belief in freedom of opportunity symbolized by the sporting competition (McBride, 2001; Evans and Herzog, 2002). Similar claims have also been made about rave or club culture, in which those in a club are formed into a group that may be characterized by values such as tolerance or freedom of expression (Malbon, 1998; Lynch, 2003). Social interaction in clubs or at sporting events may also generate a particular form of community which the anthropologist Victor Turner (1969) referred to as "communitas." Communitas is a temporary, unstructured form of community in which all participants are, for a brief time, regarded as equal.

This idealized form of human community offers a brief respite from the hier-archical nature of day-to-day society, and provides an important reminder of people's essential equality and of the importance of treating people with proper regard. Religious rituals may offer this experience of communitas. But it is also conceivable that in the crowd of sports fans or clubbers, we can see other ways in which normal social barriers are erased and communitas is created. Popular culture may therefore form an alternative means to religion to being drawn into the values and beliefs of particular communities, or of experiencing particular forms of social relationship such as communitas.

2   The *existential/hermeneutical* function of popular culture. Popular culture can be seen as providing a range of resources that shape the way in which people make sense of and experience their lives. Lyden (2003), for example, argues that film represents an important source of myth within con-temporary society. Thus, the experience of watching a film in a cinema is one of temporarily being drawn into an alternative experience of reality in which we are exposed to particular stories about basic human issues such as sex, rela-tionships, families, violence, and death. These filmic myths may at times offer idealized accounts of how human dilemmas might be resolved or how human lives might be lived, but the idealized nature of these myths can serve as a challenge to how we might conduct our lives in the real world. Films can therefore be understood as offering images of what it means to live the good life, or to act virtuously, that can act as a resource for our own everyday reflec-tions on how we should live (see Miles, 1996; Kupfer, 1999). Other forms of popular culture can also be understood as providing people with a set of values and beliefs around which they organize their lives. Lelwica (2000) and Gray-beal (2001), for example, discuss how the dieting industry functions as an important source of meaning for many women in Western society. The world of meaning offered by dieting includes ideals (e.g., being a certain, often unat-tainable, body weight), virtues (following the specific regime of one's current diet), and sins (eating amounts or types of food proscribed by one's diet).[11] Other examples of popular culture that provide meaningful systems of values and beliefs for some people include hip hop (Sylvan, 2001), the music of Bruce Springsteen (McCarthy, 2001), and Star Trek (Porter and McLaren, 1999, pp.217ff.; Jindra, 2000). People may be inducted into the ideas, values, and beliefs of different forms of popular culture through a range of structured, ritualized activities such as attending Star Trek conventions, going to dieting meetings, taking part in on-line discussion groups, or watching a film in a cinema. Holland (2001) further describes how the act of ringing into radio phone-in shows to discuss one's personal problems can also function as a ritual that inducts one into the way of looking at life offered within that particular

show. Commitment to values and beliefs offered through popular culture can also be reinforced by the celebration of cultural icons who exemplify a particular set of attitudes or understanding of life (see, e.g., Anijar, 2001). The texts and practices of popular culture can therefore function in ways that provide people with frameworks within which they make sense of the world and reflect on how to live their lives.

3   The *transcendent* function of popular culture. In addition to performing important social, existential and hermeneutical functions, some writers have also suggested that popular culture can be a means through which people may have some transcendent or religious experience. Robert Johnston (2000, pp.57ff.) makes the valuable point that theologians and scholars of religion tend to read films in terms of the "meaning" of their stories and neglect the possibility that the aesthetic experience of watching a film might serve as a means of encountering the divine. Johnston also gives particular examples of people who have had significant religious experiences in the context of watching film (Johnston, 2000, pp.19ff.). Nicholas Saunders (2000) has also suggested that dancing at raves can become a form of "walking meditation" akin to Buddhist forms of spiritual practice. Saunders' controversial belief in the role of the recreational drug Ecstasy in such spiritual experiences reflects a longer tradition in which the use of psychedelic drugs in popular culture has been associated with the pursuit of spiritual and mystical experience (see, e.g., Leary, 1998; www.ecstasy.com, 2003; www.hyperreal.org, 2003). In the same way that religious practices of prayer and worship can serve as media for religious experience, so arguably certain forms of popular culture can function as means of encountering transcendence.

Whilst there is a growing literature arguing that popular culture serves religious functions in contemporary society, it is, as ever, important to maintain a critical scrutiny in relation to these claims. There may well be considerable validity in claiming that electronic and print media provide much of the myths and symbols from which we make sense of our lives. Indeed some writers come close to advancing such claims as incontrovertible truth (see, e.g., Beaudoin, 1998; Herrmann, 2003). Establishing the extent to which popular culture does indeed serve social, existential/hermeneutical, and transcendent functions, however, will require much more detailed research into the ways in which individuals/fans and groups/audiences make use of popular culture in their day-to-day lives.[12] Indeed empirical research into the ways in which people engage with popular cultural texts and resources may suggest a complex set of factors that shape the ways in which popular culture does serve religious functions. For example, Linderman and Lovheim's (2003) empirical study of two on-line discussion groups suggests that whilst such groups may function in ways that reinforce certain values and beliefs, the extent to which this happens will depend on how safe or accepted a particular individual feels within that community. Popular culture may indeed serve certain religious functions within contemporary society, but we still need to develop clearer understandings of the ways and extent to which this happens.

## missiological engagements with popular culture

A third approach to the theological and religious study of popular culture arises more specifically out of the life and thought of the Christian Church in Western society. The notion of premodern Western society as "Christendom," in which Christianity formed the all-embracing framework within which people understood their lives, oversimplifies the complex pluralism of beliefs that existed even in premodern times. The sense of the West as fundamentally Christian, however, has been a powerful concept and even persists today in some of the rhetoric surrounding the "clash of civilizations" between Islam and the West.

The idea of Western society as fundamentally Christian was an influential one in the development of missionary activity by the European Church in the eighteenth and nineteenth centuries. Initially, mission was understood as a process of sending Western missionaries out to Africa, Asia and Latin America to bring the Gospel to non-Christian cultures. As the twentieth century has progressed, however, the Church was increasingly confronted by the secularization and "de-Christianization" of Western society, as well as the development of a much greater pluralism of religious beliefs in Europe and North America (Bruce, 1995; Schreiter, 1997, pp.90ff.). Where as missiology had traditionally been understood as the study of how to relate Christian belief and practice to non-Western cultures, there is now an increasing interest in the notion of a missiology for Western culture. For if Western culture is no longer fundamentally oriented around the concepts and practices of Christian faith, then this raises questions for the Western Church as to how it relates to the post-Christian culture within which it now finds itself.

Interest in developing a missiology for Western culture has led to a growing number of books and articles that offer analyses of the nature and dynamics of contemporary Western culture and reflect on the implications of these for Christian belief and practice (see, e.g., Tomlinson, 1994; Riddell et al., 2000; Drane, 2000; McLaren, 2002). Some writers exploring a missiology for Western culture have suggested the need for changing church structures or indeed the very concept of what "church" is, in order to allow for a more constructive engagement between Christian belief and contemporary Western culture (Hunermann, 2001; Ward, 2002). The influential missiologist David Bosch (1995, pp.27ff.) has also argued for the importance of Western Christians being overtly committed to God's in-breaking reign of justice, peace, and reconciliation, and of being able to engage critically with the non-Christian worldviews offered within contemporary culture.

Within this wider discussion about how the Church can relate appropriately to Western culture, there has also been increasing interest in how Christians should relate to different forms of popular culture. The literature in this field generally adopts two different views of popular culture. One approach tends to regard popular culture with suspicion as a potentially dangerous source of beliefs, values, and practices that are antithetical to Christian faith. The other tends to view popular culture more positively as a medium that can even help to promote new and creative understandings of Christian faith.

The first of these approaches is typically based on a conservative (often Protestant) theology and missiology that makes clear distinctions between "Christ" and "culture," and sees all human culture as inherently flawed and in need of divine transformation (see, e.g., Newbigin, 1983, 1986; Lingenfelter, 1992). At the same time, though, writers adopting this approach often see culture and the arts as a medium through which the truth and creativity given to us by God can potentially find expression. A critical approach to contemporary culture, from this perspective, does not therefore entail withdrawing entirely from all forms of popular culture, but involves thinking critically about whether a particular aspect of culture reflects God's truth and goodness or not (see Romanowski, 2001).

This approach is exemplified in Brian Godawa's (2002) book *Hollywood Worldviews*. In this book, Godawa argues that film is a significant source of cultural myths, and that through these myths we are presented with particular understandings of what it means to experience redemption in life. Godawa describes film as therefore presenting its audiences with particular "worldviews" (understandings of good, evil, health, salvation, etc.) that can be compared with the distinctive and true worldview offered by the Christian faith. Godawa is therefore interested in how films perpetuate specific worldviews, such as existentialism, postmodernism, or neopaganism, and seeks to critique these from a conservative Evangelical Christian perspective. He also goes on to explore how Christian faith is represented both positively and negatively within contemporary film, and critiques some of the assumptions that perpetuate the negative representations. Godawa's work thus exemplifies a conservative missiology of popular culture which does not reject all forms of art

and culture out-of-hand, but which seeks to critique popular culture in relation to certain conservative theological and cultural assumptions.

This approach contrasts with a more positive view of popular culture that
is exemplified by the work of the young Catholic theologian, Tom Beaudoin.
In his book, *Virtual Faith*, Beaudoin (1998) argues that popular culture has
served as the primary medium through which a new generation of Americans
have made sense of their lives. As members of "Generation X" became disillusioned with traditional sources of meaning and authority such as the State,
the educational system, the family, and the Church, so popular culture
became the "surrogate clergy" that guided and formed this generation (1998,
p.21).[13] Thus, where traditional religious symbols, concepts, and practices
failed to engage this generation, film, TV, popular music, computer games,
the internet, books, and fashion stepped in to fill the gap.

Rather than viewing this reliance on popular culture in a negative way,
Beaudoin argues that popular culture can have a valid and healthy role in
shaping and expressing people's religious quests. He goes on to suggest that a
serious theological engagement with the meanings of contemporary popular
culture could itself be a transformative experience for the wider Church. He
proposes the idea of the "sensus infidelium" (the wisdom of the unfaithful)
to suggest that "people (or forms of popular culture) who profess to know little
or nothing about the religious may indeed form, inform, or transform religious meaning for people of faith" (1998, p.34). Beaudoin notes that serious
missiological engagement with the cultures of the developing world led to the
emergence of Third World theologies that have given new insights into the
meaning of the Christian faith and tradition. In the same vein, he argues,
Western Christianity could also be renewed and transformed if it listened seriously to the aspirations, concerns, and struggles expressed through contemporary Western popular culture.

Falling between these two approaches is a growing body of popular Christian literature that argues that particular forms of popular culture mediate fundamental religious truths. Writers such as Connie Neal (2002) and Francis
Bridger (2002) have, for example, proposed that the Harry Potter books and
films constructively deal with important spiritual and moral themes, and a
similar case has been by Mark Pinsky (2001) in relation to *The Simpsons*.
Although these writers are often themselves from conservative religious back-
grounds,[14] they typically wish to distance themselves from the suspicion of
popular culture that can sometimes characterize conservative theologies and
missiologies. At the same time, however, this kind of literature tends to offer
positive accounts of popular cultural texts such as Harry Potter or *The Simpsons* precisely because they are read as supporting certain core Christian

beliefs or values. Beaudoin's notion that a serious missiological engagement with popular culture could transform Christian theology and practice is thus a more radical position than that of many of these writers. For, in contrast to Beaudoin's interest in the potential renewal of Western Christianity, this kind of literature is more typically concerned with reassuring religious audiences about the safety and validity of certain types of popular culture.

This interest in developing critical missiological engagements with Western popular culture has thus stimulated a considerable debate and literature within the Christian Church. The fundamental issues at stake here are concerned with how the Church and individual Christians should relate to popular culture. Are there certain forms of popular culture that need to be avoided or heavily critiqued from a Christian perspective? Or is it, in fact, possible to find healthy spiritual and religious stimulation from some forms of popular culture? Underpinning this debate are certain theological assumptions about the nature of goodness and truth. Occasionally these assumptions are subjected to critical scrutiny, but more commonly within this type of study of popular culture, these theological assumptions form the starting point on which popular culture is then subsequently evaluated. This is somewhat different to the final approach to the theological study of popular culture that we shall consider here, in which popular culture is used as a vehicle for reflecting on theological understandings of God, the world, and the meaning of our existence. It is to this final approach that we shall now turn.

## using the texts and practices of popular culture as material for theological reflection

Defining theology can be as complex a task as defining "religion" or "popular culture," and the emergence of a range of contextual, liberation, and post-Christian theologies since the latter part of the twentieth century has further demonstrated the wide range of forms that this discipline can take (see, e.g., Ford, 2004). In this book, I will work with a broad definition of theology as the process of seeking normative answers to questions of truth, goodness, evil, suffering, redemption, and beauty in the context of particular social and cultural situations. The breadth of this definition (which will be discussed in more detail in chapter 5) is aimed at including the wide range of people who find themselves involved in the study of academic theology today, a group that includes not only people with particular religious commitments (such as Christians, Jews, and Muslims) but also increasing numbers of people working from post-Christian or humanist perspectives. Whilst the way in which I talk about theology as a discipline in this book is intended to be as inclusive as possible, it is also realistic to recognize that "theology" is still primarily conducted by people with religious (most often Christian) commitments or who are living and working in the context of particular church or faith communities. In practice, then, theology tends to be a discipline concerned with how particular religious traditions can be related issues of truth, goodness, evil, suffering, redemption, and beauty in the contemporary world.

If we understand theology as the exploration of these kinds of questions in relation to particular religious beliefs and traditions, then it is clear that a growing number of writers are using texts and practices from popular culture as a focus for such reflection. This approach to theological reflection typically involves a critical dialogue between a particular religious text or theological concept and a specific aspect of popular culture. Through this process of critical conversation between popular culture and theological texts and concepts, writers have thus sought to use popular culture as a means of exploring issues including the nature of God, the possibility of meaning in life, the nature of sin and evil, and the nature of redemption.

There is a particularly well-established literature of this style of theological reflection in relation to film (see, e.g., Marsh and Ortiz, 1997). Indeed Margaret Miles (1996) suggests that film is an important focus for theological reflection precisely because films are an important cultural medium through which contemporary issues and concerns are explored. Some writers, notably David Jasper (1997), have questioned whether popular film is simply too formulaic and superficial to serve as a serious focus for theological reflection. But the wider trend is for theologians to focus on popular Hollywood films rather than art-house movies as the focus for their work.

Within this approach to the theological study of popular culture, the notion of dialogue is a very important one. This concept implies that the popular cultural text or practice needs to be taken seriously on its own terms (i.e., it's own "voice" needs to be heard) in order for a proper conversation between theology and popular culture to take place. As Robert Johnston puts it in relation to film:

> the danger of theological imperialism is high enough in practice that I would argue that [Christian] moviegoers should first view a movie on its own terms before entering into theological dialogue with it . . . To give movie viewing this epistemological priority in the dialogue between film and theology – to judge it advisable to first look at a movie on its own terms and let the images themselves suggest meaning and direction – is not to make theology of secondary importance . . . But such theologizing should follow, not precede, the aesthetic experience. (Johnston, 2000, p.49)

An adequate dialogue between theology and popular culture thus requires what Michael Dyson (2001, p.118) has referred to as an "ethical patience," in which the theologian does not make hasty judgments about what they find tasteful or distasteful, or try to impose their pre-existing concepts on to popular culture. One example of the latter are books and articles that attempt to identify "Christ-figures" in contemporary film (see, e.g., Malone, 1997; Bergeson and Greeley, 2000). To suggest, however, that Edward Scissorhands or the Preacher in *Pale Rider* are "Christ-figures," though, is to impose Christian symbolism on to these movies in a way that fails to hear what those movies are saying on their own terms. Serious theological reflection on popular culture goes beyond the superficial identification of religious themes and symbolism within it to a more substantial dialogue between cultural texts and practices and wider theological questions and resources.

Within the more substantial literature offering theological reflection on popular culture, three particular approaches have so far emerged.

Firstly, there are writers who *explore popular culture in relation to biblical texts*. Robert Jewett (1993, 1999) has sought, for example, to relate Pauline letters from the New Testament to contemporary film. Jewett describes his work as an attempt to establish an "interpretative arch" between film and biblical text in which a mutual dialogue can take place between the questions and concerns of contemporary culture and the questions and concerns of the first-century Church. Whilst Jewett recognizes the importance of listening seriously to the perspectives offered within contemporary film, he is also clear that he ultimately gives priority to insights that emerge out of the biblical text. This enables him, for example, to argue that the film *Amadeus* exemplifies Pauline notions of sin (Jewett, 1993, pp.31ff.) or to critique the notion of vengeance offered within the film *Pale Rider* (Jewett, 2000).

A different approach to studying popular culture in relation to the biblical text has been developed by Larry Kreitzer (1993, 1994, 2002). Rather than reading contemporary film in the light of biblical texts (as Jewett does), Kreitzer seeks to "reverse the hermeneutical flow" and to read the Bible in the light of contemporary film. Kreitzer thus suggests that a sensitive engagement with the images and meanings of contemporary films can help to stimulate our imaginative and critical engagement with the Bible. For example, Kreitzer (2002, pp.105ff.) notes recent debates amongst biblical scholars about the Synoptic Gospels' account of the crucifixion of Jesus, which began "at the third hour" (i.e., 9 a.m.) and was marked by darkness suddenly falling "on the sixth hour" (i.e., noon). These debates have encompassed discussion about the meaning of this claim about darkness falling. Is it, for example, meant to be a historical claim (for which there is no clear corroborating evidence) or is it meant to be a metaphorical statement about the unfolding struggle between Jesus and the forces of darkness? Kreitzer suggests that attention to a twentieth-century film such as *High Noon* can make us more aware of how narratives can use of images of time, light and darkness to heighten a sense of dramatic tension about an imminent conflict between good and evil. The implication is that through studying the film *High Noon*, we might be better equipped to engage imaginatively with the accounts of Jesus' crucifixion and might avoid getting into relatively fruitless debates about the historicity of specific claims of the Gospel text.

A second approach involves *exploring popular culture in relation to particular theological questions and concepts*. A good example of this approach is Christopher Deacy's (2001) book *Screen Christologies*.[15] A central concern for Deacy is the way in which contemporary films explore issues of redemption. Deacy claims, theologically, that redemption is only possible on the basis of a full and accurate recognition of the nature of the human condition. In the book of Ecclesiastes, for example, the narrator (Qoheleth) offers a detailed account of the arbitrary and apparently meaningless nature of human life. Yet is precisely out of a recognition of the bleak horizons within which we live that some kind of hope or redemption can be found. As Deacy (2001) puts it:

> Indeed, far from suggesting *rejection* of life, let alone self-destruction, Qoheleth affirms that *within* the limits of our knowledge, ability and circumstances . . . once we accept the actuality of death and the finitude of human existence without the illusions which the fear of death so easily generates, then the mind can be redeemed and set free from what amounts to a major source of crippling activity. We can subsequently learn to live authentically within the prescribed limitations and boundaries of our existence. (Deacy, 2001, p.61)

On the basis of this theological understanding of redemption, Deacy offers a critique of a range of contemporary films. He is critical of films such as Frank Capra's classic *It's a Wonderful Life*, which Deacy sees as offering an idealized, inauthentic vision of what human life is really like. By contrast, Deacy identifies the tradition of *film noir* as offering far more adequate, and ultimately redemptive, images of human existence. The *film noir* style (popularized by films such as *The Big Sleep*, *The Maltese Falcon*, and *Double Indemnity*) depicted characters who were morally ambiguous, and who were essentially powerless in the face of the arbitrary and meaningless nature of existence. At their conclusion, such films rarely offered neat resolutions of the dilemmas with which the characters had struggled. Such visions of human life are, argues Deacy, a far more authentic basis on which to begin to build genuinely redemptive responses rather than the escapist fantasies of the more traditional "Hollywood ending." Theological questions about the nature of redemption therefore provide Deacy with a framework for critically evaluating images of life offered through contemporary cinema.

A third style of theological reflection in relation to popular culture is to *explore popular culture as a source of methods for doing theology.* Anthony Pinn (1995, pp.113ff., 2000) has, for example, suggested that in the black musical traditions of blues and rap it is possible to identify a theological method of "nitty gritty hermeneutics." By this, Pinn means that it is possible within these musical genres to identify an approach to interpreting life which is committed to "telling it like it is" in the face of a hostile world. Furthermore, this "nitty gritty hermeneutics" is concerned with developing a full and honest insight of the world, even though this might mean challenging more romanticized images or unsettling existing social conventions. Such an approach to thinking about life remains important in the lives of black communities in America which continue to be blighted by racist and unjust social structures. Whilst Pinn acknowledges that rap music has not always offered the constructive social and cultural criticism that a "nitty gritty hermeneutics" should aim for, he argues that rappers still provide a number of examples of a commitment to "telling it like it is." As such, Pinn argues, theologians may have useful lessons to learn about how to engage in their own work from such examples.

Robert Beckford (1998, pp.115ff.) has also developed a similar argument in relation to the music of Bob Marley, in which he proposes that Marley's work offers important insights into what it means to undertake black liberation theology. Marley's music demonstrated his commitment to using his own experience of oppression to interpret the world, his commitment to social and psychological liberation, and his commitment to a particular discourse and cultural form (reggae music) to develop liberatory ideas and images. Marley's interpretation of the Bible was also fundamentally guided by his experience of oppression and commitment to liberation. Whilst Marley was clearly not a Christian theologian in any orthodox sense, Beckford argues that the commitments that shaped his music offer a useful guide for those who want to undertake black liberation theology. Again, popular culture can be read as providing models and methods for how theologians might conduct their own work.

## conclusion

In this chapter we have briefly noted four different approaches to the study of popular culture that have been developed by theologians and religious scholars. Arguably one of the most important questions that any theological or religious study of popular culture must face is "so what?" There are plenty of articles and books that I have chosen not to discuss in this chapter which do little to dispel the notion that such study is essentially a "lark" or the "kinky side-interest of a scholar who should really be doing something else" (Miles, 1996, p.ix). Such literature can at times struggle to reach beyond banal observations about the relationship between religion and popular culture which may be of personal interest to the author but have little impact on wider cultural analysis or criticism.

The four approaches to the religious and theological study of popular culture that I have described in this chapter do have the potential, however, to make a serious contribution to the academic, cultural, and religious life of Western society. Through studying the relationship between contemporary religion and the environments, practices, and resources of everyday life, we can develop a clearer understanding of how religion is practiced and perceived today. Analyzing the possible religious functions of popular culture can help us to understand more about the nature of life in the contemporary world and to think critically about the resources that popular culture offers us in our search for belonging, meaning, and transcendence. Continued work on missiological responses to popular culture may help faith communities to relate to contemporary society in thoughtful and constructive ways. Using popular culture as a medium for theological reflection can also provide an important means of exploring essential questions about our existence in ways that connect with the symbols, concepts, and concerns of contemporary culture. Each of these approaches, when undertaken in a reflective and rigorous way, has the potential to be able to give a confident and robust answer to the question, "so what?"

Identifying these four approaches can therefore help us to understand the range of interests and concerns that people bring to the study of theology, religion, and popular culture, as well as the potential value of this kind of study. In the latter part of this book, we will look at particular methodological issues that specifically relate to the theological study of popular culture. Before going to look in more detail at how we might engage in the theological study of popular culture, it will be important to examine how wider theories and debates in popular culture studies can provide an important framework for such theological analysis. In the next couple of chapters, then, we will examine firstly how theories of electronic media and consumer culture can help us to analyze contemporary forms of popular culture (chapter 3), before going on to examine wider debates in the critical evaluation of popular culture (chapter 4).

# Chapter 3

# machines, tvs, and shopping: the shape of everyday life in contemporary western society

## introduction

In chapter 1 I suggested that a productive way of thinking about popular culture may be to see it in terms of the environment, resources, and practices of everyday life. This raises the question of what is distinctive about the environment, resources, and practices of everyday life in our contemporary world. A wide range of academic disciplines seek to examine this question, including anthropology, cultural and communication studies, geography, political science, social psychology, and sociology. If those involved in theology and religious studies are to offer serious analyses and critiques of contemporary popular culture, it is clearly important for these to be informed by relevant concepts and debates from this wider range of disciplines.

In this chapter, we will think about two areas that social and cultural commentators have identified as particularly significant for analyzing our everyday life, namely the specific roles that both electronic media and consumption play in our lives today. These are simply two areas that can be focused on as significant aspects of the practice of contemporary everyday life – we could equally focus on issues such as changing patterns in marital and family networks, developments in contemporary urbanization, or the emerging forms of global economy. Both electronic media and consumer culture play particularly significant roles, however, in relation to specifically theological and religious concerns such as the construction of communities, identities, values, and beliefs. As we shall discover towards the end of this chapter, electronic media and consumer culture are also intertwined within the structures and processes of global capitalism in a way that raises wider cultural, political, and economic questions about what promotes or hinders human well-being in the contemporary world.

One of the dangers of this kind of social and cultural analysis is that there can be an assumption that we are living in an age that is wholly different to any other in history. Arguably the widespread use of the terms "postmodernism" and "postmodernity" over the past twenty years may have contributed to this impression, as do claims that we are living in a new "digital age" or in a new form of "consumer culture" radically different to the society that preceded it (Lyon, 1994; Lury, 1996; Briggs and Burke, 2002). The reality is more complex than this, however. Whilst technological change would make certain aspects of our existence unrecognizable to those who lived only a century ago, there are other aspects bound up with this new technology that have closer links to older ways of thinking and acting. The practice of presenting one's thoughts and feelings in written form in internet dating has some similarities, for example, with the practice of courtship by letter that would have been more common in some social groups in previous centuries. When discussing the kind of broad social changes that we are covering in this chapter, then, the challenge is to avoid getting caught up too much in rhetoric about the novelty of our age or in broad generalizations about the significance of such changes. Rather we should aim to keep as clear perspective as possible on what these social changes really do mean in our day-to-day lives and how they relate to longer historical trends and processes.

## the coming of the machine age

Although our focus in this chapter is primarily on electronic media and consumption, it is important to recognize that these have become important features of everyday life precisely because of new technologies of production that have been developed over the past two hundred years. The Industrial Revolution, beginning in Britain in the eighteenth century, was a slow and complex process. There was no overnight social transformation from an economy based on small manufacturers using hand methods of production to large-scale factory-based production using new technology. Rather the eighteenth and nineteenth centuries saw the growth of factories alongside the persistence of smaller, local manufacturers whose specialist skills remained important for various industries (see, Berg, 1994; Carnevali, 2003). By the late nineteenth century, however, industrial development in the Western world

Figure 3.1   A line of Model T automobiles awaiting further assembly at the Highland Park Ford Plant in Michigan. This production line was the first moving assembly line in the world and represented a watershed in the rapid production of mass consumer goods (© Corbis).

had reached a point where an increasing number of goods were being produced for consumption for a wider population (Slater, 1997).

As the twentieth century dawned, there was an increased awareness of the importance that industrial forms of mass production could have in transforming everyday life. In 1913, Ford started to produce its Model T car for the first time using a moving assembly line, and this became a powerful example of how new technologies of production could lead to greater affordability for new consumer goods (Woodham, 1997).

Although sales of Ford cars had been overtaken by those of General Motors by the 1920s (Misa, 1995, p.227), Henry Ford became a cultural icon through his belief in social progress through new technologies of mass production. Indeed, the term "Fordism" was coined to capture this social philosophy, and the notion of a "Fordist" society was used to refer to the idea of an economy increasingly organized around large-scale industrial production for a mass population. "Fordism" also became associated with the thought of the American engineer, Frederic Taylor, who became famous for his theories of manufacturing techniques which he set out in his book *The Principles of Scientific Management* (Taylor, 1911). Taylor argued that industrial output could be much more efficient and cost-effective if the factory was run as a "human managing machine," with each worker having a specified role, and a set time to achieve that role in the production process (Misa, 1995). The twin philosophies of "Fordism" and "Taylorism" thus came to represent a new belief in the possibility of a transformed society and economy through rational planning and the use of machine-based technologies of mass production.

By the early decades of the twentieth century, then, there was an increasing attempt in industrialized societies to come to terms with what it meant to live in a "machine age" (see, e.g., Woodham, 1997, pp.29ff.). Many saw the machine age as a new opportunity to break with unhelpful traditions of the past, and as a chance to build healthier and more egalitarian societies based on new technologies. Indeed this was a key principle of the movement in design and architecture that became known as "modernism," and which was associated with figures such as Le Corbusier, Alvar Aalto, the Dutch De Stijl group and Frank Lloyd Wright. Across Europe, there was evidence of the attempt to embrace the implications of the machine age. The Deutsche Werkebund (a leading collective of German designers) engaged in a public debate in 1914 about whether design should primarily be a process of the artistic expression of the individual designer or whether design should orient itself more to what could be achieved through industrial methods of mass production (Pevsner, 1968). Whilst not wholly conclusive, this debate tended to move German design more in the direction of working with techniques of mass production, and this emphasis took clearer shape with the formation of the seminal Bauhaus Institute in 1919. Elsewhere, in postrevolutionary Russia, the Constructivist school of design explored how geometric symbols could be used as cultural images and icons for a new age. Whilst in Italy, the Futurist movement embraced machine technology as offering an opportunity for a new virile and empowered humanity – even to the extent of celebrating new technologies of armed conflict as a new level of human evolution.

The movement into the "machine age" was not universally welcomed, however, with artists and cultural commentators raising significant objections. Ideas of mass production were closely tied, for example, to the ideas of mass culture that were the source of such concern to writers like Clement Greenberg, F.R. Leavis, and Dwight McDonald. Aldous Huxley's (1932) novel *Brave New World* famously painted a picture of a dystopian future society in which Fordism was the new religion, and in which the maintenance of a ratio-

Figure 3.2  The Terminator films are a recent example of science-fiction's explo-ration of anxiety about the threat to humanity posed by powerful and intelligent machines (still from *Terminator 3: The Rise of the Machines*, © Columbia Films).

nally ordered society based on the consumption of mass produced goods had come to displace authentic human experiences and relationships. Fritz Lang's pioneering science-fiction film, *Metropolis*, first shown in 1927, also showed the instability of a society in which the masses are simply the exploited drones of "Taylorized" systems of production. *Metropolis* also explored the theme of the threat of the machine that becomes conscious and which can take human form, and which can act in destructive ways towards humanity. This anxiety about humanity being harmed or controlled by machines continues to be a theme in popular films, as has been seen more recently in the *Terminator* and *Matrix* trilogies (see, e.g., French, 1996; Graham, 2002).

Thus, whilst being the focus of both celebration and concern, the move towards greater industrialization and reliance on machine technologies has been one of the major stories of recent Western and global history.[1] This trend has had a profoundly significant impact on the everyday lives of many people, particularly when it became possible for new technologies of communication, such as telephones, radios, and televisions to be mass produced and thus become more easily accessible in Western society. The growth of industrial output from the end of the nineteenth century onwards also produced an increasingly wide selection of household goods and other consumables for the individual to buy. In the next sections of this chapter, we will turn our attention to the implications of the increasing accessibility and use of these new electronic media, as well as the growing experience of Western society as a "consumer culture."

## electronic media and everyday life

My experience of everyday life is very much bound up with electronic media. I listen to the radio as I drive in to work and my mood is likely to be effected by whether I love or am bored by the music I'm listening to, or whether I'm amused or irritated by the banter between the DJ and her production team. When I arrive at work, I check my emails – both on my work and personal email accounts. I'm in email contact with students, colleagues, and friends who not only live locally to me in Birmingham, but who are spread across Britain and across other parts of the world. Through the day, I'll check the latest digest of messages of an email discussion group that I belong to for supporters of one of the local soccer teams, and I may well also check out the "blog" of a friend of mine who lives in New York. Through the day I will speak to people on the telephone, and will text friends on my mobile phone about arrangements that we're making for going out or just to check how they are. When I get home, I will certainly listen to some of my CD collection and may well spend time watching a program on one of the 40 cable television channels that I have access to. "The Simpsons" remains a particular favorite, if I can get home early enough, and keeping up with this also gives me a point of conversation with my young nieces who live in another part of Britain, but who are also avid watchers of the show. Some days I might also get the video games console out, and try with usually limited success to get a reasonable score on the cricket game that I play on it. Before bed, I might check my email again, surf the net, or just spend time watching a news program on TV.

Now, none of these revelations about my life are particularly unusual. But they do provide some illustration about how electronic media such as telephones (including mobile phones), televisions, radio, video games, computers, and the internet play an integral part in the way in which contemporary daily life can be structured and acted out. Since the invention of electric methods of telegraphy in the mid-nineteenth century, there has been a significant growth in the range and accessibility of electronic media in the everyday lives of many people in Western society (see table 3.1).

As these new media technologies have developed and spread, new disciplines have developed to try to make sense of their significance within society (Briggs and Burke, 2002). Media studies has emerged as an academic specialism in its own right, and has generated its own leading thinkers (see, e.g., O'Sullivan and Jewkes, 1997; Mackay and O'Sullivan, 1999). Perhaps most famous of these has been Marshall McLuhan who claimed that the world had now become a "global village" linked by electronic media which would transform our understanding of ourselves and our environment (see, e.g., McLuhan and Powers, 1989).

The work of writers such as McLuhan represents part of a much larger body of literature by commentators on the effects that the growth of electronic media have had on human society. A recent example of this can be found in Robert Putnam's (2000) best-selling sociological treatise *Bowling Alone: The Collapse and Revival of American Community*. Putnam provides a substantial range of sociological data that indicates that from the 1970s onwards, there has been a significant decline in Americans' participation in civic, social, and communal organizations from political parties, to churches, voluntary organizations, and bowling leagues. He argues that this trend has negative implications for American society as the "social capital" that is accumulated through belonging to such groups has a wide range of beneficial effects both for the individuals involved and for society as a whole. In attempting to trace the reasons for this withdrawal from public and communal activities, Putnam (2000, pp.216–46) suggests that one of the significant factors associated with it has been an increasing dependence amongst Americans upon television as a medium of entertainment. He observes that "it is precisely those Americans most marked by this dependence on televised entertainment who were most likely to have dropped out of civic and social life – who spent less time with friends, were less involved in community organizations, and were less likely

Table 3.1  Significant dates in the development of electronic and other related media

| | |
|---|---|
| 1837 | Invention of the electric telegraph |
| 1838 | Opening of 13-mile long telegraph line between Paddington and West Drayton in London |
| 1846 | Siemens develop insulation for electric wiring |
| 1849 | Telegraph link built between Berlin and Frankfurt |
| 1865 | Telegraph cable successfully laid between America and Britain |
| 1876 | Alexander Graham Bell invents the telephone |
| 1877 | Edison invents the phonograph, one of the world's first medium for sound recording |
| 1878 | First American telephone exchange built in New Haven |
| 1888 | Berliner invents the gramophone |
| 1896 | Marconi begins to publicize his work with wireless technology in London |
| 1896 | Lumière brothers give the first public showing of a film |
| 1901 | Marconi transmits wireless telegraphy messages across the Atlantic |
| 1903 | First world congress on wireless telegraphy |
| 1903 | A message from President Roosevelt circles the world in nine and a half minutes via Pacific Cable |
| 1905 | Double-sided vinyl disks for the gramophone are released |
| 1906 | Release of the first animated cartoon and the first full length feature film, *The History of the Kelly Gang* |
| 1907 | First film production companies set up in Hollywood |
| 1909 | First film newsreels produced in America |
| 1910 | Opening of the first 5000-seater cinema, the Gaumont Palace, in Paris |
| 1910 | Radio receivers in kit form are put on sale to the American public |
| 1914 | First full-length color feature film, *The World, the Flesh, and the Devil* was released in Britain |
| 1915 | Musical recital broadcast from Britain is received by listeners across Europe |
| 1919 | National Association of the Motion Picture Industry in America agrees to submit films for censorship |
| 1919 | Radio Corporation of America founded |
| 1920 | British Board of Film Censors established |
| 1921 | First full-length feature film with sound, *Dream Street*, produced in America |
| 1923 | License granted to the British Broadcasting Corporation |
| 1926 | John Logie Baird demonstrates the television in London |
| 1927 | The BBC's broadcast of the Grand National horse race becomes the world's first outdoor sports broadcast |
| 1927 | Transatlantic wire and wireless telephone service set up |
| 1928 | Disney produce the first Mickey Mouse cartoon, *Steamboat* |
| 1928 | Baird transmits television pictures from London to New York |

Table 3.1 *Continued*

| | |
|---|---|
| 1929 | A radio advertising campaign for Lucky Strike cigarettes produces significantly increased sales and demonstrates the potential of advertising through radio |
| 1929 | First Oscars ceremony held in America |
| 1930 | Baird factory made television set marketed in Britain |
| 1930 | Hays cinema code agreed in America |
| 1931 | First regular television broadcasts made in America |
| 1935 | First use of stereo sound in cinema for the film *Napoleon Bonaparte* |
| 1936 | BBC television begins broadcasting |
| 1937 | Magnetic tape recorder marketed by AEG/Telefunken in Germany |
| 1938 | Orson Welles' radio broadcast of *The War of the Worlds* causes widespread panic in America as people mistake it for a live news broadcast |
| 1938 | First television games show broadcast in Britain |
| 1939 | Frank Sinatra's record "All or Nothing at All" sells one million copies |
| 1945 | First album chart published in America |
| 1946 | Jukeboxes start to become popular in America |
| 1947 | Transistor radio developed by Bardeen, Brattain, and Shockley |
| 1948 | Long-play records and 45 rpm singles produced in America |
| 1952 | IBM produce their first computers |
| 1953 | Twentieth-Century Fox move production to Cinemascope, a system which makes use of wide curved screens and stereo sound |
| 1954 | Texas Instruments begin to sell "electronic chips" |
| 1954 | Victor market prerecorded audio tapes for the first time in America |
| 1955 | Sony market the world's first mass-produced transistor radio |
| 1958 | Income from television advertising exceeds income from press advertising for the first time in Britain |
| 1958 | Stereo vinyl records produced |
| 1959 | The Explorer VI spacecraft takes the first television pictures of Earth from space |
| 1962 | Live satellite television broadcast made from America |
| 1963 | Olsen's "mini-computer" goes on sale in America |
| 1964 | World's first discotheque, "Whisky-a-Go-Go" opens in Los Angeles |
| 1965 | First "action replays" shown on American television |
| 1966 | An estimated world audience of 400 million people watch the televising of the football World Cup finals held in Britain |
| 1969 | British television broadcasters BBC and ITV begin regular color broadcasts |
| 1969 | Sony launch videotape cassettes |

Table 3.1 *Continued*

| | |
|---|---|
| 1971 | ARPANET, a computer communication network and forerunner of the internet, begins operating from University of California Los Angeles. By 1975, this network has 2000 users |
| 1972 | Home video cassette recorders first put on sale to the public |
| 1972 | Moog synthesizer patented |
| 1974 | One of the first basic microprocessor-based games for television, "Pong," is produced in America |
| 1975 | Teletext, a television-based text information service, developed in Britain |
| 1975 | The world's first computer shop opens in Los Angeles |
| 1976 | Apple Corporation founded |
| 1979 | Sony launch the Walkman personal cassette player |
| 1980 | Atari become one of the world's leading producers of personal computers, video games consoles, and associated games, with their sales reaching $100 million |
| 1981 | Ruling in America that the home taping of broadcast signals did not constitute a breach of copyright |
| 1981 | Philips market the first compact disk player |
| 1983 | First mobile telephone system licensed in America, and despite poor reception there are one million Americans using cellular phones by 1989 |
| 1984 | Camcorders made available on sale to the public |
| 1986 | Microsoft becomes a public company |
| 1989 | Merger of Time Inc. and Warner Brothers |
| 1994 | Netscape founded |
| 1995 | Merger of CNN and Time/Warner |
| 2000 | Mobile phone sales peak in Britain: between April and June, three and a half million mobile phones are sold at a rate of one every two seconds |
| 2000 | Merger of AOL with Time/Warner |
| 2000 | More than 20% of the British population has access to the internet |
| 2000 | Microsoft fight legal battle against anti-Trust law break up of the company |
| 2001 | Merger of Disney and Fox |
| 2002 | Napster forced to introduce membership charge for its on-line musical exchange service by record production companies after its software is downloaded 57 million times by users. |
| 2003 | New wave of mobile phones marketed which combine internet access with picture messaging, music downloads, and access to gaming networks. |
| 2004 | Annual revenue for computer games ($5.5 bn) exceeds that for Hollywood films ($5.2 bn) for the first time. |

*Source*: Information drawn from Maltby, 1989, and Briggs and Burke, 2002

to participate in public affairs" (Putnam, 2000, p.246). Later, Putnam claims that television might account for as much of 25% of the social withdrawal evident in American communities since the 1970s; though the precise grounds for this kind of statistical claim are somewhat unclear (2000, p.283).

Now one of the traps that Putnam seems very close to falling into here is that of "technological determinism." This is the idea that technology *causes* certain effects to happen in the societies in which they are used, or in other words, that technology determines the nature of the society and culture within which it is used.[2] The relationship between technology and society is arguably far more complex than this, however. Manuel Castells (1996, pp.5ff.) observes, for example, that whilst technology undoubtedly influences what activities are possible within a given society, society also has a significant role in determining what technologies are developed and how those technologies are used. Raymond Williams similarly argues that it is too simplistic to imagine that television was invented in a social and cultural vacuum and that once invented it had a significant effect on the societies in which it was used. Rather, Williams suggests, the emergence of modern, industrialized societies was dependent on people being able to form into small, self-contained households that could move to different areas when changes in company location or the job market required this. The invention and dissemination of television as a medium of mass entertainment was an ideal accompaniment to the formation of what Williams (1999, p.54) refers to as the "mobile" and "privatized" home. Television was not therefore an abstract invention that subsequently shaped society, but a piece of technology that fitted in with longer social trends of industrialization and modernization that were the deeper causes of social change. Similarly it would be inaccurate to suggest that the emergence of the internet in the late twentieth century caused economic and cultural globalization. Rather the popularity of the internet can be seen in the context of a much wider social and cultural trends towards the formation of transnational networks of administration, trade, and communication that remains dominated by a relatively small cultural elite (see Castells, 1996, p.13).

It is important to be cautious, then, about assuming that technology simply causes social change. To do so risks missing the wider social and cultural trends that have led to this technology being nurtured and popularized in the first place. Having acknowledged this, however, there are certain social changes that appear to be associated with the growth of electronic media over the past hundred and fifty years. The changes that we will focus on particularly here concern our experience of community and social relations,[3] and can be thought about in terms of three inter-related issues:

1   Electronic media are associated with processes of "deterritorialization," in which people are less connected to their local communities, customs, and traditions. In premodern and early modern societies, news and entertainment would generally come through face-to-face interaction with people based in, or at least passing through, one's local community. The growing use of electronic media has been associated, however with a shift from seeking news and entertainment within the local community to receiving these within the home (the "privatization of leisure"). As people turn more to electronic media for news and entertainment, this effects their sense of relationship to their local community (see Tomlinson, 1999; Morley, 2000). Electronic media such as television, radio, film, and the internet are characterized by a separation of the contexts of the producer and their audience (Thompson, 1999). In other words, media producers need no longer come from the same geographical area or social and cultural context as their audiences. In fact, audiences will now often be exposed to media content that is produced in completely different parts of the world to where they themselves live. This can have a transforming effect on people's understanding of *place* in the world, as they no longer simply associate with, or are informed by, their local community. One of the potential consequences is that people's sense of the world is no longer shaped simply by the ideas, traditions, and customs that have been important in their local communities. This can lead to a loosening up of attitudes, as previously held certainties about the world become challenged or modified in the light of ideas from other cultures (Meyrowitz, 1999). For example, exposure to media representations of different life-choices available to women can lead some women to question traditions in their local culture that place them in a very fixed and limited social role. Electronic media can therefore be associated with a weakened sense of social bonds with local communities and cultures.

2   Weakening attachment to local communities is mirrored by growing involvement in electronically mediated communities. A weakened sense of connection with one's local community and culture, can also be accompanied by a growing sense of being part of a wider electronically mediated community. This sense of wider social connectedness may reflect an awareness of being part of a larger (sometimes global)[4] audience for media events and entertainments. Or it may involve being part of a more specific network of fans who appreciate particular programs such as *Star Trek, 24, or Buffy: The Vampire Slayer* (see, e.g., Jenkins, 1992; Jindra, 2000). Media producers will, at times, consciously shape their output to encourage this sense of community. In news broadcasts, the use of clips in which members of the public respond to news events are not intended to provide a critical analysis of these

events, but to give viewers a sense of a wider public audience that is responding to the news. At exceptional points of crisis (e.g., the death of Princess Diana, the Oklahoma bombing, 9/11), the media may also present events in a way that encourages the viewer to feel part of wider community that is shocked, confused and grieving (see, e.g., Dayan and Katz, 1992; Turnock, 2000). Internet discussion boards and email discussion lists have become another relatively recent form of electronically-communicated community (see Rheingold, 1999; and especially Campbell, 2003, on the role of internet as a source of religious community). Indeed the growing use of mobile telephones and email mean that social interaction is no longer bound by face-to-face interaction, but may be increasingly taking place through electronic means. As a sense of connection with one's local community weakens, one's sense of social relatedness may therefore be oriented much more to such electronically mediated groups and networks.

3    The concepts, symbols, images, and stories communicated within the "market-place" of electronic media play a growing role in shaping people's personal identities and understanding of the wider world. As people become less dependent on their local communities and cultures, and more absorbed into electronically mediated communities, so the way in which they make sense of life is increasingly shaped through the media content that they consume. Lifestyle television programs can thus act as a resource that people use to think about how they approach their own lives, whether in terms of their cooking, the interior design of their home, their garden, or their relationships. Fictional media entertainment also provides narratives about characters' lives that can be used as a resource for reflecting about one's own experience and aspirations (e.g., in what way do the characters in *Sex in the City* help me to make sense of my own experience of romantic relationships in contemporary urban life?). The media can also be approached as a source of information for contexts that a person might not otherwise experience. Dr Dre has, for example, commented on the popularity of hip-hop amongst white suburban audiences, saying "People in the suburbs, they can't go to the ghetto so they like to hear what's goin' on. Everybody wants to be down" (hooks, 1994, p.152). Indeed electronically mediated entertainment can even become a significant source of communal memories, with, for example, films like *Schindler's List* and *Saving Private Ryan* attempting to offer memorials of the terrible events of the Holocaust and the Second World War. Electronic media (at least within liberal democratic societies, see Postman, 1986, p.87f.) thus becomes a market-place of ideas, symbols, images, and stories from which audiences pick and choose, and draw their own meanings (Hoover, 2003). This can have the effect of "flattening out" these ideas and images,

challenging the notion that any person, idea, or institution should have an especially privileged place in society or can avoid critical scrutiny. Such "flattening out" is evident, for example, in the presence of religious groups on the internet where the construction of religious content into websites means that established institutions like the Catholic Church have no more status or authority than sites for vampire churches or the Holy Church of Moo. Immersion in electronically mediated communities thus entails immersion into an electronically mediated culture that becomes an important resource for how people make sense of themselves and the wider world.

Now these three points are important claims about the social and cultural role of electronic media in contemporary society. It is important, however, not to overstate them or accept them in too simplistic a fashion. Electronic media have not completely detached people from their local communities and traditions. Indeed electronic means of communication may be as much a way of facilitating face-to-face interaction (e.g., by texting a friend about where I will meet them that evening), as a replacement for it.[5] Attempts by media producers to encourage their audiences to think of themselves as united communities can also be resisted by members of those audiences. In his study of audience reaction to television coverage of the days following the death of Princess Diana, Turnock (2000, pp.55ff.) therefore reports that a significant number of his research respondents did not feel part of a wider community united in grief that news broadcasts made frequent references to. Indeed many of his respondents reported that they felt alienated by media reports that claimed that such overwhelming national grief existed.

In addition to this, there is reasonable evidence that people do not simply abandon their local cultural ideas and traditions in the face of ideas or stories that they encounter through electronic media. Rather the way in which people interpret electronic media is shaped by their local cultures and con-texts; see, for example, the work by Liebes and Katz (1993) on the different audience interpretations of the TV soap opera, *Dallas*, in America, Israel, and Japan. There is certainly evidence to suggest that media content can also lead people to modify their local traditions and cultures (see, e.g., Gillespie, 1995; Barker, 1999). But it is more adequate to think about this as a "glocal" process of negotiation between local cultures and electronically mediated ideas and stories, rather than electronic media simply displacing local ideas in straight-forward and homogenous ways.

Whilst it is therefore important not to overstate these claims, it remains useful to acknowledge the growing social and cultural role that electronic media play in contemporary society. Indeed understanding this role is relevant to debates about the religious functions of popular culture that we explored in the previous chapter.

Whilst contemporary community may increasingly be shaped by the technologies and content of electronic media, it is also important to avoid the notion that this is a situation in which a mass media is shaping a mass culture. The very notion of "mass" media can suggest the idea of media being used to convey a single or range of clear messages that shape the "masses" in a uniform way. Whilst such a notion may well have been important both to Nazi propagandists such as Goebbels and for the principles of public service broadcasting that underlay the formation of the BBC, it is an unhelpful concept for understanding electronic media in today's society. Today's electronic media is not a "mass" media, but a highly differentiated media that offers consumers a wide range of choice often based on specialized tastes and interests. As the twentieth-century progressed, so new technologies became available that allowed consumers greater control over what form of entertainment they wanted and when they wanted it – from audio-cassettes, to VCR's, walkmans, DVD, mini-disc, and MP-3 players. The expansion of radio and TV channels also offers consumers a much wider range of options from which to choose. As Francoise Sabbah puts it:

> In sum, the new media determine a segmented, differentiated audience that, although massive in terms of numbers, is no longer a mass audience in terms of simultaneity and uniformity of the message it receives. The new media are no longer mass media in the traditional sense of sending a limited number of messages to a homogenous mass audience. Because of the multiplicity of messages and sources, the audience itself becomes more selective. The targeted audience tends to choose its messages, so deepening its segmentation, enhancing the individual relationship between sender and receiver. (Sabbah, 1985, p.219)

We cannot therefore see the audiences of electronic media as passive recipients of a single, clear message. Rather, as we shall discuss again in chapter 8, the way in which people engage with electronic media and other popular culture resources, is a more complex interaction involving both the limitations of the message conveyed through the medium and the open-ended response of the audience. At the same time, though, an emphasis on the choice, freedom, and autonomy of the consumer of electronic media needs to be counter-balanced by the recognition that electronic media globally is increasingly controlled by a small number of transnational companies (see, e.g., Briggs and Burke, 2002). Whilst audiences may still be free in their responses to the content of electronic media, much of that media is controlled by organizations with extensive social and financial influence.

The past century has therefore seen a process in which electronic media have come to develop an increasingly important place in Western, and global, culture. We have noted here the potential role of such media in constructing our experience of community and in providing stories and symbols that interpret the world in particular ways. In the light of this, there are a range of questions that those involved in theology and religious studies will want to ask about how the media functions, how the media relates to religious traditions and concerns, and what views of the world it presents. In this chapter, though, our attention will now turn to another significant cultural trend of the past century – the emergence of consumer culture.

## "we're s-h-o-p-p-i-n-g"

"We're S-h-o-p-p-i-n-g," sang the Pet Shop Boys on their album "Actually" in 1987. The song satirized the more overtly materialistic direction that Western culture had taken in the 1980s, and that decade has indeed become synonymous with an emphasis on consumption.[6] The emergence of shopping and consumption as important cultural activities has had a much longer history than this, however. Don Slater has suggested, for example, that the roots of Western consumer culture can be seen prior to the Industrial Revolution, in the trading of nonessential items such as coffee, tobacco, and toys. James Axtell (1999) also suggests that, in the same period, a consumer revolution took place amongst Native American Indians in the eastern United States, whose economy was rejuvenated by the high price initially paid for their goods by early European settlers.

By the mid-nineteenth century, department stores were being opened in major cities such as London, New York, and Paris. With these stores came the experience of customers browsing through goods in buildings dedicated to consumption, whose architecture and design was intended to make shopping not simply a necessity but an enjoyable social activity. "Cathedrals of consumption" are therefore not a novelty of recent years, but a phenomenon with a longer social history (Crossick and Jauman, 1999; Ritzer, 1999).

For those people unable to gain access to such stores, mail order offered an alternative means of acquiring consumer goods, or at least of dreaming about what kinds of goods one would like to acquire. By the early part of the twentieth century, mail order catalogues were therefore serving an important

Figure 3.3   The Galeries Lafayette, one of the most famous department stores in Paris, was originally built in 1912. This photograph illustrates the building's Art Nouveau architecture and design that provides a spectacular environment for shopping (© Corbis).

role as means of distributing the new consumer goods being produced by the "Taylorized" factories (Woodham, 1997, pp.15ff.). The twentieth century has subsequently seen a growth in ways in which people can consume, from shopping at local-run stores in their neighborhood, to going to shopping malls and large chain stores, telephone shopping, mail order, cable TV shopping, and shopping through the internet. Shopping plays a key role in contemporary

Western culture now, and it can now be increasingly hard to find public spaces in towns and cities that are not geared in some way towards consumption.

What has the cultural impact of shopping and consumption been on the experience of everyday life, though? There is now a substantial literature to suggest that consumption does not simply enable people to meet their basic needs for food, warmth, security, and shelter, but that it serves a more sophisticated range of cultural functions as well (see, e.g., Glickman, 1999; Lee, 2000). In particular, consumption can be seen as an important way in which people express their personal and social identities, as well as their broader understanding of what it means to live a good and fulfilled life (see, e.g., Featherstone, 1991; Evans et al., 1996; Campbell, 1987; Pavitt, 2000; Lyon, 2000; Bartholomew and Moritz, 2000).

One of the first theorists to argue for the wider social and cultural significance of consumption was Thorstein Veblen. In his book *The Theory of the Leisure Class*, Veblen (1900) argued that the objects that people consume have always had an important cultural function in expressing their identity and social status. He proposed that societies naturally function at a subsistence level, in which individuals produce and consume enough in order to survive, but little more than this. In this kind of subsistence society, if a person has the resources to acquire commodities that go beyond meeting basic needs for nutrition, warmth, protection, and shelter then this acts as a social marker that they have particular significance or status within that society. Thus, if I am able to consume not just food for survival, but to eat the choicest cuts of meat, this is an indication that I have a higher social status than someone who largely subsists on vegetables. Similarly if I am able to acquire and wear clothing that does not simply keep me warm and dry, but which is also colorful or ornately decorated, this also functions as a marker of my social importance.[7]

Veblen argued that in preindustrial societies the ability to consume more than one's basic subsistence needs – what he described as the practice of "conspicuous consumption" – established a fundamental connection between the consumption of commodities and social status and identity. Furthermore, he suggested that, over time, hierarchies of commodities emerged in which particular commodities become associated with higher social status. Thus by buying certain objects (e.g., expensive jewellery) or other consumables (e.g., caviar), which have are both expensive and exclusive, a person conveys that they have a higher standing in terms of social power and wealth than a person who is unable to consume these commodities. Indeed, as Twitchell (1999, pp.13f.) notes, this hierarchy of goods was even reinforced in premodern times by the Church's "sumptuary laws" which established what kinds of commodities were allowed to be consumed by people of each social rank – thus restricting the masses' access to more exclusive goods.[8]

Certain aspects of Veblen's analysis may be questioned. His idea, for example, of relatively stable hierarchies of commodities may have been accurate in describing certain preindustrial or industrial societies, but seems less useful in postindustrial or late modern societies in which there is less consensus about what constitutes "fashion" or "cool" (Featherstone, 1991; Malbon, 1998). Thus, for example, in the context of some forms of hip-hop culture wearing a thick gold chain might be seen as a marker of status and prestige, but in another context, wearing such a chain might appear "showy," uncool, or tasteless.[9] Nevertheless, Veblen's basic argument that the consumption of commodities has a function in constructing and communicating a person's social identity and status is an important one, and underlies much of the subsequent debates about the relationship between consumption and identity.

One of the most influential theorists to have taken up Veblen's work is the French sociologist and cultural critic, Jean Baudrillard. In his book, *The Consumer Society*, Baudrillard (1970/1988) developed a theory of the significance of commodities that blends Veblen's ideas with concepts drawn from Marxism and structuralism. From Marxist thought, Baudrillard drew on the idea of the shift from *use-value* to *exchange-value* in the life of the commodity in capitalist societies. Marx had argued that valuing commodities in relation to money had a transformative effect on the cultural value and use of the commodity (see also Strinati, 1995, pp.57f.). Thus, rather, than having a cultural role and value that is defined purely by its use, the financial valuation of objects meant that commodities were placed in a different and abstract kind of relationship to each other. In terms of *use-value*, there is no relationship, say between an umbrella and a tonne of steel, as these objects have entirely different uses. When umbrellas and steel come to be defined in monetary terms, however, they become part of a whole system of interrelated commodities, in which so many umbrellas have the same *exchange-value* as a tonne of steel. The shift from *use-value* to *exchange-value*, in Marxist terms, thus means that objects are no longer defined primarily by their use but by their financial value and the cultural meaning attached to this value. This movement towards an abstract cultural valuation and meaning of an object was also developed by Marx into a fuller theory of the fetishism of the commodity which we shall return to in the next chapter.

Marxist theory therefore provided one way of explaining how commodities had a cultural meaning that went beyond their simple practical purpose. Baudrillard suggested that commodities could also be seen as having cultural meaning by understanding commodities through the lens of structuralist theory.[10] At the start of the twentieth century, the Swiss linguist Ferdinand de Saussure (1910) proposed a structuralist theory of language. Within this, de Saussure argued that individual words (or "signs") have meaning only because they are part of a larger system of language made up of other contrasting words/signs. The word "blue" thus derives its meaning from the existence of other words such as "yellow," "green," and "red" which help to define what "blue" is and what it is not.[11] Baudrillard suggested that in the same way that the meaning of words derive from the larger system of language in which a word is used, so individual commodities can be understood as having meanings that are shaped by the wider system of commodities of which they are a part. Baudrillard thus talked about the "sign-value" of the commodity, in which the commodity acts as a medium for communicating cultural meaning:

> Consumption is a system of meaning like a language . . . commodities and objects, like words . . . constitute a global, arbitrary and coherent system of signs, a cultural system. . . . Marketing, purchasing, sales, the acquisition of differentiated commodities and object/signs – all of these presently constitute our language, a code with which our entire society communicates and speaks of itself and to itself. (Baudrillard, 1970/1998, p.79)[12]

The range of commodities available within a given society therefore acts as a kind of cultural language. The cultural "meanings" associated with a Volvo car (e.g., safety, security, reliability) are, for example, different to those of a Porsche (conspicuous wealth) or a Citroen 2CV (conspicuous simplicity). By buying certain commodities (e.g., the Volvo rather than the Porsche), I am able to "say" certain things about the kind of person that I am and the kind of lifestyle that I wish to be associated with. In Baudrillard's view, then, commodities do not function simply as objects that satisfy material needs but as signs which convey particular social and cultural meanings. Indeed the American cultural critic James Twitchell has argued that in a consumer culture, commodities are no longer primarily bought for their practical uses as much for the meanings that they convey. Indeed he suggests that "such matters as branding, packaging, fashion, and even the act of shopping itself are now the central meaning-making acts in our . . . world" (Twitchell, 1999, p.14).

The idea that commodities convey cultural meanings has been consciously taken up by those involved in the design, manufacture, and marketing of commodities. Manufacturers are therefore as attentive to the cultural meaning of their products as their physical and practical uses. As one executive of the cosmetics firm Revlon is quoted as saying, "In the factory we make soap; in the market we sell hope" (Evans et al., 1996, p.6).

This awareness of the cultural meanings of commodities is particularly evident in the interest in the late twentieth century in the concept of the "brand" (see Corstjens and Corstjens, 1995; Upshaw, 1995; Klein, 2001). Again, it would be a mistake to imagine that commercial brands have only emerged in recent years. Coca-Cola has been an important brand for much of the twentieth-century, and in Britain, the construction of Odeon cinemas in the 1930s represented the creation of one of the country's first entertainment brand names. However, it is certainly reasonable to claim that widespread commercial interest in the importance of maintaining and developing "brand identity" is a more recent phenomenon (see, e.g., Klein, 2001).

The notion of the "brand" can be understood as the association of a certain set of cultural meanings, values, and aspirations, with a particular brand name or logo. Thus brand names such as Nike and FCUK conjure up certain cultural associations whether the actual commodity is a running shoe, a T-shirt, a basketball or an aftershave (see, e.g., Goldman and Papson, 1998). Thus the FCUK brand, for example, conveys a sense of youthfulness, irreverence, overt sexuality, and cheeky humor. Unsurprisingly, it tends to attract a young customer-base of people who want to be associated with these values and attitudes, or older customers who still wish to identify with youthful attitudes. Awareness of the importance of branding is even increasingly apparent in religious settings where, for example, the UK-based Alpha Course uses a range of advertising techniques to develop its brand image as an accessible and enjoyable introduction to the Christian faith (Hunt, 2001).

By attracting the consumer as much to the values and meanings of a particular brand as to a particular commodity, commercial organizations thus allow themselves a greater measure of flexibility in the commercial marketplace by not becoming too identified with a specific commodity which may become out-of-fashion or be superseded by another newer product. The role of advertising, and other related strategies (including the physical design and packaging of commodities), in the development of brand identity remains a significant area of interest for those involved in the production and selling of consumer goods (see, e.g., Pavitt, 2000.)[13]

Given that manufacturers and retailers are now consciously trying to convey certain cultural messages through their particular brands and products, it becomes even clearer how shopping can become a cultural statement of one's identity and "lifestyle." As Mike Featherstone (1991) puts it:

Rather than unreflexively adopting a lifestyle, through tradition or habit, the new heroes of consumer culture make lifestyle a life project and display their individuality and sense of style in the particularity of the assemblage of goods, clothes, practices, experiences, appearance and bodily dispositions they design together into a lifestyle. The modern individual within consumer culture is made conscious that he [sic] speaks not only with his clothes, but with his home, furnishings, decoration, car and other activities which are to be read and classified in terms of the presence and absence of taste . . . This is the world of men and women who quest for the new and the latest in relationships and experiences, who have a sense of adventure and take risks to explore life's options to the full, who are conscious that they have only one life to live and must work hard to enjoy, experience and express it. (1989, p.86)

A wide range of literature thus suggests that people in Western culture use shopping and consumption as important ways of expressing their identities and values. Indeed writers such as Ewen (1988) and Pavitt (2000) now speak about the "commodity-self," the notion that our very sense of selfhood is bound up with how and what we buy.

There is a danger that such theories of consumer culture can be overstated. Tim Edwards (2000, p.190) notes, for example, that theories of consumer culture can often be "general, theoretical and sometimes grandiose as opposed to specific, empirical and self-critical." It is worth noting that the work on consumer culture done by Veblen, Baudrillard, and Twitchell is theoretical and is not based in substantial empirical research into how people in real-world settings think about their shopping activities. Indeed Miller's (1998) major ethnographic study of shoppers in North London suggests that shopping may be concerned as much with love and altruism (e.g., shopping for groceries or gifts for one's family), as with expressing one's values and identity. Twitchell may be right to suggest that branding and shopping are important meaning-making acts for our age. But it is also possible that this may be part of a wider social trend of the "enchantment of the everyday" (Heelas and Woodhead, 2000, p.489), in which meaning is found and expressed through everyday experiences and objects, rather than an indication that society has necessarily become reduced to a consumer culture.

As with electronic media, consumer culture doubtless has a significant role in shaping the environments, resources, and practices of everyday life in Western culture. But it is important to avoid simplistic accounts of this influence and to maintain a critical approach to those theories that attempt to describe it.

## electronic media and consumer culture: seeing the bigger picture

So far, then, this chapter has suggested that our experience of the everyday may be significantly bound up with some specific cultural developments that have arisen out of the "machine age" of industrial production. The way in which we express our values and social identities seems increasingly bound up with the way we act as consumers. The ways in which we think about the world, and our experience of social relations, is also shaped by a culture in which electronic media have an increasing importance.

It is worth recognizing that these phenomena of consumer culture and electronic media are also deeply interconnected. Electronic commodities such as TV's, personal CD players, mobile phones, or computers can function as "commodity-signs" that express something about ourselves and our lifestyle. Thus, for example, early adverts for the Sony Walkman sought to associate it with cutting edge technology, youthfulness, and fashion, in the hope that it would appeal to a customer-base who would want to associate with these cultural images (du Gay et al., 1997). Similarly Apple computers have acquired cultural associations of high design, creativity, and free thinking in relation to the more "mainstream" PC. Electronic commodities such as these do not therefore simply function as bland means of engaging in electronic communication or entertainment, but are themselves carriers of cultural meanings.

Furthermore the content of electronic media is itself significantly influenced by consumer culture. One of the ways in which this influence is most evident is through the power of advertisers over the content of film, TV, and radio. Williams (1999) notes, for example, that television broadcasters (particularly public service broadcasters) have often struggled to achieve adequate funding. One of the most important sources of income for commercial broadcasters is advertising revenue, with advertising space generally sold on the basic principle of the minimum number of viewers/listeners who will see or hear the advert. Audience rating figures are therefore important in calculating how much advertisers can be charged. Put crudely, the higher the audience figures that a TV or radio program attracts the more that can be charged for the adverts that in the breaks around it. Broadcasters therefore have a commercial interest in making their programs as popular as possible, and this can have a significant influence on decisions about what kinds of programs to commission and broadcast. The quest for high audience figures can therefore lead to anxieties about broadcasters "dumbing down" program content, or focusing on the sensational, in order to appeal to as wide an audience as possible (see, e.g., Bourdieu, 1998, pp.70ff.)

Advertisers can have a much more direct influence than this on the content of electronic entertainment, however. Anderson (1995) notes, for example, that some manufacturers refuse to advertise their products during certain programs because they do not want their product associated with the content of the program. Sometimes this can reflect manufacturers' reluctance to have their products associated with programs whose content is violent or sexually explicit. But it can also extend to some manufacturers not wishing to be associated with programs whose content is satirical or contains mild political critique, such as the decision by Domino's Pizzas in the early 1990s not to advertise during *Saturday Night Live* (Andersen, 1995, p.3). Conversely manufacturers, through their advertising agencies, are increasingly interested not only in how many viewers/listeners will receive their advert but whether program content will "prime" this audience to be more receptive to positive messages about their products. This interest in the content of the program is particularly strong in instances of "product placement," where the program itself acts as a vehicle for advertising certain commodities (e.g., Kelloggs cereals in the sit-com, *Seinfeld*, or Ducati motor-cycles in *The Matrix: Reloaded*). Indeed "product placement" had become so widespread in the entertainment industries that it became a direct target of satire in Peter Weir's 1998 film, *The Truman Show*. When commissioning programs, broadcasters thus bear in mind not only the likely audience response to it, but also the responses of the marketers and advertisers who will see previews of the shows before they go out. What we see on our screens and hear through our radios is therefore significantly shaped by the interests of advertising agencies and their clients.

Engaging with electronic media will typically involve buying electronic commodities (or going to places where one can consume electronic entertainment), and the content of the electronic media is itself shaped by the wider dynamics of consumer culture. Both electronic media and consumer culture therefore function as part of a wider social and cultural system of global capitalism. The collapse of communism in Eastern Europe in the late twentieth century has left capitalism as the major global economic system. Indeed Hardt and Negri (2000) suggest that global capitalism has now become an "Empire," a dominant social system incorporating global institutions such as the International Monetary Fund and the World Bank, governments, and transnational companies. The global drift is towards societies that are based on principles of liberal democracy and free market economics, and countries that do not fit this social model risk being characterized as "rogue states" by certain Western politicians. Understanding what is distinctive about everyday life in the contemporary world will therefore inevitably involve asking about how global capitalism, as an overarching economic and cultural system, impacts on our lives.

For many people the experience in living in the context of global capitalism has significant downsides to it. For example, if personal identity and lifestyle is conveyed partly through consumption, this has clear implications for people on low incomes (see, e.g., Toynbee, 2003). As Zygmunt Bauman (2000, p.90) puts it, the flexibility of the "shopping around" type of life does not represent so much a general emancipation for society but rather involves the "redistributions of freedoms" within society. Those with sufficient income to be able to consume freely and creatively therefore have greater access to culturally meaningful symbols than those who cannot afford the right designer shoes and clothes. Alternative forms of consumption may be adopted by those on low incomes, such as the purchasing counterfeit versions of popular branded goods or buying goods second-hand at jumble sales or charity shops (see Grayson, 2000; Gregson and Crewe, 2003). But there remains a sense that poverty forms a barrier to the pursuit of meaning in everyday life. As Twitchell puts it:

> Knowing this, we can appreciate how poverty can be so crippling in the modern Western world. For the penalty of intractable, transgenerational destitution is not just the absence of things; it is also the absence of meaning, the exclusion from participating in the essential socializing events of modern life . . . When you hear that some ghetto kid has killed for a pair of branded sneakers or a monogrammed athletic jacket, you can realize how chronically poor, unemployed youth are indeed living the absurdist life proclaimed by existentialists. The poor are the truly selfless ones in commercial culture. (Twitchell, 1999, p.31)

Social injustice is evident not only in opportunities for consumption in contemporary society, but also in the processes of production of commodities. Global brands such as Nike have moved away from direct production of their commodities, and instead focus on the design, management, and marketing of their brand (Goldman and Papson, 1998). Such companies now typically "out-source" production of their goods to manufacturers in parts of the world where labor is cheap and employment rights are limited (see, e.g., Klein, 2001). As Bhattacharrya et al., comment:

> Indonesian workers who, in 1996, made 70 million pairs of Nike trainers, were earning just over $2 a day in the course of which they were forced to work six

hours overtime and were subject to beatings and sexual harassment. Whilst some of these industries appear more traditional in terms of the form of organization of work, e.g., sweatshops, there is little doubt that such production plays an integral role in global capitalism's latest phase. These developments in turn are the result of the tendency for capital to relocate in regions which can attract a cheap, non-unionized labor supply for its labor-intensive production processes. (Battacharrga et al., 2002, p.32)

If everyday life is lived within the system of global capitalism, it is evident that this system has a shadow-side to it in terms of its effects on poor and displaced people throughout the world.

## conclusion

The recent history of Western society has been significantly shaped by the emergence of the "machine age" and the new technologies of industrial production. Mass production has enabled a society to develop in which electronic media and consumer culture play a significant role. We have noted how the electronic media may influence people's experience of social relations, as well as their understanding of their personal identities and the wider world. We have also examined how consumer culture may be bound up with the process of expressing who we are, and what lifestyle and values we wish to be associated with. Electronic media and consumer culture can also be seen as part of the wider social and cultural system of global capitalism, and we have finally noted some of the problems associated with this system for those who are poor and excluded within it.

Recognizing that everyday life in capitalist societies can have a shadow-side for many people is an important step forward for the discussion in this book. When many theologians and scholars of religion write about popular culture, it is not uncommon for them to treat it as an essentially neutral phenomenon that is nevertheless interesting because of its possible religious meanings and significance. If popular culture is bound up, however, with unjust or oppressive social structures, then it is important to adopt a more consciously critical approach to the environments, practices, and resources of everyday life. This raises wider questions of whether popular culture can have damaging and dehumanizing effects on those who participate in it, and is to these questions that we will turn in the next chapter.

# Chapter 4

# can popular culture be bad for your health?

## introduction

The notion of "popular culture" can often conjure up images of fun and pleasure. Is it possible, though, that popular culture as the environment, resources, and practices of everyday life works in ways that can undermine human well-being? Towards the end of the previous chapter, we noted that electronic media and consumer culture are bound up in a larger system of global capitalism. Furthermore this capitalist system has demonstrably harmful effects on those who work in exploitative environments, who suffer from the insecurity of low-paid, casualized labor, or who find themselves excluded from the pleasures and opportunities of consumer culture through low income. The relationship between popular culture and global capitalism forms just one strand of a wider range of criticisms that have been made about the detrimental effects of popular culture that we will consider in this chapter.

Criticisms about the harmful effects of popular culture fit broadly into three different types. Firstly, there are critiques that suggest that popular culture represents a system that in some way dehumanizes or constrains those who take part in it. Secondly, there are objections that the electronic media used in contemporary popular culture have harmful effects. Thirdly, there are claims from a variety of religious and political perspectives that the content of popular culture in the form of books, TV programs, films, and music, can present damaging views of the world or encourage unhealthy or immoral lifestyles. In this chapter, we will spend time looking briefly at each of these types of critique in turn.

## caught in the matrix? popular culture as a dehumanizing system

One of the most popular film series in recent years has been *The Matrix* trilogy. A central element of the films' narrative is the notion that humanity has become enslaved in a system of control, a virtual reality world which ensures their compliance and gives them superficial pleasures but which denies them true freedom.

This central premise of the Matrix films relates very closely to critiques of popular culture which have suggested that it is also fundamentally a system of control and exploitation.

One of the writers most associated with this kind of critique is Theodore Adorno. Adorno was a leading member of the Frankfurt Institute of Social Research which was established in the 1920s, but which subsequently relocated to America with the rise of Nazism in Germany in the 1930s. Along with other philosophers and cultural critics, such as Max Horkheimer and Herbert Marcuse, Adorno's name has therefore become associated with the "Frankfurt School" of social and cultural analysis.

Adorno is arguably one of the most important cultural theorists of the twentieth-century, and despite a number of objections to his work (see, e.g., Strinati, 1995) his ideas still raise very important questions about contemporary popular culture. Adorno's popularity as a scholar has suffered in recent years, though. Partly this reflects a backlash from some writers against the left-leaning view of the world underpinning his work (see, e.g., Twitchell, 1999, p.42). Partly, it is because his work is purely theoretical and there has been a growing recognition within cultural studies as a discipline that theory needs to be held in tension with empirical studies of how popular culture functions in "real-life" settings. Partly, also, readers of his work continue to struggle with his deliberately complex writing style. Adorno's commitment to avoid the notion that one could dominate and master the world by developing an all-embracing theory led him to adopt a consciously fragmented style of advancing his arguments (see Adorno, 1991, p.8). Whilst this approach does have a certain philosophical consistency to it, it can be hard for readers to gain much initially from his writing, and secondary texts such as Strinati (1995, pp.51ff.) and Witkin (2003) can be a useful starting point for engaging with his work.

Adorno's critique of popular culture is made in what he saw as a world in which traditional religious ideas have lost their power and popular culture comes to stand in their place. Writing in 1959, he commented:

In an age of spiritual disenchantment, the individual experiences the need for substitute images of the "divine." It obtains these through pseudo-culture. Hollywood idols, soaps, novels, pop tunes, lyrics and film genres such as the Wild West or the Mafia movie, fashion substitute mythologies for the masses. (cited in Witkin, 2003, p.29)

Whilst Adorno was certainly not advocating a return to a society in which traditional religion regained its status as the source of meaningful images of the "divine," he was deeply concerned about the way in which a particular cultural system had come to fill the place of religion. Adorno labeled this new cultural system, the "culture industry," and argued that this culture industry was a significant threat to human well-being.

Adorno's ideas were formed in response to the devastating effects of the totalitarian regimes that had emerged in Germany and Italy in the 1930s. A fundamental impulse in his work was therefore a radical commitment to democracy and human freedom. Adorno saw the culture industry as a significant threat to such freedom precisely because it co-opts the vast majority of society into an exploitative cultural system over which they had no control. This system provides people with a range of manufactured entertainments and distractions, but its ultimate goal is to generate profit rather than promote human well-being.[1] The culture industry therefore functions in such a way as to preserve the basic structures of global capitalism and to pacify any attempts to challenge the way in which this system operates.[2]

Part of the way in which the culture system manages to pacify resistance is to provide people with pleasures that may be superficially enjoyable, but which fail to promote genuine human well-being or a deeper sense of happiness. As Adorno (1991, p.106) put it, "the substitute gratification which [the culture industry] prepares for human beings cheats them out of the same happiness which it deceitfully projects . . . The total effect of the culture industry is one of anti-enlightenment . . . [which] impedes the development of autonomous, independent individuals who judge and decide consciously for themselves." The culture industry therefore always ultimately fails to deliver in its promises of happiness: within its constraints "the diner must be satisfied with the menu" (Adorno, 1991, p.10).

Adorno argued that the culture industry gives people a false sense of what will bring them happiness through what he refers to as the "aestheticization" of everyday life (1991, p.11; see also Dyer, 2002, p.179). This process is one in which the culture industry maintains the illusion that happiness can be found through the resources that are already available within everyday life, such as consumer commodities or mass-produced entertainments. This illusion tends to obscure the possibility that happiness might actually be found by transforming everyday life in some way instead.

Adorno's argument here bears a close resemblance to the Marxist idea of the "fetishism of the commodity." Marx argued that within the capitalist system the working classes suffered because they had lost control of the means of production, and were therefore alienated from the process and products of their labor. He went on to argue, though, that capitalism is partly able to perpetuate itself by selling commodities back to the workers with the implied promise that it is these commodities that would make their lives happier. A "false consciousness" therefore is developed in relation to these commodities as workers come to believe that these will bring happiness, when in reality happiness could only be found through the workers challenging the very system that produced those commodities.[3] A gap therefore emerges between an understanding of the concrete social processes through which commodities are manufactured (which could be truly enlightening and potentially liberating), and the enjoyment of the more abstract cultural meanings of the commodity. As Celia Lury puts it:

> Commodities are a unity of what is revealed and what is concealed in the processes of production and consumption. Goods reveal or "show" to our senses their capacities to be satisfiers or stimulators of particular wants and communicators of behavioral codes. At the same time, they draw a veil across their own origins: products appear and disappear before consumers' eyes as if by spontaneous generation, and it is an astute shopper indeed who has much idea about what most things are composed of and what kinds of people made them. (Lury, 1996, p.41)

To give a contemporary example, a particular brand of trainers can, for example, be enjoyed as cultural symbols of style and the love of sport (see, e.g., Goldman and Papson, 1998). But to enjoy these trainers as cultural symbols in this way obscures the fact that they may have been produced using suppliers who pay very low wages and provide poor conditions for their workers. The trainers have, through this process, become a "fetishized" object in which a set of cultural symbols and pleasures ("commodity aesthetics") have been substituted for an understanding of the physical, human, and social processes through which the trainers have been produced. The Marxist concept of the "fetishism of the commodity" thus bears close resemblance to Adorno's suggestion that the culture industry functions in ways that obscure social control and exploitation through "substitute gratifications."[4]

Adorno also offered more detailed suggestions of how the culture industry maintained its hold over those who are forced to live within it. For example, he suggested that the culture industry offers a "pseudo-individualization" within the commodities and entertainments that it offers. By this, he meant that the culture industry provides a variety of products and pleasures that appear to give individuals a wide range of choice, but that this choice is illusory because people are still always choosing within the limits offered by the culture industry. Thus, for example, he argued that the range of different Hollywood stars meant that film-viewers could retain a sense of choice about who their favorite stars were, but that this choice masked the more basic fact that they had little freedom to change the capitalist cultural system that produced them.

Similarly, Adorno suggested that the culture industry pacifies its participants through a process of "standardization," in which entertainments work within fixed genres that do not demand too much of their audiences, but encourage passive or infantile responses. Mainstream pop music is, for example, highly formulaic. Indeed Jimmy Cauty and Bill Drummond (1998), founders of the band the KLF, once wrote a book titled *The Manual: How to Have a Number One Hit The Easy Way* that explained the common structure and content that a pop song would need to reach number one in the singles chart. The formulaic nature of such commercialized pop music, in Adorno's view, only serves to encourage people to think in terms of narrow, predetermined cultural categories rather than to be able to think in more independent and flexible ways.

One of the criticisms that has been made of Adorno's notion of the culture industry is that he depicts people as cultural dopes, who virtually live like automata controlled by this overarching capitalist cultural system (see, e.g., Strinati, 1995, p.78). Such a notion is hard to sustain, however, when one recognizes the range of popular cultural texts and practices that involve a conscious critique of this system. Best-selling books such as Naomi Klein's (2001) *No Logo* or Douglas Coupland's (1992) *Generation X* contain critiques of contemporary consumer culture, as do films such as David Fincher's *Fight Club* or Sam Mendes' *American Beauty*.[5] Indeed, Cauty and Drummond's manual on how to have a number one hit in the singles' chart was written precisely to demystify the working of the music industry and to make the process of record production more accessible to a wider audience. In doing so, *The Manual* sought to deconstruct certain myths about popular music; namely that it is difficult to achieve chart success and that achieving chart success will actually make any improvement to the quality of one's life.

To take another example from the context of popular music, there is a long tradition of black musicians who have used their work to offer explicit critiques of the effects of racism and social injustice within society from Bob

Figure 4.1   Advertising campaigns by the Italian clothing company Diesel frequently adopt a knowing and ironic approach to the idea that the meaning of life can be found through the commodities of consumer culture. In this poster, bearing the caption "Fun is now sponsored by Diesel," three models adopt caricatured postures of enjoyment in a stylized scene of natural beauty whilst "Danny Diesel," the somewhat disturbing corporate mascot for this campaign, lurks in the background (© Diesel Ltd).

Marley and Gil Scott Heron to more recent rap artists such as Public Enemy and Arrested Development (see Beckford, 1998; Gilroy, 1993; Pinn, 2000; Pinn, 2003). Indeed some forms of black popular music can be seen as performing an important counter-cultural function in maintaining an awareness of black history that is often ignored within white Eurocentric educational systems (Beckford, 1998).

Paul Gilroy also argues that forms of black music have positively encouraged local performers to take prerecorded tracks and use them in their own individual way in their local situation:

> The musical counter-cultures of black Britain are primarily based around records rather than live performances but the same aesthetic of performance applies. Music recorded on discs loses its preordained authority as it is transformed and adapted. In reggae, soul and hip-hop sub-cultures the disc which

appears in the dominant culture as a fixed and final product is extended and reconstructed as it becomes the raw material in a new creative process born in the dialogue between the DJ, the rapper or MC and the dancing crowd. A range of de/reconstructive procedures – scratch mixing, dubbing, toasting, rapping and beat boxing – contribute to new layers of local meaning. The original performance trapped in plastic is supplemented by new contributions at every stage. Performer and audience alike strive to create pleasures that can evade capture and sale as cultural commodities. (Gilroy, 1993, p.39)[6]

Popular culture is not therefore a monolithic system that determines how people think and act. Indeed, as we noted back in chapter 1, people can make use of "mass" culture in ways that subvert its intended meanings and challenge socially oppressive ideas (see, de Certeau, 1984; Fiske, 1989). Even obviously standardized popular music can become a focus for resistant social and cultural practices, as is evident when the pop music of boy bands ostensibly aimed at early teenage girls gets taken up and used on the dance floors of some gay nightclubs. The notion that people are simply cultural dopes is therefore hard to sustain.

In actual fact, though, Adorno's work does not offer a simplistic view of people as cultural dopes, unthinkingly shaped by the products of the culture industry. Indeed Adorno suggested that it was perfectly feasible that people would see through the techniques and manipulations of the culture industry, yet struggle to escape its control:

> It may also be supposed that the consciousness of consumers themselves is split between the prescribed fun which is supplied to them by the culture industry and a not particularly well-hidden doubt about its blessings. The phrase, the world wants to be deceived, has become truer than had ever been intended. People are not only . . . falling for the swindle; if it guarantees them even the most fleeting gratification they desire a deception which is nonetheless transparent to them. They force their eyes shut and voice approval, in a kind of self-loathing, for what is meted out to them, knowing fully the purpose for which it is manufactured. Without admitting it they sense that their lives would be completely intolerable as soon as they no longer clung to satisfactions which are none at all. (Adorno, 1991, p.103)

Consumers may well then understand that the culture industry is offering them superficial gratifications, yet struggle to conceive how their lives or society more generally could be structured in any way other than through this existing capitalist system. Furthermore, Adorno suggested that when individuals or groups do develop genuinely innovative social and cultural ideas these are quickly incorporated into the culture industry (1991, p.9).[7] Examples of this can clearly be seen in the context of popular music. The free party, "acid house" scene in Britain in the late 1980s and early 1990s was, for example, a complex cultural movement involving new trends in music and recreational drug use, entrepreneurial event-organizers, as well as elements of organized crime. At its height, outdoor raves could attract up to tens of thousands of participants. Within this movement, however, there was a more radical emphasis on the "right to party," which when it appeared to conflict with other interests of private property and keeping the peace led to the Conservative Government introducing legislation to prevent unlicensed raves (see, e.g., Collin, 1997; Garratt, 1998). This legislation contributed to the drift towards the opening of commercialized clubs in urban areas that have rarely maintained any of the early radicalism of the rave scene. In the context of hip hop culture, there have been attempts by some rap artists to resist the transformation of a black urban artistic form into a global commodity (see George, 2000; Dyson, 2001). But the same tendency for the culture industry to "appropriate" radical new forms and ideas for its profit margins is still evident even here.[8]

The way in which popular cultural industries operate has doubtless become more complex than when Adorno was producing his cultural criticism in the middle part of the twentieth century. Whilst Adorno could, for example, still talk in terms of "mass" media, contemporary entertainment industries have become highly specialized and segmented (as we noted in the previous chapter). Arguably, though, such segmentation could be seen as simply a more complex expression of the process of "pseudo-individualization" that he identified. Furthermore, there continues to be evidence that popular cultural industries have not abandoned hope of influencing the complex markets and audiences with which they work, but that they have simply devised more sophisticated means of trying to influence them (see, e.g., Rushkoff, 1999).

Whether one agrees or not with Adorno's assessment of the dangers of popular culture, his work does raise some fundamental questions that any contemporary critical engagement with popular culture needs to address. Firstly, his work raises basic questions about the relationship between popular culture and capitalism, and the extent to which capitalism is itself a force for good or ill. Secondly, his work highlights a basic debate within cultural studies about the capacity for human freedom and agency within contemporary society. Adorno's work is highly pessimistic about the capacity for humans to act freely and creatively within the constraints of the culture industry.[9] By contrast, writers such as Fiske and Gilroy emphasize the potential for resistance through the creative use of popular culture. Differences on this issue can also be detected in debates about the positive and detrimental nature of consumer culture. Mica Nava (1992, pp.185–200) has, for example, argued that consumers have retained considerable power both individually through what and how they consume, and socially through the emergence of consumer organizations and ethical consumption movements. Judith Williamson (1986), by contrast, argues that the relatively trivial pleasures and freedoms of consumption represent "an effective diversion from the lack of other kinds of power in people's lives" (p.233). Whether one sees popular culture as functioning in ways that promote or limit human freedom will inevitably have a significant role for an assessment of its political, psychological, moral, and spiritual effects.

A final point to be made about Adorno is that he never offered any clear or easy ideas about how we might escape the culture industry or what a post-capitalist society might look like. Rather he saw cultural criticism as a complex dialectical process in which it was necessary both to have some working theories about how society and culture function more generally, whilst also developing specific analyses of particular cultural products and practices (which, for him, included film, jazz, and newspaper horoscopes). There is an acknowledgement within his work that there is no perfect vantage-point from which the cultural critic is able to offer self-righteous judgments on contemporary culture. Indeed cultural criticism is more like walking with bare feet across hot sand; there is no place at which one can rest comfortably or complacently, and all one can do is attempt to move forward as best one can.

There is a humility in Adorno's work which recognizes that we are all compromised in systems and process that dehumanize ourselves and others. As he noted, all forms of culture, including the work of the cultural critic, "ekes out its existence only by virtue of injustice already perpetrated in the sphere of production" (Adorno, 1991, p.17). The challenge of cultural criticism is to attempt, at least, to understand these dehumanizing systems and processes in the hope that some form of resistance against them may be possible.

## amusing ourselves to death? the dangers of electronic media

As we noted in the previous chapter, the relationship between society and technological change is complex. It is too simplistic to imagine that new technologies simply emerge out of the creative genius of individual inventors, and that once invented they subsequently transform society. Technological change is typically bound up with a much wider range of social and cultural processes.

So, for example, the encouragement of the technologies of radio and television broadcasting can be seen as part of the wider drift towards the "mobile privatization" of households in modern, industrial societies.

Although technological change is doubtless shaped by wider social and cultural factors, it is also conceivable that technology can also influence the nature of society as well. In the previous chapter, we saw how the emergence of electronic media has arguably been associated with certain social changes such as "deterritorialization" and the undermining of local customs and traditions. Within the debates about the potentially harmful nature of popular culture, there has been considerable discussion about whether the growing significance of electronic media within Western society has had damaging effects. Partly these debates have been concerned with whether representing certain images or ideas through film, television or popular music can be damaging to the audiences who are exposed to them. We will explore these issues in the next part of the chapter. Before that, though, it is important to note the criticism that the very way in which electronic media functions as a means of communication can also be socially and culturally harmful.

One of the most important critiques of the effects of electronic media as a means of communication has been Neil Postman's (1985) analysis of the effects of television upon contemporary Western society. Central to Postman's argument is the idea that the content of what we communicate is shaped by the medium through which we communicate it (an idea reflected in Marshall McLuhan's aphorism, "the medium is the message"). To take a simple example, smoke signals can be an effective way of communicating basic information, but are not an effective medium for enabling complex philosophical discussion. A culture largely dependent on communication through smoke signals would therefore be very unlikely to produce and discuss the philosophical ideas of writers such as Plato and Aristotle.

The media that we use do not simply influence the complexity of the content that we can communicate through it, however. Rather the media we use influences the ways in which we make sense of the world. Oral cultures, for example, will tend to encourage stories and proverbs that maintain the wisdom of that culture in a way that can easily be communicated and remembered through spoken communication. Knowledge, in oral cultures, thus tends to have a "narrative" shape to it. By contrast, literate (or "typographic") cultures tend to focus more on knowledge that can be communicated through written texts. One of the features of texts is that they allow for more abstract and generalized forms of communication (e.g., philosophical discussion, scientific enquiry, legal codes). This difference is evident in the context of religion, for example. In oral cultures, myth, ritual, and visual symbols have a central role in religious practice. In literate cultures, myth, ritual, and symbols, may still play an important role, but these become supplemented and shaped by written resources such as established Scriptures, codes of law, or fixed systems of doctrine and creeds. The way in which religion is practiced and experienced, then, will be shaped by the media through which that religion finds expression.

The heart of Postman's critique is that television (as part of a longer tradition of electronic media) has transformed the way in which we think about and experience the world in just a radical way as the shift from oral to literate culture did in the past. He argues that, in the context of Western culture, written texts tended to encourage a way of thinking about the world that encouraged rationality, objectivity and the logical ordering of ideas and arguments (see, ibid., pp.53ff.). The popularity of reading in eighteenth and nineteenth century America was therefore associated with a culture in which significant parts of the population were able to deal with substantial arguments and debates. Postman notes, for example, that in the nineteenth century public political debates could often involve speakers taking up to three hours to present their arguments, generally reading from written texts and allowing their respondents a similar length of time to make their rebuttals (ibid., pp.46ff.).

It is hard for us to imagine a contemporary Western audience being prepared to sit and listen to this kind of debate for that length of time. Postman argues that this is because electronic media (and television in particular) have transformed Western culture from a focus on objective, rational discourse to a focus on entertainment. Television, he claims, has the effect of transforming any content that it communicates into entertainment, and cannot sustain the level of sustained analysis that written texts can offer. This is not so much of a problem if we simply use television as a medium for entertainment (e.g., watching sitcoms or soap operas), but he argues that television has become a dangerous social force precisely at the points where it attempts to deal with "serious" content (ibid., pp.16f.). Indeed television has trained us to approach areas such as politics, education, religion, and the law as potential sources of entertainment rather than helping us to think critically or substantially about these vital areas of public life.[10]

A further problem is that the drive for entertainment and superficial pleasure does not only effect society when people sit in front of their television sets, but that it distorts wider cultural structures and practices. In a culture dominated by television, the details of a politician's ideas becomes less important than their media image or their ability to communicate effectively through media-friendly "sound-bites." Similarly in the context of religion, there can be an increasing pressure to lead religious services in entertaining ways (evident, for example, in the "Seeker Services" model developed by the Willow Creek Church).

As society increasingly perceives life on the basis of what is, or is not, entertaining, the cultural consequences of this are potentially devastating:

> When a population is distracted by trivia, when cultural life is redefined as a perpetual round of entertainments, when serious public conversation becomes a form of baby-talk, when, in short, a people become an audience and their public business a vaudeville act, then a nation finds itself at risk; culture death is a clear possibility. (ibid., p.161).

Or as Bourdieu (1998, p.2) puts it, we find ourselves in a world "ruled by the fear of being boring and anxiety about being amusing at all costs."

Now initially it might sound as if Postman is simply a reactionary critic bemoaning the decline of contemporary culture in the face of technological change. There are reasonable grounds to support his claims about television, however. The chapter that you are currently reading comes to over 8500 words in length. I imagine (if you don't daydream too much whilst reading it) that you could read it from start to finish in about half an hour to an hour. A script for an hour-long television documentary would be much closer to 1500 words in length. So if this chapter were converted into a TV script, it would normally take five to six times as long to cover the same material. So although television may give the impression of exploring issues in a substantial way, it is actually a much less efficient medium for communicating ideas and arguments than written texts. Indeed the script of a half hour television news broadcast will contain fewer words than would be contained on one page of a broadsheet newspaper.

This is not simply a question of volume of material, though, but also its complexity. Television scripts tend to be written in a much more simple style than academic books or serious newspapers. A while ago, I visited the newsroom of one of the main daily television news programs for my region of Britain. I was surprised by the simplicity of the script that the presenters were going to use that night. The journalist who was showing me round explained that this was their typical practice. Their policy was that scripts should contain no complex words, have no sentences with subclauses, and should generally be written in a way that could be understood by the average twelve-year-old child.

Where television is arguably more effective as a medium is in presenting material that is aimed at generating an emotional response from its audience.[11] A short news item about a famine, for example, will often contain a range of visual images intended to draw a sympathetic emotional response from the audience. This might include pictures of listless children covered in flies, babies sucking at the empty breasts of their mothers, or crowds gathering at oversubscribed feeding stations. What such news items are often less effective at, however, is communicating a detailed and memorable explanation of the social and political factors that have caused this famine (see Tester, 2001, pp.8–10). Now evoking an emotional response to such images can have some positive consequences, such as inspiring the work of telethons or other public charity events such as the Live Aid concerts in 1985. But such emotional responses, detached from more serious social and political analysis, can have serious limitations. Without an understanding of sociopolitical factors that cause global poverty, a fatalistic perception can emerge amongst viewers that certain parts of the world are somehow destined to experience such suffering and a sustained response to this poverty can become hard to maintain. This leads into the complex debate as to whether a continual focus on emotive images of human suffering through television and other media can actually produce "compassion fatigue" both amongst journalists and their audiences (ibid., pp.13ff.).

Postman and others have suggested that as wider society becomes more oriented to thinking about life in terms of entertainment and emotional response so this in turn brings a new set of pressures on the media to ensure that their content is indeed entertaining. As we noted in the previous chapter, commercial broadcasters are heavily dependent on revenue gained through advertising which, in turn, means achieving good audience ratings figures. The economic logic of the media industries is that "you only get your share of the audience by offering people something that they want" (Postman, 1986, p.123). If the wider culture is oriented towards entertainment and emotional response then the pressure is for broadcasters to produce increasingly sensationalist material to keep their audiences interested (see, e.g., Bourdieu, 1998, pp.51f.). Indeed broadcasters and journalists may even increasingly believe that it is part of their moral and professional responsibility to try to provoke emotional responses from their audiences (Tester, 2001, pp.39ff.). This pressure may not only be felt amongst television broadcasters, but also amongst related media such as newspapers that might adopt an increasingly populist and tabloid style to appeal to their readers. The danger here is that a cycle is set up in which television promotes a wider culture of entertainment and emotional stimulation that in turn places pressure on the media to offer increasingly sensationalist material.[12]

There are a number of weaknesses in Postman's analysis. Firstly, it is another example of "technological determinism." Postman assumes that the drift towards entertainment in contemporary culture is something that is simply *caused* by television, rather than arising out of a more complex range of social processes such as changing work patterns that blur the distinction between work and leisure (Dyer, 2002, pp.179ff.).[13] Secondly, his argument that the literate culture of nineteenth-century Western society encouraged an objective, rationalist approach to public life neglects trends such as the Romantic movement which used written texts to develop nonrational perspectives on life. The distinction between the rationality of the literate culture and the hedonism of the television culture is thus too strongly exaggerated (see Dahlgren, 1995, p.58). Thirdly, Postman's (1986, p.88) view of watching television as a passive and unskilled activity also gives insufficient credit to the complex skills that are needed to learn to "read" any visual text.[14] Finally, his theoretical account of how television functions as a medium does not produce adequate accounts of how television audiences actually respond to programs. Whilst many people watching a news item about a war or famine may only respond emotionally (with despair, indifference, or outrage), others may be prompted by this item to find out more about this crisis through reading other relevant material. Television may indeed be most effective in trying to provoke emotional responses from its audiences, but this does not mean that television audiences will only seek to respond emotionally to what they see.

Nevertheless, despite these limitations, Postman's critique of television still provides a useful illustration of the way in which electronic media can be seen to have harmful social effects through the way in which they function as means of communication.

## bad visions: criticisms of the content of popular media

"The following program contains coarse language and due to its content it should not be viewed by anyone." So runs the satirical opening caption for the TV show, *South Park*, which jibes at a culture which it perceives as too highly sensitive about the content of its popular media.[15] Controversy about the content of the popular media (including programs such as *South Park*) has been present ever since electronic media such as radio, TV, and film started to become widely used in the early twentieth century (see, e.g., Carter and Weaver, 2003, pp.43ff.). Indeed such debates predate electronic media and can be seen in nineteenth-century anxieties about the potentially harmful effects of popular theatre and the press (Murdock, 2001).

Concern about media content can often reflect an underlying belief that the ideas and images we receive through the media can in some way shape our own thoughts, attitudes, and actions. bell hooks, for example, notes the capacity of audiences to interpret and respond to the content of films in their own idiosyncratic way. But she also argues that to emphasize the freedom and autonomy of audiences is to miss an important point about how movies seek to induct people into a particular way of looking at the world:

> The fact that some folks may attend films as "resisting spectators" does not really change the reality that most of us, no matter how sophisticated our strategies of critique and intervention, are usually seduced, at least for a time, by the images we see on the screen. They have power over us and we have no power over them. Whether we call it "willing suspension of disbelief" or just plain sub-mission, in the darkness of the theater most audiences choose to give them-selves over, if only for a time, to the images depicted and the imaginations that have created those images. (hooks, 1996, pp.3.)

Now, it may be that film is a particularly persuasive medium in this respect. Watching a film in a darkened cinema, in which our visual field is directed purely to the images on the screen, suggests that we are deliberately allowing ourselves to submit to an experience provided for us by the film-maker. This can be quite a different experience to watching television in the home, when the TV program may at times be a direct focus of attention, but can also be a background accompaniment to other activities like conversation or doing the ironing (see Gray, 1992). Nevertheless, hooks' point about film here does reflect a wider concern the content of popular media can "seduce" us, and influence the way we see the world or the way in which we behave.

Concern about the content of the media is something that is voiced by cul-tural critics from both the political left and right. Those writing from a more left-leaning perspective typically raise concerns about the "representation" of characters, experiences, and social groups in the media. The notion of "representation" is an important concept here. It draws our attention to the fact that stories and symbols do not simply describe the world "as it is," but offer particular views of the world that make sense within the conventions of a particular culture (see Hall, 1997).

Left-leaning cultural critics typically focus on how the representations of characters and experiences in popular media can serve to reinforce ideas that support prevailing political and cultural ideologies or preserve negative per-ceptions of vulnerable or minority social groups (see, e.g., Miles, 1996).[16] For example, Dorfman and Mattelart (1991) have written on how Disney comic books have served, at times, to support a conservative capitalist political ide-ology. Thus, in Disney comics published in Chile in the early 1970s around the time of the left-wing social reforms of President Allende, Donald Duck cartoon strips contained stories of evil characters who sought to steal property from the wealthy but who could be resisted through the use of arms. This, tragically, proved to be prophetic as a military coup led by General Pinochet removed Allende from power and reversed his attempts at social and economic reform.

Another good example of concerns about cultural representations from a left-leaning perspective is offered through Spike Lee's film *Bamboozled*. The plot of the film focuses on the decision by a TV network to raise its flagging audience figures by reintroducing an old style minstrel show, starring a range of clownish black characters. Lee uses this as an opportunity to explore the tradition in American popular culture of black people being used as the entertainers of the white population, a practice which dates back to black slaves on the plantations being required to provide entertainment for their white slave-holders. In a striking five minute sequence at the end of this film, Lee provides a montage of clips from American films and cartoons from the 1930s onwards which consistently reinforce images of black characters as comic, slow-witted, primitive, and subservient to whites. This montage provides a powerful example of how traditions of cultural representation can reinforce stereotypical images that support existing power structures and dehumanize those who fall outside the cultural elite.

The content of the popular media can also be a source of concern to critics who adopt a far more conservative cultural and political stance than critics such as bell hooks or artists like Spike Lee. A good example of this is the film critic Michael Medved, whose best-selling book *Hollywood vs. America* sought to provide a sustained conservative critique of the content of contemporary popular culture (Medved, 1993). Medved's central argument was that the American popular cultural industries had become fixated with presenting audiences with a range of salacious material in the belief that this would achieve critical acclaim and high audience ratings. Whilst many critics might welcome much of this material, Medved claimed that the majority of the American population was fundamentally alienated and offended by it. He commented:

> Our fellow citizens cherish the institution of marriage and consider religion an important priority in life; but the entertainment industry promotes every form of sexual adventurism and regularly ridicules religious believers as crooks or crazies.
>
> In our private lives, most of us deplore violence and feel little sympathy for the criminals who perpetuate it; but movies, TV, and popular music all revel

in graphic brutality, glorifying vicious and sadistic characters who treat killing as a joke.

Americans are passionately patriotic, and consider themselves enormously lucky to live here; but Hollywood conveys a view of the nation's history, future, and major institutions that is dark, cynical, and often nightmarish.

Nearly all parents want to convey to their children the importance of self-discipline, hard work and decent manners; but the entertainment media celebrate vulgar behavior, contempt for all authority, and obscene language – which is inserted even in "family fare" where it is least expected. (Medved, 1993, p.10)

Medved's concern with the content of the popular media was therefore that this salacious content undermined "traditional" values such as respect for religious and political institutions, maintaining conventional personal and sexual morality and supporting traditional institutions such as marriage and the family. At some points, Medved's critique is concerned with issues of representation. Thus, for example, he raises concerns about the lack of positive images of priests and clergy in recent Hollywood films (ibid., pp.50ff.), arguing that consistent representations of religious figures as conmen or clowns serves to encourage skepticism towards religious institutions. At other points, though, it is clear that Medved's critique rests on the belief that certain actions and images are simply unsuitable to be covered by entertainment media in any context. He thus regards explicit sexual and violent content to be inherently unsuitable as a focus for entertainment.

By contrasting cultural critics like Dorfman and Mattelart, and Michael Medved, we can see how objections to the content of popular media are motivated by the critic's particular cultural and political commitments. At times, these cultural and political commitments become polarized in a very public way. The "culture wars" of early 1990s America, for example, involved a fierce public argument between conservatives and those adopting a more liberal or radical stance about the kind of content that was appropriate for the popular media (see, e.g., Romanowski, 1996).[17]

At the same time, however, neat divisions between conservative and liberal/radical cultural criticism can obscure a more complex picture. A left-leaning artist such as Spike Lee has himself been subject to criticism from the cultural left for the representations of women in some of his films (see hooks, 1996, pp.227ff.). Conservative and radical cultural critics will also sometimes share similar concerns. Thus Michael Medved's objections to rap lyrics that endorse violence and exploitation of women would also be shared to some extent by more radical critics such as Michael Dyson and bell hooks. What remains an important difference between such critics, however, is their wider social and political philosophy that provides a framework through which they evaluate popular culture. Thus Dyson and hooks' critique of rap lyrics is informed by their wider understanding of what it means to be black in a racist society (see, e.g., hooks, 1994, pp.115ff.; Dyson, 2001). Medved (1993, pp.31, 192f.), however, treats violent lyrics as having the same social and cultural significance regardless of whether their author is a young black rapper, a white singer in a heavy metal band, or a member of the Klu Klux Klan. In this case one's theory of culture and race has a significant bearing on how one evaluates the content of popular media.

The notion that the content of popular media can have a negative influence on its audience has found a more specific focus in debates concerning the representation of violence in the media. In my home city of Birmingham, UK, in the early hours of 1 January, 2003, two young women were shot in an inner-city area, apparently caught in gun-fire between rival gangs. In the aftermath of these shootings, one politician publicly blamed the celebration of violence in "gangsta rap" for promoting a culture of gun violence in inner city areas that ultimately led to these innocent deaths.[18] This claim is part of a long tradition of violent content in popular media being blamed for causing violent responses from members of its audiences (see, e.g., Murdock and McCron, 1997; Murdock, 2001). Recent examples of these have included claims that the film *The Basketball Diaries* inspired the Columbine High School shootings, that Marilyn Manson's music led to two Italian teenagers killing a nun, and that the horror film *Child's Play III* motivated two ten-year-old boys to murder the two year-old toddler James Bulger in Liverpool.[19]

Public debates about the effects of violent content in the media are often conducted in the face of the "commonsense" view that exposure to violent media content increases (some) people's tendency towards violent actions. As one journalist commented following the Bulger murder, "God protect us from the 'ologists' . . . I sometimes think that a degree in some sort of 'ology' blinds you to common sense. We all know that violence begets violence" (quoted from Petley, 1997, p.193).

This "commonsense" view draws support from a tradition of psychological studies which have sought to establish the effects of exposure to violent media content.[20] Exponents of the "media effects" theory have claimed that this psychological research has conclusively proven a link between violent media and violent behavior. The reality is somewhat more complex. The methodologies are many of these psychological studies are vulnerable to critique (see, Petley, 1997; Barker, 2001, pp.39ff.; Gauntlett, 2001, pp.55ff.). For example, psychological studies such as these are normally conducted in laboratory

Figure 4.2   Nu-metal star Marilyn Manson, here performing at the House of Blues in Las Vegas. Manson's music has been accused by some critics in Europe and North America of inciting people to violence (© Corbis).

environments rather than studying people's reactions to media in real-world settings. The findings of studies are sometimes overstated: does the evidence from one study that children were more likely to burst a balloon than play with it after watching a violent film really indicate that violent media would cause them to act aggressively towards other people? Furthermore, this long tradition of psychological research has also generated contradictory findings that do not clarify what kind of audience is more likely to be susceptible to violent media content (Barker, 2001, p.40). Claims that "research" has conclusively proven a direct link between violent media and violent behavior need to be made with much greater caution than is often the case when the popular press try to use the media as a scapegoat for the latest newsworthy killing.

In contrast to this psychological body of research, there is a growing number of sociological studies that suggest that individuals do not respond to media violence in common and predictable ways. Rather the way in which individuals respond to violent media content is likely to be influenced by a range of factors including their gender, ethnicity, class, and previous experience of exposure to violence (Carter and Weaver, 2003, pp.89ff.). There is also little evidence that children, who are often depicted as particularly susceptible to the effects of media violence, respond by simply imitating that violence. Conversely, children often have complex strategies for thinking about media violence, and when exposed to violent media content are more likely to identify with the victim than the perpetrator (see Barker and Petley, 2001, pp.11ff.; Buckingham, 2001).

Indeed "media effects" theories are open to critique on the grounds that they often carry hidden ideological assumptions (often under the cover of their "common sense" position). Typically supporters of the notion that media violence causes violent behavior assume that those most likely to imitate violent media content are from social underclasses rather than respectable middle-class households. As one cultural critic commented in the wake of the Bulger murder, "would you allow an ill-educated, culturally deprived, unemployable underclass unlimited access to violent pornography?" (quoted from Petley, 1997, p.193; see also Petley, 2001). Anxiety about the effects of violent media thus form part of a longer historical process of mainstream society demonizing poor, excluded social groups, who then become an object of fear (Murdock, 2001). Such a process enables mainstream society to project notions of violence and threat into social underclasses, rather than face more complex questions about how violence and injustice are implicated in wider social structures. Moral panics about the content of gangsta rap, for example, thus focus attention on the lyrics of a handful of popular musicians rather than on the social conditions that do much more to blight the lives of the black, urban poor (see, e.g., hooks, 1994, pp.115ff.; Beckford, 2004).

If there is little evidence to suggest a simplistic view that media violence causes violent behavior (and good reason to be skeptical about ideological assumptions within such a view), does this mean that the media has no role in shaping its audience? If that were the case, then the concern with issues of representation amongst left-leaning cultural critics would seem to be as misplaced as Michael Medved's belief that violent films make for a more violent society. In other words, if the media does not really have any effect on its audience, does it matter how women, black people, or gay men and women are represented through the media?

There are reasonable grounds for suggesting that such representations do indeed matter. Research on audience responses have suggested that people are likely to adopt the way of understanding the world that is offered to them through the media unless they have some other experience or way of interpreting the world that contradicts this media perspective (see Barker and Petley, 2001, pp.18ff.). If this is indeed the case, then the way in which the media represents society and different groups within it has considerable importance. If I receive media representations of Muslims as aggressive fundamentalists or black men as violent criminals, without having experiences or frameworks for critiquing these representations, then the risk is that I will simply absorb these negative representations as a true reflection of how the world is. Ironically, then, whilst violent media content is unlikely to promote violent behavior, "media effects" theories are more likely to have more of an impact on audiences when they are presented in the popular press as the "common-sense" way of understanding contemporary violence. David Gauntlett (2001) thus aptly titles his discussion of these issues, "The worrying influence of 'media effects' studies."

The content of popular media can indeed, then, have a role in shaping society. Those working within theology and religious studies who are concerned with social transformation therefore need to develop methods and tools for thinking critically about media content, and we shall return to explore these in more depth after the next chapter.

## conclusion

In this chapter, we have explored the idea that far from being a neutral phenomenon, popular culture can be bound up with structures, practices, and ideas that can be dehumanizing or can threaten the basic fabric of human culture. Through this chapter we have noted three different types of critique of popular culture. Firstly, the structural critique offered by Adorno and other writers argues that popular culture functions in ways that ensnare people in a wider capitalist system (the culture industry) that deprives them of true human freedom and happiness. Secondly, the critique of electronic media offered by writers such as Postman and Bourdieu claims that the very nature of such media encourages a culture focused on entertainment and emotional stimulation, in which serious critical thinking comes to be seen as too boring or difficult. Thirdly, we have noted different kinds of objections to particular examples of the content of popular media, either because they offer dehumanizing representations of social groups or because they undermine "traditional" values.

Running through all of these criticisms and debates are two questions which are central to serious reflection on the potentially harmful aspects of popular culture.

Firstly, what is the nature of appropriate and healthy forms of pleasure? At the very start of this chapter, we noted that the notion of popular culture is often associated with ideas of pleasure and enjoyment. Yet as this chapter has progressed, it is clear that at least some of the pleasures that may be associated with popular culture are, at best, ambivalent. From Adorno's perspective, for example, popular culture may provide people with immediate superficial gratification, but this is different to the more substantial pleasures of free and creative human communities. From Postman's perspective, television may also offer immediate pleasures of the emotional response from watching an amusing comedy, a well-constructed drama, or a tightly fought sports contest. But such pleasure is again superficial and dangerous, if it becomes detached from an ability to think critically about the nature of the world. Finally, cultural critics from bell hooks to Michael Medved argue that what may appear superficially enjoyable in the media can in fact influence our perceptions and values in dangerous ways.

In some classes that I have taught on popular culture, some students have objected that I am asking them to take a particular film or TV show too seriously. "It's only meant to be seen as a bit of fun," some of them protest. The critiques we have noted in this chapter, however, show that the ideas of "fun" and "pleasure" are by no means straightforward. Indeed, if there is any validity in these critiques, then it is clear that what might be experienced as pleasurable could at the same time be dehumanizing, entrapping, or morally dangerous. This observation should challenge us to think more critically about the nature of pleasure and to ask what it would mean to seek constructive and authentically human forms of pleasure through the environments, practices and resources of our everyday lives.[21] We will return to think about this issue in terms of debates about the aesthetics of popular culture in the final chapter of this book.

The second question concerns the nature of human freedom in relation to popular culture. Is popular culture, as Adorno suggested, ultimately a cage that entraps us, and in which we can only find some space for maneuver through the practice of cultural criticism? In a culture organized around television are we inevitably attracted to superficial, short-term stimulation? Are we fundamentally influenced by the content that we are exposed to through the media? To reply "yes" to these questions suggests that human agency in the face of these wider cultural structures and resources is very limited. Yet it may be, as writers like de Certeau, Gilroy, and Fiske have suggested, that individuals and groups still retain significant power and freedom to resist and challenge dehumanizing forces in society.

Our perspective on this issue will be important in shaping the tone and content of our cultural criticism. Writers such as Adorno and Postman sound a highly pessimistic note in their assessment of contemporary culture, and perhaps this is realistic. But an emphasis on the persistent possibility for humans to resist forces that limit and diminish them is a more optimistic and hopeful perspective. Perhaps a balanced assessment is Stuart Hall's (1981) notion that popular culture remains a site of struggle between powerful and resisting forces, and that neither side wins any final or conclusive victories. From a theological perspective, notions of transcendence, or indeed of the inbreaking kingdom of God, might also influence one's judgment of how pessimistic or optimistic one should be in the face of contemporary culture.[22]

In this first part of the book, then, we have explored a range of issues that set the wider context for the theological and religious study of popular culture. We have examined the significance of different definitions of popular culture, and explored the range of questions and interests that those involved in theology and religious studies bring to the academic study of popular culture. We have also looked at how an understanding of the role of electronic media and consumer culture might contribute to a wider analysis of everyday life in a contemporary world shaped by global capitalism, as well as wider debates about harmful aspects of popular culture. Understanding the issues at stake in each of these areas is important for developing serious academic analyses and critiques of particular forms of popular culture. For without a clear sense of the issues involved in defining popular culture, a clear grasp of why we are studying popular culture or a clear understanding of relevant concepts and debates in the analysis and critique of popular culture, we are unlikely to produced well-focused or convincingly argued work. In addition to these wider issues, though, it is also important to understand more specific methodological approaches that those involved in theology and religious studies might adopt in studying popular culture. In the second part of the book we will turn our attention, firstly, to how we might think about the process of developing a theological critique of particular forms of popular culture, and then to different methodological approaches that can be used to develop a clearer analysis of the meaning or significance of particular forms of popular culture as part of this type of theological study.

# Chapter 5

# developing a theological approach to the study of popular culture

## introduction

Back in chapter 2 we explored four different ways in which people involved in theology and religious studies have explored popular culture. The first two approaches that we considered – studying religion in relation to everyday life and studying the religious functions of popular culture – are primarily concerned with the critical analysis of forms of contemporary religion. As such these approaches can be seen as fitting within the concerns and methods of the discipline of *religious studies*. By contrast, the latter two approaches – missiological engagements with popular culture and theological reflection in relation to popular culture – are more concerned with engaging with popular culture in relation to particular religious questions, beliefs, and values. As such, these approaches can therefore be seen as fitting more within the scope of the discipline of *theology*.[1]

Now at the time of writing this book, the more substantial academic work within these different approaches has tended to be undertaken by those whose interests and methods are drawn from the field of religious studies. Whilst there have been good examples of serious theological engagements with popular culture (of which we have noted some in chapter 2), the literature on missiology, theology, and popular culture has tended to be written for more popular audiences. Writing theology in an accessible way for a wider audience is an important responsibility for those working within this discipline. But inevitably more popular texts tend to give less focused attention to theoretical and methodological issues, and as a consequence can lack depth and have little impact on wider social and cultural criticism.

One of the central aims of this book is to help readers to think about what it means to develop a rigorous approach to the theological study of popular culture. In particular this will involve thinking about what kinds of questions it is important to ask from a theological perspective in relation to popular culture, as well as what kinds of methods will help us to answer these questions. In this chapter, I will present an overview of these issues before going on to explore particular methods in more depth in the following chapters. This overview will include a discussion of different ways in which a "dialogue" can take place between theological norms and popular culture, as well a particular model for understanding the process of reflecting theologically on popular culture. Before going on to these issues, however, we first need to begin by asking basic questions about the very nature of theology as an academic discipline.

## what is theology?

Understanding the distinctive contribution that theology has to make to the wider task of social and cultural criticism requires us to have a clear understanding, first of all, of the nature of theology as a form of study and reflection. As a starting point for this, I want to suggest the following definition for theology:

> *Theology is the process of seeking normative answers to questions of truth/meaning, goodness/practice, evil, suffering, redemption, and beauty in specific contexts.*[2]

There are three aspects of this definition that it is particularly important to emphasize. Firstly, *theology is a normative discipline*. As Peter Hodgson (1994, pp.3ff.) comments, the primary focus of theology should be "Theos" or "God." The notion of "Theos" can be seen in terms of a "personal subject who enters into relations" (ibid., p.4), or in more abstract terms as the principle of the "Absolute," "transcendence," or "ultimate concern" (see, e.g., Tillich, 1953, p.15). With either understanding, however, the notion of Theos/God implies an absolute reference point for our existence. Theology can therefore be understood as a discipline in which we reflect on the nature of existence in relation to this absolute reference point. It is a *normative* discipline in the sense that it requires us to reflect on how we can speak truthfully or meaningfully about life in relation to this absolute, what it means to live our lives in a good or just way in relation to it, and what concepts such as evil, suffering, redemption, and beauty mean in the light of it. Theology is not therefore simply a descriptive exercise (e.g., presenting a history of religious ideas). Rather it involves trying to find ways of understanding the absolute reference point of existence, and reflecting on the nature and significance of our existence in relation to this absolute.[3]

Thinking about theology in this way inevitably raises the question as to whether theology can only therefore be practiced by people who are committed to particular understandings of "God" or who indeed find the concept of "God" meaningful at all. The definition of theology that I gave at the start of this section is intended to be as inclusive as possible. In the context of Western societies in which increasing numbers of people do not have any active commitment to a particular religious tradition, it is important to think of theology as a discipline that is potentially open to anyone interested in asking questions about meaning and value in life.[4] An interest in "Theos" need not imply any prior commitment to belief in a personal God, but simply a willingness to contemplate the nature and possibility of an absolute reference point for life. At the same time, however, it is realistic to acknowledge that most people with an interest in "theology" usually have some form of religious commitment.[5] At this point, it is important simply to recognize that theology is fundamentally concerned with exploring how we can best understand existence and live good and just lives.

A second important element of my definition is the notion that *theology is a contextual discipline*. As a discipline, theology focuses on questions that can be seen as having a universal significance for all people. What is the truth of existence? What does it mean to live a good and meaningful life? What limits or harms existence, and in what ways can existence be healed or redeemed? At the same time, however, the answers that theology provides are inevitably shaped by the language, symbols, concepts, and concerns of the particular context in which those questions are asked.[6] For example, the creeds of Nicea and Chalcedon, which might appear to be timeless statements of Christian doctrine, are more accurately understood as attempts by the early Church to express biblical tradition in the light of the philosophical concepts of its day. Similarly, in the twentieth century, the strongly contrasting theologies of Karl Barth and Rudolf Bultmann can be seen as attempts to reflect on the significance of the Christian tradition in the light of a Western society scarred by the horrors of the First World War.

The twentieth century has seen a growing amount of work by theologians in non-Western cultures who have sought to explore how the Christian tradition can be interpreted and expressed in ways that are meaningful and constructive in those cultures (see, e.g., Bevans, 1992; Sugirtharajah, 1993; Parratt, 1995). The emergence of theologies of liberation, as well as contemporary forms of practical theology, have also demonstrated the significance of beginning theological reflection from the point of one's own experience (see, e.g., Pattison and Lynch, 2004). Thus, the experience of being a woman, black, gay, or disabled, can all provide a distinctive starting point for asking exploring theological issues in ways that may not be adequately addressed in theologies typically developed by white, able-bodied, heterosexual men. If theological answers are to be relevant to the lives and experience of people raising theological questions, then it becomes harder to imagine that theology can generate universal, timeless concepts that will be equally valid or helpful in all times and places. Rather theology needs to be conducted in ways that take seriously the particular context and experiences of those engaging in theological reflection.

A third important notion within this definition is that *theology involves a dynamic process of reflection*. If the discipline of theology does not provide people with a set of "ready-made" answers that can simply be imposed on all people, contexts, and societies, then this implies that theology involves a *process* of reflection. Rather than studying theological ideas as a static body of knowledge that is universally applicable, theology is better understood as a process of exploring traditional theological resources in the light of contemporary questions, beliefs, values, practices, and experiences. In recent years, people working within the disciplines of theological education, as well as pastoral and practical theology, have sought to clarify some of the important elements of this process of reflection (see, e.g., Green, 1987; Groome, 1987; Lartey, 2000). We shall look at a particular model of this process of theological reflection later in this chapter.

It is possible that this process of reflection will generate clear answers for a particular context to which an individual or group is deeply committed. Luther's statement, "Here I stand. I can do no other," illustrates this position. At the same time, though, it can be helpful to recognize that the answers generated by theological reflection are provisional and open to further change and development. As Stone and Duke put it:

> To engage in theological reflection is to join in an ongoing conversation with others that began long before we ever came along and will continue long after we have passed away . . . We are called only to do the best we can, given who and where we are. This is actually the best that theologians manage, not only because as humans they are limited and fallible and because times change, but because the final word is God's alone. (1997, p.4)

Thinking of theological reflection as an on-going conversation can also alert us to the importance of listening to others' contributions to that conversation.

This is particularly important if we are to avoid assuming that our theological conclusions may necessarily be appropriate to the experiences or contexts of people different to ourselves. Indeed, given that academic theology has traditionally been dominated by the perspectives of white, Western, hetero-sexual, able-bodied men it can be particularly important to listen to the con-tributions from those who fall outside this small theological "elite" (Poling, 1996).

The definition of theology that I am offering here, then, emphasizes the *normative*, *contextual*, and *dynamic* nature of theology. Whilst this definition might be criticized by those who argue that theology simply involves the assertion of fixed, objective theological truths, my emphasis on the contextual and dynamic aspects of theology fits within a growing con-sensus on the nature of this discipline within both religious organizations and the academy.

## the relationship between theology and popular culture

Having explored a basic definition of the discipline of theology, this raises the next question of how theology can be related to the study of popular culture. We have already noted that theology is a contextual discipline. The relation-ship between theology and popular culture can be clarified further if we think of popular culture as a particular context within which theological reflection takes place. This kind of theological activity can therefore be understood as *the process of seeking normative answers to questions of truth/meaning, goodness/practice, evil, suffering, redemption and beauty in relation to con-temporary popular culture.*

In the first part of this book we have seen how popular culture represents a range of structures, texts/resources, and practices that provide a framework for everyday life. This framework includes ideas about the nature and meaning of existence, values (such as images of what it means to live the good life), practices, experiences, and different types of human relationships. So, for example, electronic media convey particular interpretations of our exis-tence. Branded commodities are intentionally associated with particular values and "lifestyles." Furthermore, popular cultural activities involve a range of practices and relationships – some of which, as we have seen, involve social injustice and inequality. In addition to this, popular culture also becomes a means through which people potentially enjoy a range of experi-ences – including experiences of pleasure, beauty, and transcendence.

Each of these popular cultural beliefs, values, practices, relationships, and experiences are of relevance to the discipline of theology. If theology is a process of seeking normative answers to issues of meaning, value, and practice, then it is appropriate for theology to engage with the way in which these issues are explored through popular culture. Whilst it is important for theology to understand and describe values, beliefs, practices, and experiences within popular culture, theological reflection cannot stop at this point. Rather, as a normative discipline, theology will involve asking critical questions about how true, good, or constructive these particular values, beliefs, practices, and experiences are. As we have seen, theology involves a process of negotiation between understandings of the absolute reference point for life and the particular concerns, aspirations, and practices of our particular culture and context. Asking theological questions about popular culture therefore requires us not only to identify the values, beliefs, practices, and experiences of popular culture, but also to think critically about these in relation to our understandings of the absolute.

This kind of theological critique involves three broad types of question:

1   do popular cultural understandings of God, suffering, evil, and redemption offer a true, adequate, or meaningful account of existence in the light of the absolute reference point for life? (ontological enquiry)
2   to what extent does popular culture involve just relationships between people, enable people to lead good and authentic lives, or promote human well-being? (ethical/liberationist enquiry)
3   to what extent does popular culture offer constructive experiences of pleasure, beauty, and transcendence? (aesthetic/spiritual enquiry)

Asking these kinds of questions can be understood as a form of dialogue between theological concepts and resources and the values, beliefs, practices and experiences of popular culture. As we noted back in chapter 2, a serious theological study of popular culture demands sufficient "ethical patience" to understand popular culture on its own terms before subjecting it to critical scrutiny in relation to our understanding of the absolute. Once we have "heard the voice" of popular culture, this raises further questions about how we go on to conduct the conversation between our understandings of the absolute and these popular cultural perspectives and experiences. In the next part of the chapter we will now go on to consider different ways in which theologians have conducted this kind of dialogue.

## different models of conversation between theological norms and popular culture

Notions of how one might appropriately hold a dialogue between theological norms and popular culture will inevitably be shaped by certain presuppositions about the nature of the relationship between the absolute reference point of existence and human cultures. Reflecting on these assumptions can lead to the development an explicit *theology of culture* that provides a framework within which more specific theological analyses of particular forms of culture can take place.

One of the classic summaries of different approaches to the theology of culture was provided by H. Richard Niebuhr (1951) in a series of lectures entitled *Christ and Culture*.[7,8] Niebuhr's central argument was that there was no agreed Christian perspective on how human cultures should be understood. Indeed, within the history of the Christian Church, Niebuhr identified five different approaches to understanding culture which lead to Christians developing strongly contrasting views of their contemporary cultural context. Interestingly, Niebuhr did not suggest that any one of these five views was ultimately correct, but rather suggested that through their partial perspectives, a greater truth could emerge:

> Christ's answer to the problem of human culture is one thing, Christian answers are another; yet his followers are assured that he uses their various works in accomplishing his own. It is the purpose of the following chapters to set forth typical Christian answers to the problem of Christ and culture and so to contribute to the mutual understanding of variant and often conflicting Christian groups. The belief which lies back of this effort, however, is the conviction that Christ as living Lord is answering the question through the totality of history and life in a fashion which transcends the wisdom of all his interpreters yet employs their partial insights and their necessary conflicts. (ibid., p.2)

The five approaches that Niebuhr identified were as follows:

1   *Christ against Culture*. This position was characterized by drawing a clear opposition between the absolute truth embodied in Christ and the particular forms of contemporary culture. Christians adopting this approach have therefore tended to emphasize an either/or choice between following Christ or engaging in contemporary culture. At times this can take the form of a physical separation of Christian communities from the wider culture (e.g., in the case of some Anabaptist communities), or more commonly a sense of psy-

chological and spiritual differentiation between God's people and the "world."

2  *The Christ of Culture*. The polar opposite to the "Christ against Culture" position, this view adopts a far more positive view of the potential of human culture. Christ's life and teachings are thus seen primarily as achievements of human culture, and certain forms of culture (e.g., democratic institutions or Marxist societies) are seen as embodying Christ's truth.[9]

3  *Christ above Culture*. This third approach interprets Christ as the completion of human culture. Whilst human culture may indeed have significant positive elements within it, and whilst culture may point people towards Christ, the ultimate consummation of our cultural aspirations comes from Christ. This approach is associated with forms of Catholic sacramental theology which emphasize the potential of human culture to be a mediator of truth and grace, but which ultimately locate this truth and grace as gifts of God rather than in human achievement.[10]

4  *Christ and Culture in Paradox*. In this approach Christ and culture are seen as separate and autonomous parts of human life. This approach is exemplified in Luther's belief that the State, whilst still a flawed part of human culture, demanded respect and obedience in one's civic life as the Church demands obedience in one's personal religious life. Human culture, despite its flaws, is thus something that must still be tolerated and worked within during the constraints of this life and this world.

5  *Christ the Transformer of Culture*. This final approach shares the belief of the first and fourth of these approaches in the fundamentally flawed nature of human culture. But unlike the Christ against Culture model, it advocates engagement rather than withdrawal from culture. The truth embodied in Christ thus becomes a resource with which contemporary forms of culture can be critiqued and challenged in the hope that they may be transformed.

Between these five different positions it is possible to identify certain basic issues that are at stake in the theology of culture. Foremost amongst these is the question of whether human culture can, in any sense, be seen as a force for goodness and truth. The "Christ of Culture" and "Christ above Culture" hold different, but basically positive views of human culture as a resource for truthful and authentic existence. By contrast the other approaches draw a much stronger distinction between the truth revealed in God and the flawed truths and practices of human culture. Other key questions relate to how truth is revealed to us (e.g., simply through specific religious resources or through more diverse cultural forms), whether participation in human culture could be seen as a creative opportunity, duty, or threat, and how optimistic we might be that human culture can be changed in constructive ways.

Niebuhr's overview makes it clear that the notion that there can be a constructive dialogue between theological norms and popular culture is not necessarily accepted in all theologies of culture. The perspectives of "Christ against Culture," "Christ of Culture" and "Christ and Culture in Paradox" do not allow for any such dialogue. In the case of "Christ against Culture" this is because culture is seen as fundamentally compromised and beyond redemption. By contrast, in the case of "Christ of Culture," it is because Christ essentially becomes identified with certain cultural forms, and the potential of a critical dialogue between theological tradition and these cultural forms becomes weakened. Similarly with "Christ and Culture in Paradox," no substantial dialogue is possible between theological norms and culture because they operate in fundamentally different realms of human existence.[11]

The remaining approaches of "Christ above Culture" and "Christ the Transformer of Culture" give greater weight to the value of critical theological engagement with culture. Whilst there are clear differences between these approaches in terms of how positively they view human culture as a mediator of goodness and truth, both also see theological reflection as making a constructive contribution to interpreting and critiquing cultural values and practices.

Niebuhr's typology is very useful in identifying core issues and different perspectives in the theology of culture, but it is of limited use however in helping us to think in detail about how a dialogue between theological norms and popular culture might be conducted.[12] Indeed Niebuhr's overview of "Christ and Culture" can usefully be supplemented by an understanding of four different ways in which a dialogue between theological tradition and popular culture might be conducted.

The first of these approaches can be described as an *applicationist* one. In this approach, popular culture is subjected to a critique on the basis of certain fixed theological beliefs and values.[13] A basic assumption of this approach is that it is possible to identify core theological truths from a particular source (e.g., the Bible or Church tradition) and then apply these critically to the beliefs and values of popular culture. Having identified these religious beliefs and values, popular culture is then evaluated positively or negatively to the extent that it fits with this particular religious view of the world. Thus, for conservative film critics such as Michael Medved, religious injunctions against adultery mean that screenwriters and directors should not attempt to represent adultery in a positive light in films and TV programmes. In the film, *Shirley Valentine*, Shirley's brief adulterous affair on holiday is represented in this story as a constructive and helpful part of her journey towards a more liberated and authentic life. Yet from a conservative, applicationist perspective, this would tend to be seen as an inappropriate celebration of an inherently sinful act.

The applicationist approach is the least dialogical of the three approaches to be considered here. At best the "voice" of popular culture is taken seriously and heard on its own terms, but the ultimate arbiter of truth and goodness in this conversation comes from preformed theological beliefs and values.

A second approach to the dialogue between theology and popular culture can be described as a *correlational* one. This approach is particularly associated with the work of Paul Tillich (1959; see also Bulman, 1981). Tillich proposed that the basic task of theology was to provide a response from religious tradition to the particular concerns and predicament of contemporary life. Theology thus becomes a process of *correlating* the questions raised by contemporary culture with *answers* revealed through religious tradition.

Initially this correlational method may sound as if it shares a good deal of common ground with the applicationist approach. In practice, though, Tillich's method gave much greater weight to the voice of contemporary culture in its dialogue with theology. Partly this is because in his method contemporary culture is allowed to set the focus for the conversation, in contrast to applicationist approaches which simply evaluate contemporary culture on the basis of a preformed theological agenda. Thus the concerns which are being wrestled with in contemporary culture become the questions that theology has to address. Partly also, Tillich's approach gave contemporary culture an important role in how we interpret religious traditions in seeking to answer these questions.[14] For example, he saw existentialism as a key tool not only for analyzing the key struggles and dilemmas of contemporary life, but he also used existentialist thought as the framework through which he interpreted Christian ideas back into this context. Thus, for Tillich (1952), God becomes the "ground of our being" who makes it possible to live in ways that are courageous and imaginative in the face of the uncertainties and suffering of our existence.

In the dialogue between theological norms and popular culture, Tillich's correlational method thus gives much greater weight to the "voice" of popular culture than applicationist approaches. At the same time, however, Tillich was clear that the answers to these concerns came ultimately from religious tradition rather than contemporary culture. He commented:

> [T]heology must use the immense and profound material of the existential analysis in all cultural realms . . . But theology cannot use it simply by accept-

ing it. Theology must confront it with the answer implied in the Christian message . . . The answer cannot be derived from the question. It is said *to* him who asks, but it is not taken *from* him. Existentialism cannot give answers . . . To give such answers is the function of the Church not only to itself, but also to those outside the Church. (Tillich, 1959, p.49)

Tillich's position here raises the question again of where we might reasonably expect to discover authoritative insights into the nature of truth and goodness. Tillich was clear that these ultimately resided in religious tradition, yet at the same time he did not dismiss the possibility that wider culture beyond the Church may have an important and constructive role in shaping our understanding of existence. Tillich clearly saw the role of the Church as that of maintaining a prophetic voice in the midst of wider society. But he also recognized that prophetic voices may also come from that wider society which might challenge distorted beliefs and practices in the Church. He thus wrote about the "latent Church," made up of people who had no formal religious affiliations, but who had important insights to offer on the nature of truth and goodness (ibid., p.51). This acknowledgment opens up the possibility that popular culture might have a constructive role in shaping our views of existence in addition to religious tradition. This possibility is explored more fully in a third approach to dialogue between theological norms and popular culture.

This third approach can be described as a *revised correlational* method. This method, associated with the work of theologians such as David Tracy (1981) and Don Browning (1991), is influenced by Tillich's correlational method but develops it in two important respects. Firstly, rather than seeing theology as a process of correlating questions raised by culture to answers offered by religious tradition, a revised correlational approach envisages a more complex conversation involving questions and answers from both culture and tradition. As Don Browning puts it:

[A revised correlational approach] envisions theology as a mutually critical dialogue between interpretations of the Christian message and interpretations of contemporary cultural experiences and practices. Stated more explicitly, Christian theology becomes a critical dialogue between the implicit questions and the explicit answers of the Christian classics and the explicit questions and implicit answers of contemporary cultural experiences and practices. According to [this approach], the Christian theologian must in principle have this critical conversation with "all other answers" from wherever they come. (1991, p.46)

This kind of dialogue is not therefore simply characterized by seeking religious answers to cultural struggles and dilemmas. Rather it becomes a process in which questions that have previously been regarded as important in religious tradition can be put to contemporary culture (e.g., the eschatological question of what end we believe the universe is moving towards). Equally it becomes one in which the often implicit answers to contemporary struggles that are offered within popular culture are also treated seriously as a resource for thinking about issues of meaning and value.

This broader and more complex understanding of the conversation between theology and contemporary culture leads to a second important development of Tillich's correlational method. This is the notion that contemporary culture can be a mediator of truth and goodness in its own right, and that contemporary culture can generate insights that require us to challenge or revise ideas and practices that have been an established part of religious tradition. As the pioneering pastoral theologian Seward Hiltner (1958, p.223) commented, theology should be seen as a "two-way street" in which religious tradition and contemporary culture can learn from each other, rather than the "one-way street" model adopted by Tillich.

The fourth and final approach to be considered briefly here is a *praxis* model of conversation between theology and culture exemplified by the range of liberation theologies that have emerged in recent decades (see Bevans, 1992, pp.63ff.). This approach shares the openness of the revised correlational approach to seeking truth, meaning, and value wherever it may be found, whether in religious tradition or popular culture. What distinguishes the praxis approach, however, is its commitment to critiquing religious and cultural beliefs and practices on the basis of their ability to promote liberation and well-being. Unlike the applicationist model, which evaluates popular culture on the basis of a preformed notion of theological orthodoxy, the praxis model evaluates both religious tradition and popular culture on the basis of "orthopraxy" (or their capacity to promote right action). The praxis model thus treats conversation partners of theological tradition and popular culture with equal regard, but also opens both up to critical scrutiny about the kind of lives and practices that both make possible.

To summarize, then, the applicationist, correlational, revised correlational, and praxis approaches represent four different models for conducting a conversation between theological norms and popular culture. The applicationist approach proceeds from the basis of a preformed theological agenda and set of beliefs and listens to the "voice" of popular culture simply with the intention of evaluating the extent to which it fits this agenda or those beliefs. A correlational approach, by contrast, attempts to listen to popular culture to discern the primary struggles and concerns of contemporary society. It then seeks to analyze what religious tradition might have to offer by way of answers to these concerns, and to present these religious answers in ways that are intelligible and relevant to that contemporary context. A revised correlational approach values a complex conversation between the questions and insights of both religious tradition and popular culture, and allows for the possibility that both religious tradition and popular culture can be usefully challenged and transformed through this process. Finally, the praxis model seeks to evaluate both theology and popular culture on the basis of their capacity to promote lives and practices that promote liberation and well-being. Of the various writers that we considered in chapter 2, Michael Medved and Brian Godawa are good examples of writers who adopt an applicationist approach. Robert Jewett and perhaps Christopher Deacy can be seen as working within a correlational method. Larry Kreitzer, Tom Beaudoin, and Anthony Pinn work within a revised correlational approach, as they give greater emphasis to the possibility that religious tradition can learn from popular culture. Finally, Robert Beckford, Anthony Pinn (again), and Margaret Miles can be seen as demonstrating a praxis approach in their work.

Earlier in this chapter we noted that theology involves a dynamic process of reflection. Each of these models of conversation between theology and popular culture involves a process of reflecting on the meaning of theological resources and popular cultural beliefs, values, practices, and experiences. In the final part of this chapter, we will think in more detail about how we can understand the process involved in following through one of these particular conversational models.

## the process of theological reflection on popular culture

The particular conversational model that I want to explore further in this section, and which will provide the basis for our discussions in the rest of the book, is the revised correlational approach. The particular conversational model that one adopts will inevitably be shaped by one's own experience, context, and religious commitments. In my view, the revised correlational approach is a constructive one precisely because it recognizes that truth and goodness are not the sole possession of one particular religious tradition or world-view. Such a recognition is important in the context of a pluralist society in which we are confronted by a range of different beliefs, values, practices, and experiences. The challenge of living in a pluralist society is that of learning to think critically about these different perspectives and practices in a way that can value what is positive within them whilst challenging that which is damaging. The revised correlational approach offers one way of thinking about a theological engagement with contemporary culture that invites a wide range of participants into the conversation and which values truth and goodness wherever it may be found.

Having said this, the revised correlational approach also needs to be informed by the praxis model. The praxis model is invaluable in reminding us that appropriate theological reflection should ultimately inspire ways of living and acting that are liberating and transformative. At its worst, the revised correlational approach risks becoming a form of abstract theological debate that does not lead into any tangible outcomes for the way in which people live their lives. From a praxis perspective such abstract debates are, not unreasonably, regarded with suspicion as superficial explorations of issues of meaning and value that do nothing to relieve suffering or counter injustice. The revised correlational approach should therefore take seriously the praxis model's concern for the effects of theological reflection. If it is able to do so then it holds the potential to meet the three key challenges of contemporary theology, namely taking seriously the insights of religious tradition, making constructive contributions to debates in a pluralist society and acting in solidarity with those who suffer (see Kamitsuka, 1999, p.4).

So if we adopt a revised correlational approach to the dialogue between theology and popular culture, what does this mean in practice? How do we work through the process of this kind of conversation?

Following Don Browning's (1991) work on the revised correlational approach, it is possible to identify three main stages to this process. Firstly, we need to engage in what Browning refers to as *descriptive theology*. This involves trying to understand the "horizon" of the particular example of contemporary popular culture that we are studying. Such understanding is developed by trying to discover the meanings of this aspect of popular culture on its own terms without bringing any religious or ethical judgments to bear on it. This may involve asking the following questions. What questions or issues is this form of popular culture concerned with? What understanding of life does it offer? What values and beliefs seem to be associated with it? What does this form of popular culture mean in people's day-to-day lives? What kind of lifestyles and practices is it associated with? What kind of experiences do people have in relation to this form of popular culture?

Through asking these kinds of questions we may be able to develop a clearer *description* of the concerns, beliefs, values, practices, and experiences associated with this aspect of popular culture. Developing this description may also involve studying how religious groups have responded to this form of popular culture. Examining these religious responses may generate new insights into the meanings of popular culture, and equally may also alert us to how religious groups have misunderstood popular culture or made premature and uninformed judgments about it.

When we have gained a clearer understanding of the meaning and significance of the particular aspect of popular culture that we are studying, it is then necessary to move onto the second stage of this process which Browning refers to as *historical theology*. Browning comments that the central question for this stage is to ask "what do the normative texts that are already part of our effective history *really* imply for our praxis when they are confronted as honestly as possible" (ibid., p.49)? In other words, this stage involves taking a serious look at our particular religious or philosophical tradition and asking what relevance it might have to the particular form of popular culture we are studying. This may involve reflecting on whether one's tradition raises important questions that are neglected in this aspect of popular culture. Or it may involve identifying core beliefs, values, symbols, or stories from one's tradition that address similar concerns or issues to those being explored in popular culture. As with the initial stage of describing popular culture, though, this investigation should not be undertaken superficially. Rather it involves serious scrutiny of how one's tradition might best be interpreted given the different situations and contexts through which it has been developed.

The first two stages of this process of reflection therefore aim at establishing two "horizons" for the conversation.[15] One of the horizons (clarified by descriptive theology) is that of the meaning and significance of the particular aspect of popular culture that we are studying. The second horizon (clarified by historical theology) is that of the questions and perspectives raised by our particular religious or philosophical tradition that are relevant to this form of popular culture. The third stage of this process, which Browning refers to as *systematic theology*, involves bringing these two sides or horizons together in a mutually critically conversation.

Writing as a Christian theologian, Browning describes the central task of this third stage as being "the fusion of horizons between the vision implicit in contemporary practices and the vision implied in the practices of the normative Christian texts" (ibid., p.51). This "fusion of horizons" involves asking critical questions of both popular culture and religious tradition. From the perspective of the normative beliefs and values of our particular tradition we may want to ask the following. In what respects does popular culture offer a truthful or constructive account of existence? To what degree are the values evident in popular culture good or healthy? Are the practices of popular culture just and do they promote well-being? Are the experiences associated with this form of popular culture adequate or constructive experiences of beauty, pleasure, or transcendence?

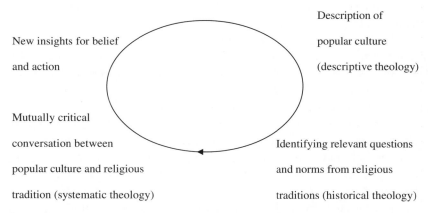

New insights for belief
and action

Mutually critical
conversation between
popular culture and religious
tradition (systematic theology)

Description of
popular culture
(descriptive theology)

Identifying relevant questions
and norms from religious
traditions (historical theology)

Figure 5.1    A model of the process of theological reflection on popular culture.

Equally, from the perspective of popular culture, we could ask whether the questions and insights of popular culture might lead us to revise our understanding of our particular religious or philosophical tradition. Does popular culture raise questions that have been inadequately explored by our tradition? Does it generate insights that help us to interpret our tradition in new ways? Or do particular perspectives on truth and goodness within popular culture challenge us to reject aspects of our tradition that may themselves be inadequate or damaging?

Through asking this range of questions, it is therefore possible to set in motion a mutually critical conversation between religious tradition and popular culture which has the potential to transform both our understandings of that tradition and the way in which we think and act in contemporary culture.

In summary, then, the revised correlational approach places a high value on taking time to understand both popular culture and religious tradition on their own terms. It is only through taking both seriously that a substantial and critical conversation between the two becomes possible.

A complex set of issues surrounds the question of how we can judge whether or not the outcomes of this conversation are truthful, good, and constructive. It is not possible to provide a simple answer to these issues in a way that will satisfy everyone. Some people undertaking this approach will still want to have this conversation guided by certain basic theological concepts that are seen as non-negotiable within a given religious tradition (orthodoxy). Others will judge the outcome of such conversations by the extent to which they generate liberating and healing practices and lifestyles (orthopraxis). Another possibility is that there can be no clear external criteria by which we can confidently judge the outcomes of such conversations, and that we are left instead to rely on the capacity of those involved in it to act in ways that are humble, rigorous, imaginative, and critical.[16] Ultimately these questions form part of the wider background of theological assumptions that a person or community brings to this kind of reflection, and will need to be addressed as part of more general theological discussions about how we know the nature of truth and goodness.


## conclusion

This chapter has addressed a number of complex issues, and in conclusion it will be helpful to summaries the main elements of a theological approach to the study of popular culture that I have set out here.

Firstly, understanding what it means to study popular culture from a theological perspective requires us to have a clear understanding of the nature of theology. In putting forward my own definition, I have suggested that theology needs to be seen as a normative, contextual, and dynamic discipline. Theology therefore involves a process of exploring how contemporary questions about meaning, values, and practice can be related to our understanding of the absolute reference point of life.

Based on this definition, I then proposed that popular culture can be seen as a particular context in which theological questions are explored. A theological study of popular culture thus means thinking critically about issues of meaning, value, and practice in popular culture from the perspective of particular theological beliefs, values, and concepts.

This kind of study can be usefully thought about in terms of a dialogue or conversation between religious tradition and popular culture. How one approaches this conversation – or whether one believes such a conversation should even be attempted – will be influenced by a range of basic assumptions that make up one's implicit or explicit theology of culture. We noted Niebuhr's summary of five different models of theology of culture which involve different perspectives on the potential value of a dialogue between religious tradition and culture. We also noted basic issues at stake in developing a theology of culture such as whether human cultures can be a source of goodness and truth, whether participating in culture should be seen as a creative opportunity, duty, or threat, and how optimistic we can be that culture can be transformed in positive ways.

Working on the assumption that there may be some validity to a critical conversation between theological norms and popular culture, we then identified four different approaches that such a conversation might take. The applicationist approach seeks to critique popular culture on the basis of pre-formed theological concepts. The correlational model seeks to correlate questions raised by popular culture with answers sensitively derived from religious tradition. A revised correlational approach advocates a more complex conversation between questions and answers offered both by religious tradition and popular culture. This approach also raises the possibility that popular culture may inform and challenge the beliefs and practices of religious tradition in the same way that theological norms may challenge popular culture. Finally, we noted a praxis model that evaluates both religious tradition and popular culture on their capacity to promote liberation and well-being.

In the last part of the chapter, we looked in more detail at the process involved in engaging in one of these conversational approaches – the revised correlational method. Here we noted that this process of reflection initially involved learning to understand and describe popular culture on its own terms. This then led to a process of investigating our religious or philosophical tradition to establish what relevance it might have for the particular popular cultural beliefs, values, practices, and experiences that we are studying. Finally, this process involves bringing together our understandings of popular culture and our understandings of our particular religious or philosophical tradition into a mutually critical conversation in which both "horizons" can inform and challenge the other.

These ideas about what it means to engage in a theological study of popular culture provide the basis on which the discussions in the remaining chapters of this book take place. In chapters 6–8 we shall now look in more depth at particular methods and approaches that can help us as we try to develop more rigorous and satisfying conversations between theological norms and popular culture.

# Chapter 6

# an author-focused approach to studying popular culture: eminem and the redemption of violence

## introduction

One of the themes that has emerged in the last couple of chapters has been the importance of listening to popular culture on its own terms before making any theological evaluation of it. Arguably one of the reasons that theology has made a limited impact on wider cultural debates is that, fairly or unfairly, religious responses to popular culture are sometimes perceived to be reactionary, superficial, or ill-informed. Whilst there is some excellent work on popular culture being undertaken by those working in theology and religious studies, there are also examples of work being produced in this field based on very limited knowledge of key issues, theories, and methods in popular culture studies.

If theological and religious critiques of popular culture are to be taken seriously in the wider academic and public arena then they need to begin from a substantial understanding of the forms of popular culture being studied. Indeed, as we noted in the last chapter, the first stage of a serious theological engagement with popular culture will be to understand the "horizon" of popular culture on its own terms. One of the most important tasks for the theological study of popular culture, at the moment then, is to develop a clearer understanding of specific ways in which we can "read" and make sense of popular culture. Even some of the better work being done in this field is at times vague about what methods are being used to study popular cultural texts or practices. By clarifying the range of methods that we could use in making sense of popular culture, we are able to see some of the assumptions and blind-spots that we might be bringing to our work. We can also become clearer about the range of different approaches that we can use in such study and the distinctive strengths and limitations of these approaches.

In the next three chapters we will be adopting a case-study approach to look at how different approaches to exploring popular culture can inform theological analyses of specific forms of popular culture varying from Eminem, *The Simpsons*, and club culture. The methods being presented here are not offered on the basis of a hierarchy in which some methods are seen as being intrinsically more useful than others. Rather it is more useful to think of these in terms of network of different methods that are helpful for illuminating popular culture in different ways. By limiting ourselves simply to one method, we limit the insights we can gain about our field of study. But through learning about popular culture by using a range of methods, we can begin to build up a richer and more complex understanding of our subject.[1]

In this chapter, we will begin by exploring an overview of this network of methods, and briefly consider those methods that will not be discussed in more detail later in these chapters. We will then turn our attention to the first of the methods of studying popular culture that we are going to examine in more depth, namely an "author-focused" or "auteur" approach. Finally we will explore how this approach can contribute to the theological study of popular culture by using it as the basis for a discussion of the redemption of violence in the music of Eminem.

## an overview of key approaches in the study of popular culture

To introduce this network of methods for studying popular culture, I want to begin with a diagram (figure 6.1).

This diagram highlights three different approaches to understanding popular culture, an author-focused approach, a text-based approach, and an ethnographic/audience-reception approach. Each of these approaches brings a different set of questions and methods to the study of popular culture, as we shall see more clearly in these coming chapters. Put simply, an author-focused approach is interested in exploring how a particular piece of popular culture (e.g., a film, novel, or piece of music) reflects the background, status, personality, and intentions of its particular author or authors. This approach assumes that by understanding more about the author we will be able to gain a clearer picture on some of the core meanings of the form of popular culture that we are studying. Secondly, a "text-based" approach explores how we can

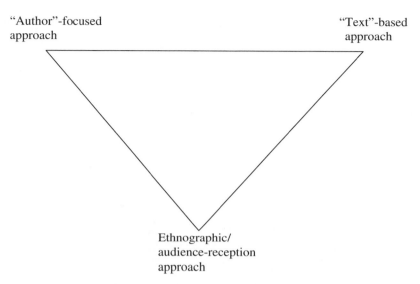

"Author"-focused
approach

"Text"-based
approach

Ethnographic/
audience-reception
approach

Figure 6.1   Key approaches to analyzing popular cultural texts and practices.

read the meaning of popular cultural "texts" (which could include anything from TV programs to fashion) without any reference to the thoughts or intentions of the people involved in creating them. This approach is thus less interested in the mind of individual authors, and more interested in how language and symbols convey cultural meanings. Thirdly, an ethnographic or audience-reception approach focuses on what meanings popular culture has for people in real world settings. This might include what meanings people take from watching particular films or TV programs, or from taking part in popular cultural activities like shopping, clubbing, playing sports, or going traveling. This approach is therefore less interested in what a popular cultural "text" might mean in abstract terms, and more concerned with what meanings popular cultural "texts" or "practices" have for people in their day-to-day lives.

Whilst these three different approaches set the broad framework for popular culture studies, there are other important methods that have also been used to study authors, texts and audiences. We can include these by developing our initial diagram in the following way (figure 6.2).

Psychoanalytic criticism, ideological criticism, and genre criticism are all important methods for studying popular culture. Whilst there is not enough space for us to consider each of these in as much detail as the author-focused, text-based, and ethnographic methods, it will be helpful to give at least some introduction to them.[2]

"Author"-focused                                                    "Text"-based
approach                                                            approach

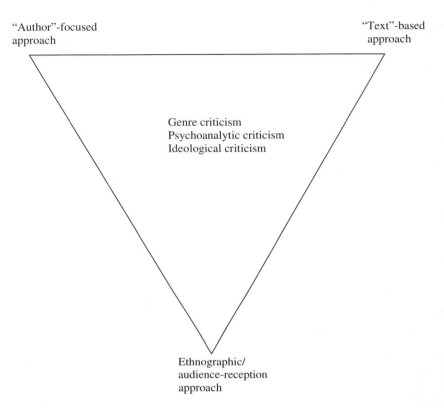

Genre criticism
Psychoanalytic criticism
Ideological criticism

Ethnographic/
audience-reception
approach

Figure 6.2   Further approaches to the analysis of popular cultural texts and
practices.

*Psychoanalytic criticism* uses concepts from psychoanalytic theory to
analyze the meanings and functions of popular culture. The psychoanalytic
movement, which began with the pioneering work of Sigmund Freud, has itself
been a complex one and psychoanalytic theory has taken a number of specialized forms. Reflecting this, cultural critics have sought not only to draw on
Freud's theories, but also notably on the work of writers such as Carl Jung and
Jacques Lacan who developed their own original psychoanalytic approaches.

Psychoanalytic theories and methods have been used to study popular
culture in a variety of ways (see Creed, 2000, for a good summary of these).
For example, psychoanalytic ideas can be used to explore how an individual
author's psyche has been shaped by their early experiences, and how this influences their later creative work. One of the first examples of such a psychoanalytic study of a creative artist was Freud's (1910) own analysis of the

significance of Leonardo da Vinci's childhood on his subsequent work. Secondly, psychoanalytic ideas can be used to make sense of particular themes or events in popular cultural texts such as films or TV programs. Thus, the character of Norman Bates in Alfred Hitchcock's film *Psycho* can be interpreted in psychoanalytic terms as a story about the damaging consequences of a man failing to resolve his Oedipal desires for his mother.[3] Thirdly, psychoanalytic theories have also been used in a variety of ways to examine how people interact with popular culture, what makes it pleasurable for them, and how popular culture structures pleasure in certain ways. One of the most well-known studies of this type is Laura Mulvey's (1975) article "Visual pleasure and narrative cinema" which draws on psychoanalytic concepts to explore how films typically reinforce a "male gaze" on the world. What each of these approaches share is a common belief that psychoanalytic theories and methods form a useful way of interpreting texts and experiences that enable us to see things within them that we might miss without these psychoanalytic tools.

*Ideological criticism* shares a similar belief that understanding popular culture requires us to begin from particular theoretical and cultural standpoints. Indeed psychoanalytic and ideological forms of criticism can be seen as both working on the basis of a "hermeneutic of suspicion" that uses particular theoretical concepts and methods to get beyond the biases and distortions of "common sense" interpretations of the world. Ideological criticism actually embraces a range of different, though at times overlapping, approaches. Each of these approaches begins from the assumption that "normal" everyday understandings of the world tend to hide certain vested interests and the realities of social inequalities or oppression. These understandings thus have an *ideological* function in maintaining the status quo in a given society or in hindering attempts to change society in ways that are more equal and liberating.[4] However, through analyzing culture from a certain perspective, ideological critics argue that it is possible to see beyond these distorted understandings, and to think in ways that give a more accurate analysis of unjust and oppressive social structures and practices.

The main approaches to have developed within ideological criticism are Marxist, black, postcolonial, and feminist methods of cultural criticism. Marxist approaches emphasize the importance of social and economic relationships in shaping our view of the world, and in particular how capitalist societies function in ways that tend to protect vested economic interests. Black cultural criticism begins from the starting point of acknowledging racial injustice and identifies how the assumptions and practices of white-dominated societies have tended to neglect black experiences and perceptions.

Postcolonial criticism focuses on how cultural texts and practices may either reproduce or resist the dominant assumptions of Western Europe or North America, and obscure or emphasize perspectives from cultural contexts in other parts of the world. Feminist criticism recognizes the patriarchal nature of contemporary society, and seeks to highlight how contemporary culture can function in ways that marginalize women's experiences and interests. It is important to recognize that these approaches are not necessarily discrete entities, though. Indeed contemporary ideological criticism will often draw insights from each of these approaches (and others, e.g., gay and lesbian criticism and queer theory) in developing critiques of distorted and damaging cultural assumptions and practices. For seminal examples of these forms of ideological criticism in the context of theology and religious studies, see Gutierrez (1973) on Marxist criticism, Cone (1970) on black cultural criticism, Radford Ruether (1983) on feminist criticism, and Sugirtharajah (2002) on postcolonial criticism.

Ideological criticism can be applied to popular culture studies in a range of ways. It can be used to explore the ideas and motivations of particular authors (e.g., to what extent do they seek to replicate or challenge damaging cultural assumptions and practices?). Equally, it can be used in the study of popular cultural texts, for example in the critical analysis of the ways in which oppressed or marginalized groups are represented in those texts. Similarly, ideological criticism can also be used to explore the forms of popular culture in day-to-day life. For example, does popular culture function in ways that simply maintain the injustices of a capitalist system, or can people make use of popular cultural resources in ways that are genuinely liberating?

The third approach to be considered briefly here is *genre criticism*. Genre criticism is normally used in relation to popular cultural texts such as films, TV programs, books, and music. A basic assumption is that it is possible to identify broad categories (or "genres") that many such texts fall into, and that these categories share certain basic characteristics and conventions that both writers and audiences have grown used to. Thus, in the context of film, we are familiar of the concept of broad genres such as the Western, horror, science-fiction, romantic comedy, or film noir (see, e.g., Dick, 2002, pp.117ff.). Similarly, in the context of TV, we are also used to distinctions such as period drama, sitcom, or documentary. As a method of analyzing popular culture, genre criticism explores the significance of the relationship between a genre and a particular author, text or audience. For example, what do we know about how a particular author understands their work in relation to the broader genre within which they are working? What can we learn about a popular cultural text from the ways in which it supports or subverts the conventions of a particular genre? Or what might the popularity of a particular genre tell us about the context and concerns of the audience that enjoys it?

Genre criticism is not a straightforward approach, however. Popular cultural texts, at times, do not fit easily into any given genre or fall across several genres. The notion of genre may not always be helpful in particular instances as well. Is film noir, for example, really a genre or more an attitude towards the representation of life in film (see Deacy, 2001)? Furthermore, whilst a cultural critic may find it helpful to think about a particular popular cultural text in terms of its genre, the audience for this text may approach it with a quite different set of interpretations (see Tudor, 1976). Whilst these points should make us cautious about adopting simplistic approaches to genre criticism, analyzing popular culture in terms of genres can at times produce some useful insights into our field of study.

Psychoanalytic, ideological, and genre criticism all represent important tools that can be used to make sense of popular cultural texts and practices. Central questions in the study of popular culture, however, surround the issues of the significance of authors, texts, and everyday practices for making sense of popular culture. It is to the question of the significance of the author that we will now turn.

## an auteur approach to the study of popular culture

There is a long tradition in Western culture of placing a high value on the creative abilities of the individual artist. In 1550, Giorgio Vasari first published his book *The Lives of the Artists* in which he celebrated the creative genius of a range of Renaissance artists, amongst whom Michelangelo was depicted as the greatest talent. This book, which became a founding text for the discipline of Western history of art, presented these artists as creative individuals, blessed by God, who had ushered in a golden age of artistic achievement. This emphasis on the individual artist has also found expression in romantic and neoromantic understandings of art as the process of expressing the artist's inner world (Johnston, 2000, p.132f.). Thus, from this perspective, art is best understood as an attempt by the artist to communicate their own particular thoughts, feelings, and perceptions.

Given this emphasis on the individual artist in Western culture since the Renaissance, it is unsurprising that one broad approach to understanding popular cultural texts such as film, music, books, websites, or TV programs is to explore their meaning in relation to the author or authors who created them. For if these texts are in some way an expression of the thoughts, feelings, and intentions of their author, then understanding more about the author should tell us more about the text itself. This interest in the author of popular cultural texts has been developed in most detail in the context of film studies. What became known as the *auteur* approach to film criticism developed initially in postwar France, and in particular in the 1950s through the French film journal *Cahiers du cinema* (Stam & Miller, 2000, p.1). This approach was subsequently taken up in other countries, notably by the film journal *Movie* in Britain and by the film critic Andrew Sarris in America (Caughie, 1981, p.9).

At the heart of this approach was the suggestion that critics should evaluate films on the basis of the artistic skill of those responsible for "authoring" them. The author in this context quickly came to mean the director of the film, though less commonly scriptwriters or film stars have also been thought of as of "auteurs" (see, e.g., Phillips, 1996). Not all directors were judged to be auteurs, however. It was claimed that a good auteur-director would be able to rise above the constraints of working within a commercialized film industry, and be able to impose something of their distinctive personality, concerns or vision on their films. Andrew Sarris (1992, p.586ff), for example, argued that an auteur would be a technically competent director, who could stamp their mark on their films and bring a consistent personal perspective whatever the specific content of their work. This would produce what Sarris (1976, p.246) describes as a "meaningful coherence" across the body of that director's work, and make it possible to think about the meaning of his[5] films in terms of this particular style. Directors who could achieve such standards were regarded as auteurs. A director who produced work which was formulaic or which lacked signs of individual creativity tended to be designated as a "metteur-en-scene": competent craftsmen as opposed to creative artists, whose work was of less artistic and critical significance (see, e.g., Wollen, 1972).

Inevitably this distinction led to heated debates about which directors qualified for auteur status and which did not, as well as charges that this approach led to work produced outside this canon of auteurs being neglected (see Phillips, 1996, p.151). Despite the difficulties in resolving these disputes, auteur critics maintained that attention to the style and concerns of a particular author was a helpful strategy for interpreting the visual art offered through film.

Since its initial hey-day in the 1950s and 1960s, auteur criticism has faced a range of objections. Many of these reflect a basic concern that thinking about a film (or indeed similar popular cultural texts such as TV programs or popular music) in terms of the creative output of a single individual author is too simplistic (see Tasker, 2002, p.3). For example, the process of producing such popular cultural texts is highly collaborative, with many different people involved in their composition and production. Whilst some particular auteurs may indeed be able to dominate the production process as Sarris suggested (e.g., Stanley Kubrick), there is a danger that focusing on the individual director or musician, for example, oversimplifies our understanding of this process. Similarly too strong an emphasis on the personality of the auteur may lead us to make too strong a connection between the content of their work and their own personal background. Or it might be equally tempting to emphasize the unity of styles and themes across their work, rather than focus on what is discontinuous or different within it. Placing too much emphasis on what authors might have to say about the meaning of their own work risks obscuring the fact that they themselves may not be fully aware of its possible meanings. Furthermore, as film production companies and record labels stress the integrity of the auteur as a means of promoting their work, we may need to be conscious that the idea of the auteur in contemporary popular culture may be as much a marketing tool as a theoretical concept. Such marketing practices can distort our understanding of artists' work, as for example in the case of musicians who are credited with writing their own material by record companies when it is in fact largely written by someone else (see Shuker, 2001, p.130).

Ultimately, though, auteur criticism fell out of fashion in the 1970s and 1980s with the emergence of new, poststructuralist approaches to cultural criticism that placed a much stronger emphasis on the ways in which language, symbols, and texts construct meaning (for a further discussion of this, see chapter 7). Indeed Roland Barthes (1977), whose work was seminal in this movement, proclaimed the "death of the author" and argued that the meaning of the text came from our reading of it and not from what we imagined the author's intended meaning to be. From this perspective the author of a text was reduced to a messenger of predetermined cultural meanings, rather than an individual creator of meaning (see Caughie, 1981, p.126).

This trend has subsequently reversed – with some skeptics noting that whilst poststructuralist writers proclaimed the death of the author, some of them became international academic celebrities and certainly kept collecting their royalty checks (Stam & Miller, 2000, p.4). The debate about the role of authorship and the meaning of texts remains a complex one, and indeed raises questions of subjectivity, agency, and interpretation that are at the heart of contemporary debates in cultural theory. Nevertheless, there is a greater willingness amongst many contemporary cultural critics to think about the significance of the author as one figure involved in the construction of meaning in popular cultural texts. The contemporary interest in authors, however, places a strong interest on the significance of authors in the context of wider historical, social, and cultural forces that influence their work (see Andrew, 2000; Toynbee, 2000).[6]

Whilst we need to be cautious, then, about adopting too simplistic an understanding of the role of the author in shaping the meaning of a popular cultural text, what kinds of questions can we usefully ask about popular cultural auteurs? Four different types of question can be suggested here:

1    *Contextual/cultural questions.* What is the author's social and cultural background? How might this context influence the style and content of their work? In what ways is the author's background and context similar or different to our own, and how might this shape the way in which we interpret or respond to their work?

2    *Questions of authorial intent.* What do we know about the author's own views on what they were trying to explore or communicate through their work? How do they interpret what it means? If they are seeking to work within a particular genre, how do they understand their relationship to that genre (e.g., attempting to support, revise, or subvert it)?

3    *Questions relating to the author's wider body of work.* How does this particular piece of work relate to other work done by this author? What is its significance in the context of this wider body of work? In what ways is it similar or different to other work done by this author, and what significance can be attached to these similarities and differences?

4    *Psychological/psychoanalytic questions.* What can we reconstruct about the author's psychological history? What do we know about their formative, early experiences? What is the relationship between the individual author's psyche and their creative output?

From our discussion above, it is clear that some caution needs to be taken in answering these questions. The notion of the author as creative individual artist can be such a seductive one in the context of Western culture that we can be tempted to ascribe greater coherence or significance to an author's background, intentions or style than may be justified. Nevertheless, if these types of question are answered on the basis of rigorous analysis of what we know about a particular author, then this can provide some useful perspectives that can help us to develop an interpretation of particular popular cultural texts.

In the final part of this chapter, we will now examine how this author-focused approach might contribute in practice to a theological analysis of the music of Eminem.

## studying a rap auteur: eminem and the redemption of violence

"So much anger aimed in no particular direction/ it just sprays and sprays . . . (lyrics from "White America," *The Eminem Show*)
   My music is my psychiatrist. My microphone is my psychiatrist, it listens to me talk. Once I've got it out, I'm not mad anymore. (Eminem quoted in Weiner, 2002, p.78)

Eminem has arguably been one of the most remarkable phenomena in Western popular music of the past decade. Since the release of his *Slim Shady LP* in 1999, this previously obscure white rapper has received extraordinary levels of public and critical interest in his work. Indeed in 2002, Eminem's name attracted more enquiries by people using the Google internet search engine than any other American musician. This public interest has been reflected in the high sales figures for his music. Each of this three albums, *The Slim Shady LP*, *The Marshall Mathers LP* (released in 2000), and *The Eminem Show* (released in 2002) have all sold several million copies, as has his soundtrack to the 2002 movie *8 Mile* (Bozza, 2003, pp.34ff.). In its first week of release *The Marshall Mathers LP* sold just over two million copies (not quite an industry record), and when *The Eminem Show* sold 1.3 million copies in its first week it bucked the trend of an otherwise depressed music market[7]. *The Eminem Show* subsequently went on to become the best-selling popular music album of 2002.

   Eminem's fame, or notoriety, is far from being simply down to his impressive record sales, however. His meteoric rise to fame has been dogged by a range of controversies. As a form of popular music, rap developed in poor black communities in America in the 1970s, and has traditionally been associated with black performers.[8] The fact that Eminem, as a white performer, has enjoyed greater commercial success than most other black rappers has led some people in the hip hop community to regard him as the new Elvis Presley – someone who "steals" black music and who profits from it by virtue of being white. Unflattering comparisons have also been made between Eminem and Vanilla Ice, another white rapper of the early 1990s who enjoyed commercial success amongst white audiences that few critics felt his music genuinely merited. It is arguably too simplistic to see Eminem simply as the creation of record companies who wanted to broaden the appeal of rap amongst a white audience. He did, after all, live most of his teenage years in a predominantly black neighborhood in Detroit and was genuinely engaged in the black hip hop culture of that city, helping to form the rap group D-12 in which he is the only white performer. Furthermore, before coming to fame, Eminem also worked hard for several years in trying to win credibility with black rap audiences who were deeply skeptical of the idea of a white rapper, and towards the end of that time was earning recognition for his writing and performance skills (Hasted, 2003, pp.35ff.). Nevertheless, Eminem has remained an ambiguous figure in the hip hop community, and despite his commercial success and Grammy awards, his work still receives a mixed reception at best in the rap music press (see, e.g., Bozza, 2003, pp.87ff.).[9]

Suspicion towards Eminem amongst some in the hip hop community has been a relatively minor controversy compared to the public reaction to the content of his lyrics, however. The recurrent violent stories, fantasies, and threats within his songs have attracted criticisms from politicians, pressure groups, and journalists who have questioned whether this kind of material is suitable for public consumption. More specifically the frequent references to violence against women (including rape), and the mocking attitude towards gay men and women, have led to the charges that his music is dangerously misogynistic and homophobic and that it encourages violence towards these already vulnerable groups. As one spokesperson for a gay rights group commented, Eminem's lyrics were "the words that kids hear in school hallways before they get beat up" (Huxley, 2000, p.145).

The controversy about the violence in Eminem's songs, and his own attitudes towards this content, provide a useful case example for an author-focused approach to the study of his music. Making sense of this violent lyrical content, and reflecting theologically on its significance, can be usefully informed by understanding more about Eminem's own background and how he understands his music relating to his own life experience. As we shall see in more detail shortly, it is clear that Eminem regards his artistic treatment of violence as personally cathartic, and in this sense sees his working of violent emotions and fantasies into rap songs as a redemptive way of dealing with his sense of rage at the world. Perhaps surprisingly, given the content of his lyrics, some commentators who would otherwise be regarded as liberal or left-leaning have agreed with him (for example, Maureen Dowd (2002) of the *New York Times*). Whether the treatment of violence in Eminem's music is indeed constructive or not is a central part of the cultural controversy that surrounds his work. By exploring Eminem's social and psychological background, as well as his own understanding of his music, we can develop clearer insights into his work that can then provide a basis for exploring theological questions about how constructive and redemptive his artistic treatment of violence really is.

Figure 6.3   Eminem during his performance at the Docklands Arena, London in 2001. Wearing the hockey mask and carrying the (unplugged) chainsaw is another example of the way in which Eminem plays with images of himself as a violent threat to society (© Corbis).

Within this author-focused approach, then, we need to develop an interpretation of Eminem's work by trying to understand more about him as a person and performer. A brief biography will be a useful starting point for this.[10]

"Eminem" is one of the aliases of Marshall Bruce Mathers III, who was born in Kansas City on 17 October 1972.[11] Marshall's father was only 23, and his mother 17, when he was born, and his parents' youthful marriage proved short-lived with his father moving out of the family home never to return when Marshall was only six-months old. Marshall never had any further contact with his father. As an older child he tried to write to him but never received any response. Even more painfully, he would sometimes stay at relatives of his fathers and would be there when his father telephoned them, yet his father never asked to speak to him on the phone (Hasted, 2003, p.20).

Marshall was subsequently raised by his mother, Debbie, with whom he appears to have always had a strained relationship. The precise details of his childhood are the focus of a bitter dispute between them, which led to his mother initiating a $10 million law-suit against him in September 1999 for allegedly defamatory comments he made about his upbringing in press interviews.[12] His mother has publicly characterized herself as a loving parent, trying to offer the best home for him she could under difficult circumstances. By contrast, he has depicted her as emotionally unstable, dependent on prescription drugs, and unsupportive. Doubtless, some of his accounts of his childhood are inflected with the exaggeration that can typify the self-presentation of rap performers. It is hard to know, for example, what to make of his claim that he suffered Munchausen's syndrome by proxy at his mother's hands (made in the lyrics of "Cleaning out my closet" in *The Eminem Show*). Nevertheless, it is clear that he regards his childhood as a painful time for him for a number of reasons.

Marshall's childhood years were certainly marked by insecurity and poverty. During his childhood his mother never found regular employment, though did at some points receive an income by fostering other children. Her low income meant that much of Marshall's early childhood was spent living in different homes – either those of her relatives or in other rented accommodation before they defaulted on rent and had to move on. From when he was eleven, they lived in different poor areas in Detroit, eventually settling in a poor predominantly black neighborhood in which Marshall would at times be bullied for being white. This bullying was a regular feature of Marshall's childhood, which at times took highly dangerous forms. When he was ten, an older boy who had often bullied him pushed Marshall into a snow bank during a fight. Hitting his head on the compacted snow caused a head injury that developed a few hours later into a life-threatening cerebral hemorrhage.[13] Attacks continued into his teenage years, with Marshall being shot at on one occasion, and being forced to strip to his underwear at gun point by a gang another time before being rescued by a passing truck driver who was himself armed with a gun. Marshall's accounts of his childhood and teenage years reflect a sensitive and vulnerable person who did not begin to make real friends until he was a teenager. His sense of an unstable and unsupportive home, and an unsafe and dangerous world beyond it, provided considerable emotional impetus for his subsequent musical work.

Marshall Mathers left school at the age of fifteen, having failed ninth grade for the third time as much, he later claimed, because of his poor attendance as his limited educational ability. His decision to leave appears to have been influenced by strong pressure from his mother for him to find a job to bring some money into their household. From this point on he then began a series of low-wage jobs, the one which he held most regularly being a short-order cook at a nearby suburban restaurant. For the next ten years, he worked in these jobs whilst at the same time continuing to hone his skills as a rap writer and performer. Despite a hostile reception from some parts of the black hip hop community in Detroit, he enjoyed some degree of success in building up his musical profile. He had signed to a local production company at the age of fifteen, when the owners heard him rapping on a local radio station. In time this led to the release of his first album, *Infinite*, in 1996, which sold few copies and received no critical attention. Despite winning rap contests on a regular basis, he was receiving no significant income from his music and had to continue working long hours in his low-paid jobs to survive. These financial pressures increased when his developing relationship with Kim Scott (originally one of his mother's foster-charges) led to Kim giving birth to their daughter, Hailie Jade on Christmas Day, 1996. The struggle to pay rent on their home, or even pay for basic necessities such as diapers for Hailie, dominated the following year and reached a low point when Marshall lost his job five days before Christmas Day in 1997. His attempt to take a drugs overdose at that point, in the midst of his depression, was subsequently reflected in frequent references to suicide and self-harm in his later lyrics.

In the midst of this particularly difficult period, a remarkable transformation took place in Marshall Mathers' fortunes. He was approached by the production company Interscope (who also produced the music of Marilyn Manson) to sign a record deal in which his music would be produced by Dr Dre. Dre had previously established a high-profile musical career through his membership of the controversial gangsta rap band N.W.A. (Niggaz With Attitude) and through his own solo work. At the point of signing Eminem, though, Dr Dre's career had itself stalled, and the collaboration between these two artists proved decisive in ensuring subsequent commercial success for both as well as artistic credibility for the largely unknown white rapper.

Whilst the transformation from urban poverty to musical superstardom could appear to be a fairy tale ending for Marshall Mathers, in reality it opened a new chapter of difficulties for him. His use of alcohol, marijuana, Ecstasy, and other prescription medication became much heavier. The law suit initiated by his mother in 1999 led to a complete breakdown in relations between them. His relationship with Kim (whom he married in 1999) also proved to be fragile. Even when Hailie was a few months old, Kim found a new partner and was threatening to take out a restraining order to prevent him from seeing Hailie Jade. Whilst Kim and Marshall were reconciled at this point, their relationship continued to be fraught and he initially sued for divorce after she slit her wrists in August 2000. The couple eventually divorced in 2002, taking shared custody of Hailie Jade.

From this brief biography, it is clear that the early life of Marshall Mathers has involved considerable hardship. Consistent themes have been the struggle with urban poverty and effective homelessness,[14] being a victim of violence, feeling let down by parental and authority figures,[15] and experiencing dysfunctional and conflictual relationships with the women with whom he was closest in his life. This range of traumatic experiences has become a basic, indeed relentless, resource in his subsequent musical output, and through understanding this background we can begin to develop more insight into the varying significance that violent images and stories play in his music.

Whilst violent content pervades much of Eminem's songs, it is important to distinguish the different forms that this takes. Firstly, there is content (mainly on *The Slim Shady LP*) in which the violence is absurd and cartoonish, and evidently intended to be humorous. One example of this is the violent fantasy scene on the track "As The World Turns" in which Eminem pursues a woman to her home, who tries to seduce him, then bites his leg off before he finally kills her by penetrating her with his "go-go-gadget dick." Whilst this humor may not be to everyone's taste, this content clearly has a surreal element more in keeping with children's cartoons than with any suggestion of reference to reality. A second type of violent content in his music are images and threats that fit more generally within the genre of gangsta rap. This can be seen in songs in which Eminem talks up his interest in guns and his willingness to resort to violence to protect his interests (e.g., "I'm Shady" on *The Slim Shady LP* and "Soldier" on *The Eminem Show*). This content can be seen more in terms of Eminem trying to project an image of himself that fits within this gangsta genre, rather than reflecting his own life experience in any sense. Indeed, far from the macho image of the gangsta rapper, the young Eminem appears to have been physically frail and shy. Despite the despair that he felt at times in the midst of his poverty, he never resorted to crime such as drug dealing as a means of getting money. His only real dealings with the police arose when, as a teenager he got into a fight trying to protect his mother, and more notoriously, in June 2000, when he assaulted a man outside a club whom he believed had been kissing Kim. Some of the violent content in his music therefore needs to be read not as a reflection of his life or personality, but as a form of lyrical expression that fits within the genre of music within which he is working and that is popular with the often white, suburban audiences who buy it.[16]

A third category of violent content in Eminem's work appears to arise much more directly out of his experience, however. His work is remarkable for its consistent attacks on a range of people whom he perceives as having person- ally let him down, disrespected, or hurt him. As Eminem has put it, "I run on vengeance" (Hasted, 2003, p.28). These figures include his father and mother, Kim, school bullies, teachers, erstwhile friends, critics in the hip hop community, other rappers and pop musicians, politicians, and feminist and gay rights protestors. In different ways each of these become the focus for violent threats or fantasies. The most explicit of these are typically reserved for those in his family. "My Name Is" contains a reference to Eminem slitting his father's throat in a dream. "Kill You" includes lyrics about raping and killing his mother. As we shall discuss in more detail shortly, the songs "Bonnie & Clyde '97" and "Kim" give detailed accounts of him slitting Kim's throat and then dumping her body in a lake with the help of Hailie Jade.

It is clear that Eminem himself regards this violent content as a helpful and constructive way of dealing with the emotions of hurt and frustration he feels at his past experiences and his continuing struggles. As he comments:

> Writing is definitely therapeutic for me. My shit is like therapy, not only when I'm writing it, but also when I'm in the booth saying it. It's a way to get shit off my chest. (Weiner, 2000, p.78)

Eminem thus sees his music as providing a creative outlet for powerful emotions and desires for vengeance that might otherwise find expression in more destructive ways, either through physical harm to himself or others. In this sense, his understanding of his work could be seen to reflect Freud's notion of the value of the destructive impulses of the id being subliminated into more constructive forms of expression such as humor or one's work (see Jacobs, 1992, pp.38f.). The fact that Eminem regards his music as a con- structive way of dealing with his aggressive impulses is further indicated by the fact that he played Kim tracks in which he recounted violent fantasies about her, and appears genuinely surprised that she reacted badly to them. For Eminem, then, his music provides a means of containing and expressing emotions and impulses that would be more dangerous were they to be acted out.

There are two important strategies that Eminem uses to separate out the expression of his personal desires for vengeance and the acting out of violence in the real world. One of these is the use of a particular persona, "Slim Shady," to act as the mouthpiece of these fantasies. Eminem describes Slim Shady as the "dark, evil, creatively sick" part of himself (Weiner, 2000, p.10).[17] But unlike the Marshall Mathers who was rejected and bullied, or the Eminem who just tries to be a nice guy, Slim Shady is set on a mission to destroy all those who have wronged or hurt him, and then to cause further chaos simply because he wants to. Through adopting the Slim Shady persona, Marshall/Eminem becomes able to say how he feels about the world and what he would like to do to people who have damaged him.[18] Yet precisely through using this persona, it becomes possible to see these fantasies as the product of a disturbed mind, rather than as literal statements of what Marshall/Eminem intends to do. Indeed Eminem is at pains to distance his real self from the violent image he portrays of himself in his music. As he raps on "Sing for the Moment," "if my music is literal, then I'm a criminal – how the fuck could I raise a little girl? I couldn't, I wouldn't be fit to."

A second strategy for distancing the music from real violence is Eminem's relatively sophisticated analysis of media effects theories that suggest a connection between violent media content and violent behavior. He consistently critiques the idea that the image that he portrays of himself in the music should be taken as a role model for people in any sense. In "My Name Is," he asks a class of children if they want to be like him, and "fuck their lives up" as well as he has done (their response is somewhat bemused). Similarly his track "Role Model" begins ironically with Eminem saying he is going to drown himself and asking whether his audience would like to copy him at this too. His songs also make frequent reference to the difference between representing violence in the media, and actual violent behavior in the real world. On "Sing for the Moment," on *The Eminem Show*, he comments that music can certainly create moods and evoke feelings, but asks if music can load guns and pull triggers. If it could, he goes on, then anyone before a judge on assault charges in the future can simply blame his music and not need to take any responsibility for their own actions.

Eminem therefore clearly understands his music as a creative form that allows him to explore violent thoughts and fantasies in a way that does not create more violence in the real world. He consistently claims that his music is not to be taken "literally," either as a reflection of his own lifestyle or as a form of encouragement to actual violent behavior. Nevertheless, it provides him with a means of expressing powerful feelings and fantasies that continue to haunt him out of his deprived past and his continuing struggles with some of his relationships in the present.

This understanding of his work is evident in three tracks that relate to his fantasies about murdering Kim. In the summer of 1997, only a few months after Hailie's birth, Kim was threatening to move in with another man and his son, and to get a restraining order preventing Marshall from seeing his daughter. He responded by writing "Bonnie & Clyde '97," in which he narrates a conversation with Hailie Jade as he drives with her to the lake with Kim's dead body in the trunk of the car. He tries, in turn, to persuade her that this is just a game (that the red stain on Kim's shirt is just ketchup and that Kim just wants to go for a late night swim), and to explain why he has murdered Kim (Kim made him real mad and was trying to stop him from seeing Hailie Jade). Eventually they arrive at the lake, and he seeks Hailie's help as they push Kim's weighted body in and he asks her to help with "a couple more things in the trunk" (the dead bodies of Kim's new partner and his son). An arguably more disturbing follow-up to this song came with the track "Kim" on *The Marshall Mathers LP*. This offers a fantasy of the actual argument between Marshall and Kim (with Eminem playing both voices), that leads eventually to Kim having her throat cut. The track begins with him confronting Kim about leaving him, and the confrontation becomes more aggressive and accusatory on his part until she is reduced to pleading for her life and he kills her. In the real world it became clear that Kim found the brutal treatment of her in these songs profoundly distressing, and her attempt to kill herself in August 2000 came only a few weeks after the album containing the track "Kim" was released.

At the same time as expressing these violent thoughts and fantasies, Eminem also distanced himself from them in another related track on *The Marshall Mathers LP*. Following the opening track "Kill You" (which is one of the most violent and misogynist tracks on arguably his darkest album) comes the remarkable track "Stan."[19] The lyrics of "Stan" present an unfolding story of a fan who is obsessed with Eminem, and who feels slighted because Eminem does not return his letters and does not sign an autograph for him after a concert. Enraged the fan decides to get drunk and to drive his car into a river with his pregnant girlfriend locked in the car trunk. The final verse of the song returns to Eminem who has now got round to writing to Stan, apologizing for not replying before and explaining that he hadn't intentionally ignored him after the concert. Eminem goes on to write about how important it is for Stan to maintain a good relationship with his girlfriend and to seek counseling help his various problems. The final denouement comes with Eminem realizing that a recent radio report of a man driving a car into a river with his girlfriend locked in the trunk – in a rough copy of the fantasies in "Bonnie & Clyde '97" – was in fact about Stan, and that his letter of advice and consolation has just come too late.

Taken together "Bonnie & Clyde '97," "Kim," and "Stan" provide a good illustration of how Eminem seeks to deal redemptively with violence in his music. The first two of these tracks are essentially vehicles for Eminem to express his rage at Kim's threats to leave him and prevent him seeing his daughter. He sees them as cathartic releases of the genuinely destructive feelings he had in response to her actions. Yet, through the track "Stan," he makes it clear that he has no intention of acting these fantasies out, and that he is sickened and saddened by those who would. Rap music thus becomes the means through which the hurt, insecurity, and rage of Marshall Mathers can be contained, expressed creatively and thus, in his view, redeemed.

So far, then, we have thought about the issue of the redemption of violence in relation to the "horizon" of Eminem as a rap auteur. Theological engagements with popular culture do not stop simply with descriptions of the "horizon" of popular culture, however, but involve bringing the "horizon" of theological norms and resources into critical conversation with popular culture. In the final part of our discussion here we will think about how two different understandings of salvation in Christian theology might inform our reflections about Eminem's treatment of rage and violence in his work.

The first of these understandings of salvation is taken from the work of the contemporary British theologian, David Ford. Ford (1999a, pp.167ff.) suggests that the Christian view of salvation is one that emerges out of the encounter with the face of Jesus. Through the person of Jesus, God has redeemed the world, and it is through encountering the face of Jesus that we are challenged to live in ways that fall in line with the divine intent to redeem creation.[20] This raises the question of what kind of redemption is conveyed and inspired through the face of Jesus. Ford (ibid., p.175) comments that this redemption is characterized by "trust, adoration, love, joy, repentance, attentive listening, and ultimate hope." Though such is the richness and complexity of this redemption that "any notion of precision which requires and overview and appraisal is absurd" (ibid., p.175). Our understanding of the redemption inspired and made possible by the face of Jesus is further developed when we recognize that this face is that of a man who has experienced death. The dead face of Jesus thus acts as a symbol both of someone utterly committed to fulfilling their responsibility before God, as well as representing an absence that we are challenged to fill by meeting our own responsibilities (ibid., p.206). Furthermore the resurrection of Jesus Christ becomes a divine affirmation and underwriting of the process of redemption that has begun in him.

How does this Christian theology of redemption, described by Ford, relate to Eminem's attempts to redeem his rage and suffering through his music? One immediately striking point is that whilst Eminem may regard his music as personally cathartic – this is "his therapy" – it seems to lack a sense of responsibility for those around him. Writing about "Bonnie & Clyde '97" he has commented:

> I was also tryin' to piss Kim off. I put a lot of my personal shit out there. But I don't care. See, it's like every time someone disses me, I'ma talk about them. It's kind of like if you piss me off, I'ma respond in my songs. Okay, Kim, you're going to piss me off? Then I'ma make you look stupid in front of all these people. But I don't limit this attitude to Kim . . . I mean anybody. (Eminem, 2002, p.31)

Whilst his music may indeed provide an outlet for rage and frustration, there is also a sense of lack of concern for others in this process. Ford's description of a Christian theology of salvation indicates that redemption is bound up with a proper sense of concern and responsibility towards the other. Yet by comparison, Eminem's sense of redemption in his music is narcissistic – it is redemption for him alone. Whilst Eminem might, at times, lament the capacity for words to "teach hate,"[21] his attacks on his family and casual misogyny[22] and homophobia do little to convey a sense of responsibility to those around him.[23]

A more sympathetic understanding of Eminem's work could be developed from an alternative theological view of redemption, however. Delores Williams (1993) has developed a womanist theology that places an emphasis not so much on liberation as on survival. Taking the stories of Hagar from the book of Genesis as her focus, Williams argues that the experiences of this African slave-woman continues to provide a valuable framework for understanding the nature of salvation for black women in postslavery America. The Genesis stories explain that Hagar, according to custom, was used by Abram to conceive his first son because his wife Sarai was unable to conceive at that point. On becoming pregnant, however, Hagar finds herself mistreated by Sarai and runs away from her owners. God intervenes at this point, though, telling Hagar to return to Abram and Sarai (presumably because she has a much better chance of survival if she does so). At a later point, when Sarai gives birth to Isaac, Hagar and her son Ishmael are sent away by Abraham. Once again, though, at the point where Ishmael is about to die in the wilderness with his mother, God intervenes to underwrite their survival. Ultimately the salvation of Hagar is not one of liberation from oppressive social structures or of her being accepted within society, but it is the basic physical survival of herself and her son. At times, then, an experience of salvation at the hands of God may not be a dramatic transformation of one's attitudes, circumstances or relationships, but it may simply be the resources to continue living day-to-day.

Now there are a number of regards in which the story of Hagar can be seen to resonate particularly with historical and contemporary experiences of black women (e.g., the use of black female slaves to bear or nurture the children of white slaveholders, see Williams, 1993, pp.15ff.). For me to apply Williams' theology of redemption as survival to the experience of a white man such as Eminem inevitably leads to the loss of these associations. Nevertheless, I would suggest that her notion of redemption as survival may have some value in developing a theological response to his music. Whilst we may indeed want to question how constructive some of his lyrical content is, there is undoubtedly a sense that Eminem's music has been essential to ensuring his psychological and material survival. His story is certainly one in which his emotional and physical well-being have at times been dangerously threatened, and yet through his music he aspires to survive his deprived background and to try to offer a better life for his daughter Hailie Jade. Eminem's musical treatment of rage and violence may not therefore be redemptive in the fuller sense of the term used by David Ford, but if this music has enabled him to survive then it could be seen as a form of base-level redemption on which more positive developments could be built in the future.

Even this theological reading of Eminem's work could be seen as too generous, however. Whilst Delores Williams talks about redemption in terms of survival, she does not see Hagar's survival at being at the expense of Abraham, Sarah, or Isaac. Yet, as we have seen, within Eminem's desire for his and Hailie Jade's survival there is an apparent willingness to harm anyone who threatens or harms him (including Debbie and Kim). This might lead us to question the extent to which Eminem's desire for survival is redemptive. On the one hand his survival seems to come at a price to some of those close to him. Yet, on the other hand, can some of his anger be seen as justifiable and can his desire to support Hailie Jade be seen as evidence of a more redemptive impulse?[24] Perhaps the most plausible conclusion is that Eminem is an ambiguous figure whose music combines lyrical skill, intelligence, sensitivity, and yet also a narcissistic disregard for others.

Ultimately this raises the question about how we much we can reasonably expect of Eminem at this point in his development. Given his family and social background, it is not surprising if his music is angry, unforgiving, and narcissistic. We may wish to question Eminem's assumption that his music is as redemptive as he seems to believe it is. We might wish that his treatment of violence in his music might take more account of Michael Dyson's (2001, p.129) criticism of gangsta rap's "tired, cliché-ridden exploration of a subject [violence] that demands subtlety, artistic courage and the wisdom to refrain from using a sledgehammer where a scalpel will do." But questions of redemption need to be asked not only of Eminem, but also of his audience and of the wider society that shaped Eminem's formative years. If redemption, to use Ford's concept, involves learning to face our responsibilities for the other then we might want to ask how redemptive it is for white suburban audiences to derive pleasure from musical forms that stereotype white and black urban poor as misogynistic and violent criminals. Similarly, we might want to ask what the challenge of redemption means for a society that allows a section of its community to languish in the despair of the poverty-trap or in which children are raised in emotionally deprived or insecure surroundings. If we want to ask questions of redemption in relation to Eminem's work, then we need also to ask questions about what it means to redeem the society that raised him. As Tupac Shakur once commented, "the hate you gave little infants fucks everyone" (Dyson, 2001, p.115). The anger and violence that characterizes Eminem's music thus challenges us to think what it means to redeem society in ways that does not place so much hate in the hearts of those that it claims to nurture.

## conclusion

In this chapter, then, we have developed an overview of a network of methods that can help us to interpret specific forms of popular culture. We noted that there are three main approaches which focus on the *author* of a piece of popular culture, a particular popular cultural *text* and the way in which popular culture is used by particular *audiences* or by people in *real everyday settings*. We also looked briefly at how three more specific ways of analyzing popular culture – psychoanalytic criticism, ideological criticism, and genre criticism – could also help us to understand more about authors, texts, and audiences.

In this chapter we have gone on to look in more detail at the author-focused, or auteur, approach to studying popular culture. We have noted how this approach developed in relation to film criticism, and some of the strengths and limitations of this particular approach. Finally we explored how an auteur approach could be used in the theological critique of popular culture through the case example of the redemption of violence in the work of Eminem. By raising questions about Eminem's background, psychological development, and intentions about his work, we have been able to develop a clearer view of how and why he approaches his music in the way that he does. Such an understanding can help us to develop a more substantial analysis of the meaning of his work before we go on to reflect on it in relation to particular theological norms and resources.

In the next chapter, we will adopt a quite different approach to analyzing popular culture, which does not ask any questions about the author at all but rather invites us to think about what it means to see popular culture as *text*.

# Chapter 7

# text-based approaches to studying popular culture: "homer the heretic" and civil religion

## introduction

In the previous chapter we introduced a range of different methods for ana-lyzing popular cultural texts and practices. In particular, we focused on how the study of the author(s) of a popular cultural text might help us to under-stand more about how to interpret that text and place it in a wider context. In this chapter we shall now explore a second major approach to the analy-sis of popular culture which seeks to study the qualities and structures of texts without any reference to their authorship. The particular methods that we will examine here are semiotic, narrative, and discourse approaches to text analysis. Having introduced each of these different methods, we will then see how they can be used to interpret a specific episode of *The Simpsons*, "Homer the Heretic," and this will then lead into further theological reflection about some of the understandings of religion that can be read from this particular popular cultural text.

The type of text-based approaches to studying popular culture that we will consider here are not concerned with speculating about the "mind" or "inten-tions" of the author. Rather they focus on how the form and content of a text function to construct a range of possible meanings. Whether by studying the significance of contrasting characters or images within a film, the way in which the narrative of a TV sitcom is constructed, or the kinds of language and cultural images used on a website, these methods focus on how spoken, written, "visual," and "auditory/musical" language constructs meaning.[1]

Such text-based approaches to studying popular culture can be an impor-tant supplement to auteur criticism. As we noted in the previous chapter, the author(s) of a popular cultural text may not have intended, or indeed be conscious of, all of the meanings that are constructed by their text. By studying the text itself, we may therefore gain a wider perspective of the meanings within it than we get simply through exploring what the author themselves has said or written about it. These text-based approaches will also be important in situations where it is difficult to gain much knowledge about the author of a particular text. This would include studies in which we might simply have little information about an author (e.g., where we know nothing about the author, say, of a particular web-site or we are studying a film whose director has had little written about them or who has said little about their work). Similarly these text-based approaches can be important for analyzing texts for which it is very difficult to identify clearly the influence of specific authors. In major American TV comedies, for example, such as *Friends* or *The Simpsons*, the storyline and script is produced by a team of writers with different writers exerting differing degrees of influence on separate episodes. The composition of this writing team may even change within the same series of shows. Similarly the process of major film production may mean that the work of the director is subject to a wider range of influences (e.g., budget and marketing requirements, feedback from test screenings) that make it harder to see the final text as the product of a single dominant "authorial hand."

For a range of reasons, then, text-based approaches to studying popular culture can be an important supplement to auteur criticism and a key method of study when we simply lack the information to conduct an adequate author-focused approach to our study.

In addition to the practical advantages we might see in using these kinds of text-based approaches, there has also been a strong movement within literary and cultural criticism since the late 1960s which argues on theoretical grounds that the text rather than the author that should be the proper focus of critical analysis.[2] This "poststructuralist" approach to cultural and literary criticism has been associated with the influence of continental European writers such as Paul de Man, Jacques Derrida, Michel Foucault, and Roland Barthes.

Barthes' essay "The death of the author," originally published in French in 1968, was a seminal piece of work in setting out core assumptions of this poststructuralist approach. In this essay, Barthes argued that Western culture since the Reformation had placed an increasing emphasis on the importance of the mind, attitudes, and conscience of the individual. In terms of literary criticism this naturally led to an interest in the role of the mind, personality, and intentions of the author in shaping their narrative or text. As Barthes (1977, p.143) put it, "the explanation of a work is always sought in the man or woman who produced it, as if it were always in the end . . . the voice of a single person, the author confiding in us." By contrast, though, Barthes noted that non-Western cultures have placed much less emphasis on the importance of the personality of the author. Indeed some non-Western cultures associate the act of story-telling with shamanic or other mediating figures who are seen more as vehicles through whom the story expresses itself, rather than as individual figures who shape that narrative in distinctive ways. This raises the possibility that an interest in the author is not necessarily the most "obvious" or "natural" way to think about the text, but rather that the interest in the personality of the author may be more an expression of particular Western cultural assumptions. It is these cultural assumptions that Barthes sought to challenge in this essay.

Barthes drew on the structuralist linguistic theory of Ferdinand de Saussure to make the observation that language conveys meaning not because the author "puts" meaning into their words, but because words carry meaning as a result of the larger linguistic system of which they are a part. From this perspective, the meaning of this current sentence that you are reading is not communicated by some mystical process from my consciousness (as author) directly to yours (as reader), but it arises out of the way in which particular words are ordered within it. On this basis Barthes suggests that rather than thinking about authors as preceding language and texts, we should think in terms of language preceding and finding expression through the author. Authors do not create entirely new meanings, but simply act as channels through which language expresses itself. As Barthes put it:

> We know now that a text is . . . a multi-dimensional space in which a variety of writings, none of them original, blend and clash. The text is a tissue of quotations drawn from the innumerable centres of culture . . . [Should the author] wish to *express himself* [sic], he ought at least to know that the inner "thing" he thinks to "translate" is itself only a ready-formed dictionary, its words only explainable through other words, and so on indefinitely. (1977, p.146)

Barthes argues, then, that when we engage with a "text" (whether a novel, film, TV program, pop song, etc.) we are not engaging with the mind of the author but with a specific arrangement of words, images, and sounds that make sense to us because they work within existing cultural conventions. The act of interpretation, of finding meaning in a text, is not therefore made possible by discerning the mind or intentions of the author, but by the act of reading the collection of signs, symbols, images, and sounds in front of us. This view therefore places a much stronger emphasis on the importance of the act of reading a text, than of the role of the author in constructing it. Or as Barthes (ibid., p.148) put it, "the birth of the reader must be at the cost of the death of the Author."

The key implication of this poststructuralist approach is that meaning is an "effect" of language or other cultural means of communication. The meaning that we get from watching a film arises out of the way in which particular words, images and sounds have been collected together which are then "read" by the audience. The personalities of individual characters, the emotional mood of the film, even the sense of horror, amusement, or wonder that a film may evoke, are all constructed through the language of the film. To imagine that we are engaging with "real" characters, or even the "real" mind of the director behind the film, is therefore from this perspective an illusion generated by the film text. Poststructuralist criticism has therefore sought to analyze how the meanings that we experience in different media including art, TV, film, literature, and music are therefore produced by the particular qualities and content of the text. Poststructuralism rejects auteur criticism because the notion that we can perceive and understand the authorial mind behind the text is simply a fantasy produced by the text itself.[3] All we are left with is the text, and our ability to understand the text rests in our ability to see how the text works to create certain meanings for the reader.

Even the notion that texts produce single, clear meanings universally accessible to all readers is also open to criticism. Stanley Fish (1980) has, for example, argued that the meaning of texts is fundamentally influenced by the context of the text's interpreter. Language, in Fish's view, does not have a single, stable meaning, but the meanings of language arise out of particular social and institutional contexts in which a phrase or concept has a particular significance. Pursuing this line of thinking, we might speculate about whether there is such a thing as "a" text that can be interpreted, but whether texts have quite different meanings and significance depending on the context in which they are experienced and interpreted. Thus in the context of our discussion in this book, we might think about the different ways in which a gangsta rap song might be heard and interpreted by members of a street gang, students in an academic seminar on popular culture, and participants in a church youth-group discussion. Whilst the methods discussed in this chapter are useful in clarifying meanings generated by the structure and content of texts, we may need to be cautious in assuming that such methods can generate interpretations that will be agreed upon by people across a range of different contexts. The way in which we interpret texts will be profoundly shaped by the specific preunderstandings that we draw from our own context, and to aspire to achieve some kind of neutral or universal perspective on the meaning of a text is unrealistic.

Poststructuralist criticism has proven useful in developing our understanding of how texts work in constructing meaning, but more recently the dominance of poststructuralist approaches to cultural and literary criticism have started to weaken. There has, for example, been a growing on emphasis on the ethical responsibility of both authors and readers which recognizes that the author is not simply a notion constructed by the text, but a moral agent with responsibility for the text that they create (see Newton, 1995; Gibson, 1999). This idea has been discussed particularly in relation to the early career of the poststructuralist critic Paul de Man. De Man's emphasized the importance of the rhetorical effects of the text, and the illusion of engaging with the "mind" or "personality" of the author. His ideas came under heightened scrutiny, however, when it was discovered that, as a young writer in Nazi occupied Belgium, he had contributed anti-Semitic articles to a collaborationist newspaper (Burke, 1992, pp.1ff.). This discovery has led to extensive debates about how de Man's original act in writing these articles should be understood, as well as whether his subsequent academic career should be seen as an attempt to correct or to hide his past. What is fascinating, though, is that at the heart of this debate is the assumption that de Man as an author was in some sense accountable for his actions in writing anti-Semitic work for a Nazi sympathizing newspaper. De Man's poststructuralist theory had sought to make the author "disappear," yet his own personal history subsequently demonstrated that the author could not be written out of the process of making sense of texts quite so easily.

Whilst the dominance of poststructuralist approaches to literary and cultural criticism may be starting to wane in academic circles, it is important to recognize that these approaches still have important benefits. Poststructuralism is a useful corrective against naïve assumptions about how the text may simply be an expression of the mind or personality of the author. The range of methods to be discussed in this chapter therefore represent a further useful element of a multimethodological approach to interpreting popular culture.

## semiotics: interpreting the signs and symbols of the text

Semiotics is the study of how meaning is constructed through the content and ordering of signs within a text. Thwaites et al. (2002, p.9) define a "sign" as "anything which produces meanings." If we use this definition when we are thinking about popular cultural texts, it may be possible to see a sign as encompassing written and spoken words, the representation of physical actions, material objects, visual images, and sounds (including music). Each of these things can act as a medium for meaning, and a semiotic study of a text will seek to explore the particular meanings that are created when certain words, images, actions, and sounds are placed in relationship to each other.

Semiotics has developed into a sophisticated method of textual analysis which explores a range of different ways in which signs construct meaning (including the way in which they create the sense of an author, reader and wider social context for the text). The semiotic analysis of contemporary media has also led to a growing literature on particular conventions that are used to construct meaning in different media such as film, television, or advertising. It is not possible within the constraints of this chapter to give a detailed overview of different concepts and methods that have developed within semiotics, nor of the current debates about semiotic conventions within contemporary media.[4] Rather we will focus on two particular concepts within semiotic analysis that will help us to begin to understand how we can use this approach to make sense of popular cultural texts.

The first concept that we will explore here is the idea that signs gain their meaning because they function as part of wider systems of "difference." As an approach to textual analysis, semiotics has been heavily influenced by Saussure's theory of linguistics.[5] As we have already noted back in chapter 3, Saussure suggested that individual words (or "signs") derive their meaning from the fact that they are part of larger systems of words, and that it is the relationship of that individual word to the other words in that system that generate the meaning of that specific word. So if we think about words referring to emotion, the word "sad" derives its meaning from the fact that it refers to something different to "angry," "happy," or "indifferent." Indeed the more specific sense of the word "sad" is determined by its relationship to more closely related emotion-words such as "depressed," "grieving," "wistful," "discouraged" or "despairing." If the word "wistful" were to be removed from the English language this would then slightly change the meaning of other emotion-words as the linguistic means for differentiating between difference senses of "sadness" would be lost to a certain degree. The meaning of a word/sign is not therefore it's own unique, permanent, "private" property, but rather the meaning of a word/sign is determined by the specific role that it plays in relation to other word/signs in a larger system of language.

The key implication of this idea for semiotic analysis is that it is possible to think about what meanings a particular sign within a text conveys by thinking in terms of its relationships and differences to other signs within that text.

This point can be illustrated more clearly through using the example of Umberto Eco's (1981, pp.144ff.) semiotic analysis of Ian Fleming's novels about 007, James Bond. In this, Eco argues that Fleming's novels about Bond consistently use certain oppositions or differences between characters' allegiances, personalities, appearance, and actions to communicate particular meanings. The oppositions that Eco identifies include four types of different relationship:

1   Bond – M;
2   Bond – Villain;
3   Villain – Woman;
4   Woman – Bond.

Through the "binary oppositions" of these different relationships, Fleming further emphasizes other oppositions and differences that these characters symbolize. Amongst these Eco includes:

1   Free World vs. Soviet Union;
2   Great Britain vs. non- Anglo- Saxon countries;
3   ideals vs. cupidity;
4   love vs. death;
5   moderation vs. excess;
6   perversion vs. innocence;
7   virility vs. sexual deviance;
8   loyalty vs. disloyalty;
9   attractiveness vs. ugliness/disfigurement.

Eco therefore suggests that the meaning of Ian Fleming's novels is communicated through a series of contrasts between different characters and the attitudes and values which they represent. One important such contrast is between James Bond (who represents the free world, Britishness, virility, loyalty, and attractiveness) and the Villain (who typically represents the Soviet Union or another part of the non-Anglo-Saxon-world, cupidity, death, sexual deviance, disloyalty, and ugliness). Although this contrast between Bond and the Villain is simply one of the central contrasting relationships in the novel, we can see how this single contrast sets up a broad set of meanings and associations within the text. Thus we can see how Bond (as the good character) is identified with a particular national identity, political system, sexual orientation, and set of attitudes, which through their association with him are also implicitly seen as good. The simple contrast between Bond and the Villain therefore sets up a much wider set of meanings about what is seen as right and healthy in Fleming's novels.

By analyzing the differences, contrasts, and oppositions within a particular text, it is therefore possible to see how the text is attempting to construct a particular image of the world. The particular contrasts that are used within a text help to communicate what is important, good, desirable, or worthy of our attention, and it is through these contrasts that the text clarifies the meanings and issues that it focuses on. We will return to this idea later in the chapter when we explore the significance of the contrasting representation of characters in *The Simpsons*.

A second important concept within semiotics to be briefly noted here is the concept of metonymy. Metonymy is a process of association between signs in which a sign symbolically represents an object or concept of which it is a smaller part. To refer to a car as my "motor" or my "wheels" is therefore to use the signs "motor" and "wheels" as metonyms for the larger object of the car. In a more abstract sense, a visual image of a family with two parents and two children in an advert can be seen as a metonym for the wider concept of family life or the members of society whose life is ordered within clear nuclear family structures. Metonymy is therefore the process in which the part comes to serve as a symbolic representation of the whole.

Recognizing that signs can refer to objects or concepts much greater than themselves can help us to understand that the meanings of signs can be complex and varied. In addition to the immediate (or "denotative") meaning of an individual sign, a sign may also bear a much wider range of associations (or "connotative" meanings). Again one of the seminal studies to explore the connotative meanings of signs was Roland Barthes' (1972) collection of essays titled *Mythologies*, which were originally published in French in 1957. In *Mythologies*, Barthes argued that a wide range of cultural objects from wine, the latest Citroen car, wrestling, soap powder, and the face of Greta Garbo, were signs that represented not only an immediate reality but also a wider, arbitrary set of cultural meanings. Thus, for example, in French culture, Barthes argued that drinking red wine came to represent wider cultural values such as virility and patriotism.[6] Such an association between an alcoholic drink and an attitude to national identity is clearly arbitrary, but Barthes argued that the ability of individual signs to communicate wider cultural myths remains an important part of how signs convey meaning. Again, when we turn our attention to *The Simpsons* we shall see how particular characters and objects within the show serve metonymic functions in referring to greater social or conceptual realities, as well as representing (and indeed challenging) particular cultural mythologies.

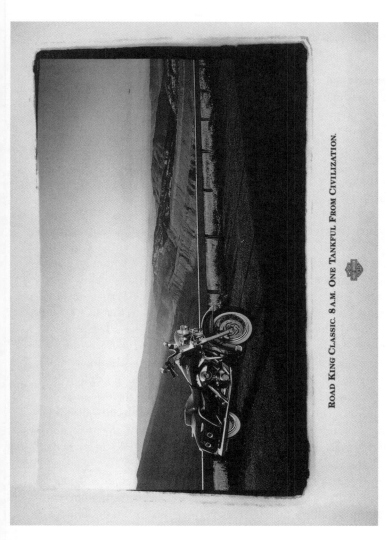

ROAD KING CLASSIC. 8 A.M. ONE TANKFUL FROM CIVILIZATION.

Figure 7.1 This 2002 advert for the Harley Davidson Road King Classic is a good example of metonymy and the connotative meanings of signs. The stunning view of a sunrise over the open landscape can be read as a metonym for 'nature' and the great outdoors. By being associated with "nature" in this image, the bike acquires connotative meanings of being both a tool that enables its owner to experience the open expanses of nature as well as an object that shares in the beauty of the natural world. Given the importance of nature in American culture (see, for example, the importance of American landscape painting following the tradition of Thomas Cole), this image can also be read as having particular resonance with American cultural discourses about nature as a source of meaning and identity for the American nation.

## the narrative analysis of texts

A second approach that can be helpful in the analysis of texts in addition to semiotics is drawn from narrative theory, or "narratology." Interest in the study of narrative has become a particularly important part of philosophy, theology, and cultural criticism over the past century. This broad interest in narrative has included discussions of how "narrative truth" forms an alternative way of understanding existence to scientific or propositional truth (Spence, 1982; Bruner, 1986), as well as how narratives construct our sense of personal and communal identity and provide us with a framework for thinking what it means to act morally (MacIntyre, 1981; Hauerwas, 1981; Gergen, 1991).

In addition to these wider debates about the philosophical, moral, and psychological significance of narrative, literary criticism has also engaged in more specific debates about how we might analyze and interpret particular narratives (e.g., in the form of novels and films). In the mid-twentieth century, theorists such as Vladimir Propp (1968) and Northrop Frye (1971) suggested that there were certain core narrative structures and conventions that formed the basis for all individual stories. Such attempts to identify universal "templates" for constructing and interpreting narratives have subsequently been treated with skepticism by poststructuralist and postmodern critics who focus more on how individual texts function (see Currie, 1998). It is not possible within the constraints of this chapter to give a detailed account of the way in which narratology has evolved over the past few decades. Nevertheless it will still be useful to identify some basic concepts and tools that can help us to think about the structure and content of particular popular cultural narratives that we may wish to study.[7]

The first observation to be made about narratives is that they are not neutral or objective depictions of events, but edited versions of events that are constructed in ways that tend to offer certain perspectives on them. Thus, for example, if I tell you the story of my journey to work today, I would be unlikely simply to give a detailed account of every physical movement and space that I traveled through. If I did you would most probably find this story dull or bizarre because it would lack a clear focus or point. Rather, I am more likely to tell a story about my journey to work in a way that focuses around a particular point, such as how I survived nearly being run over by a car or how I noticed that the trees were shedding their leaves and how this made me recognize that the year was passing. The particular events that were narrated in that story about my journey to work would therefore reflect the wider meanings that were being communicated through that story. A basic task within narrative analysis can therefore be to explore how a particular story is constructed, and through this to identify the wider meanings that the story raises.

To undertake this analysis there are certain concepts that can help us to identify different elements of a narrative (for a more detailed discussion of these, see Lothe, 2000). Firstly, we can think in terms of the *events* or *"fabula"* of narrative. These are the literal situations and actions that are presented in the narrative. These can be distinguished from the *plot* or *"sujet"* of the narrative, which is the way in which these events are presented and linked together in a way that conveys particular meanings to the audience. Thus, for example, in a story about my journey to work, the basic events might be: I walked to work, I did not see a car coming towards me when crossing the road junction, the car nearly ran me over, and the driver sounded his horn and waved his fist at me. These basic events could be placed in different plot-lines, however, which could either emphasize that I was preoccupied with a particular problem and so was inattentive whilst crossing the road, that the road junction has bad visibility and is a dangerous place to cross, or that the driver was going too fast and was engaging in mild road rage. The *events* of a narrative therefore form the basic elements out of which a story is constructed, but it is the way in which these *events* are shaped into a particular *plot* that gives the events their particular meaning or inflection. Or as Paul Ricoeur puts it, "plot makes events into a story" (Lothe, 2000, p.74). The way in which events can be narrated differently within a particular plotline include the kinds of details that are given about a particular event (e.g., what is said about the different participants involved in the event), the degree of detail in the description of the event, and the location of the event in the order of events narrated in the story. In the case of this last point, the film *Pulp Fiction* provides a well-known example of how narrating events out of chronological order can help us to see the significance of an event in a particular way. Thus the conversation between Jules and Vincent in the diner which comes at the end of the film – but which chronologically comes partway through the actual timeline of events narrated in the film – emphasizes how certain decisions made by these characters shape their eventual fates.

In addition to the notions of events and plot, three other concepts can help us to identify different elements in the way in which a narrative has been constructed. These are *narration, characters,* and *characterization.*

*Narration* is concerned with the perspective from which events or views are communicated to the audience. Does the story, for example, have a narrator who addresses the audience directly (e.g., as in *Bladerunner* or *American Beauty*) or does the narration occur indirectly through the way in which events and characters are presented in the narrative (e.g., as in *Kill*

*Bill*)? Does the audience have an overview of the different events and relationship in the narrative that is not available to any individual character in the story (e.g., as in *The Lord of the Rings*), or do we perceive events from the perspective of one particular character (as in *Forest Gump*)? Furthermore, if we are seeing events from the perspective of a particular narrator, to what extent can we trust that they are perceiving events in a good or truthful way (see, for example, *A Clockwork Orange* or *The Sixth Sense*)? What does the way in which a story is narrated tell us about what is being emphasized within that particular narrative?

*Characters* refer to the agents who act or who are acted upon within the narrative. Rather like the events of the narrative, the characters form a basic element in the structure of narratives, and it is through the interactions between characters that the plot of the narrative is able to unfold.

The meanings of a narrative will be significantly shaped, however, not only by the plot or style of narration, but also through the *characterization* of those involved in it. Again the notion of *characterization* highlights that characters are not presented in neutral or objective ways, but are rather presented in ways that fit within the particular plotline of a given narrative. Thinking about the *characterization* of those involved in a particular story thus involves thinking about what we learn about characters from the manner of their actions and reactions to events, from direct references to them by a narrator or by other characters, or through our knowledge of their internal emotions and motivations or their external appearance (e.g., their style of dress, movement, posture, speech, etc).

By thinking about the relationship between the events, plot, narration, characters, and characterization of a given narrative, it may be possible to identify how the particular way in which a narrative is constructed tends to generate certain meanings. Again, it is worth noting that this method of analysis does not require us to speculate about the mind or intentions of the author, but rather to focus on how different elements of a narrative function in ways that convey certain meanings. We will explore how these methods can work in practice shortly in this chapter when we move on to an analysis of a particular episode of *The Simpsons*.

## discourse analysis

Discourse analysis offers another useful tool for analyzing the ways in which meaning is constructed and represented in particular texts. As a term, "discourse analysis" actually covers a range of different approaches to analyzing the way in which language and other forms of social interaction construct meaning (see, e.g., Burr, 1995). The particular approach to discourse analysis that we will focus on in this chapter, though, relates primarily to theories of discourse developed by the French philosopher and historian, Michel Foucault.

Foucault's main intellectual project was an attempt to develop a theory and history of knowledge. In a range of seminal books such as *The Order of Things* (1970) and *The Archaeology of Knowledge* (1972), Foucault sought both to develop theoretical accounts of the ways in which knowledge is developed and functions, as well as specific historical accounts of the structure and development of knowledge in Western culture. In addition to this, Foucault undertook specific studies of the ways in which understandings of insanity, sexuality, and criminality had developed in Western Europe.

Central to Foucault's theory of knowledge was the concept of "discourse."[8] By "discourse," Foucault was referring not simply to language but to the way in which language (in association with particular symbols, objects, practices, and institutions) constructs our understanding of reality. Foucault argued that all human knowledge is grounded in discourse. Whilst there is a reality that exists beyond human discourse, our capacity to think about or engage with that reality is wholly dependent on the particular discourses that our available to us in our particular time and culture. Furthermore, Foucault argued that discourse is fundamentally a form of social practice. It is developed and maintained through the specific acts of individuals, groups, and institutions, whose actions are in turn shaped by discourses that make sense of those actions. Human knowledge is not therefore primarily created through the inner workings of the private, individual mind. Rather knowledge is formed, reinforced and challenged through social processes such as writing, conversation, debate, protest, and scientific enquiry, in which different discourses are brought to bear on our understanding of the world.

The knowledge of human culture at a given point in history will reflect a particular field of assumptions, patterns of thinking, and sources of tension and disagreement (Foucault referred to this as the "episteme" of a culture). Within this wider epistemic framework, specific discourses develop within human cultures that offer different ways of thinking about, and acting in, the world. In every culture there will therefore be a range of different "discursive formations" that compete against each other, offering different interpretations of life and different versions of what it means to act in appropriate ways. In contemporary society, for example, we can identify different discourses of health-care based on medical science and on alternative health-care practices such as faith healing, Reiki, and healing through crystals. These different discourses of health-care offer different understandings of pathology and different ideas of what is needed to promote human health. These discourses do not exist in a vacuum but are supported or challenged by different journals, books, magazines, institutions, and health practitioners who may view one of these discourses as fundamentally correct and the other as, at best, deeply limited. Furthermore, these discourses have not suddenly appeared in our culture overnight, but are part of longer cultural histories in which particular discourses of the body, health, and disease have evolved over a period of centuries.

For our purposes here, the key point is that popular cultural texts are places in which different discourses are expressed, developed, and challenged. In the film, *One Flew Over the Cuckoo's Nest*, for example, we see competing discourses about mental illness – one a heavily medicalized discourse that supports the power held by the staff in the hospital, the other a humanist discourse that emphasizes the dignity, rights, and potential of the patients. These discourses are reflected in the way in which characters think of themselves, speak to each other, act, and are allowed to act or not allowed to act in a particular institutional context. An understanding of this film can therefore usefully pay attention to the different discourses that shape the way in which the world is understood within it. It is not simply more complex popular cultural texts, like films or novels, though, that reflect wider cultural discourses. Even apparently mundane cultural objects are meaningful to us because of particular discourses associated with them. Ian Parker (1994), for example, shows how the instructions on a tube of toothpaste reflect wider cultural discourses concerning medical expertise and the responsibilities and powers of adults in relation to children. The language, symbolism, design, and use of popular cultural texts therefore reflects wider cultural discourses that shape the way in which we think about the world.

The practice of discourse analysis, in this Foucauldian approach, is therefore concerned with examining texts to identify how particular discourses operate within them. Following Parker (1994), this method involves looking both in detail at the particular language and concepts present in a text, thinking about what ways of thinking and acting are encouraged or prohibited by the text, and identifying the wider cultural discourses that the text draws upon. In more detail, we can see this process of analysis in terms of the following stages:

1   converting "text" into written form (note issues if we are not working with the text in its primary form);
2   reflecting on wider associations of the particular words and phrases used in the text;

3   breaking the text down into specific linguistic elements (e.g., nouns) and identifying recurring words/concepts/descriptions;

4   identifying the "subjects" (i.e., persons) within the text, what kind of actions are ascribed to these subjects, what kind of constraints there are on their actions and what kinds of relationships are described between these subjects;

5   thinking about how the particular descriptions and relationships presented by this text "address" the reader. What do they say (implicitly or explicitly) about how the reader should respond, act, view the world/particular relationships? What are the implications of not acting in the way encouraged by the text?

6   identifying the wider cultural discourses that are reflected in the particular way that this text constructs reality/relationships, and potential tensions between these discourses;

7   thinking about the cultural roots of these discourses, and how they have come to be seen as "natural" accounts of the world;

8   reflecting on the way in which these particular discourses support or subvert certain social institutions;

9   identifying the potential positive and negative effects of the discourse(s) used in this text (including asking who benefits and loses out from this kind of discourse, and what people would gain from supporting or challenging it).

This approach to discourse analysis therefore invites us to identify how popular cultural texts reproduce, develop, or challenge particular cultural discourses, and to think critically about the implications of the discourses presented in these texts. We will explore how this approach works in practice, along with the other approaches described in this chapter, by now turning our attention to an analysis of an episode of *The Simpsons*.

## analyzing *homer the heretic*

Since the showing of its first episode in 1990, *The Simpsons* has become one of the most popular comedy programs for a global TV audience. Each of the animated episodes focuses on the day-to-day life of the Simpson family which is made up of the father, Homer, mother, Marge, and children, Bart, Lisa, and Maggie. The family live in Springfield, a small American town whose work-force is largely employed in the local nuclear power station, and figures such as the nuclear plant owner, the school principal, the local bar-tender, and minister of the local church all feature regularly in the program. Other regular figures in the program are the Flanders, the Simpsons' next door neighbors, whose devout Christian attitudes and lifestyle often strongly contrast with the more worldly and self-interested approach to life demonstrated particularly by Homer and Bart.

The particular episode we will analyze here, "Homer the Heretic," first aired in the US on 8 October, 1992.[9] Whilst *The Simpsons* provides a useful range of stories for different kinds of theological and philosophical analysis, I have chosen to focus on "Homer the Heretic" because it raises interesting issues about the representation of religion that we shall think critically about later in this chapter.

A useful starting point for this textual analysis of this episode of *The Simpsons* will be a narrative analysis. This will introduce us to the story that we are presented with, as well as highlight significant themes and issues within it that can also be thought of in terms of semiotics and discourse analysis.

Firstly, then, what is the *fabula* of this narrative? Or, in other words, what main events are presented within the narrative? These can be summarized as follows:

> On a freezing cold Sunday morning, Homer decides not to go to church. He thoroughly enjoys himself at home (watching TV, making his favorite fattening breakfast, winning a radio phone-in competition, and finding a penny), and comes to the conclusion that he has had the best day of his life by choosing not to go to church. On the basis of this experience, Homer decides not to go to church again. He subsequently has a dream in which he explains his decision to God, and God accepts that Homer doesn't have to go to church. A variety of people (Marge, Lisa, the minister Reverend Lovejoy, the Flanders) try to persuade Homer to come back to church, but are unsuccessful. One Sunday morning though, when Homer is asleep, he accidentally sets the house on fire. Ned Flanders saves him from the burning house and his friends and neighbors help put the fire out. Recognizing that it is the faith of the friends and neighbors that has motivated them to help him, Homer agrees to go back to church. Next week, asleep in church, Homer has a dream in which God consoles him that nine out of ten new religions fail in their first year.

This summary presents the central events of this narrative, around which various running jokes through the series relating to different characters are played out. As we noted earlier in the chapter the *fabula* of a narrative are the specific events that take place within it. The *sujet* of the narrative, however, is the underlying plotline of the narrative according to which these events are presented in particular ways to make a certain point.

The *sujet*, or organizing plot-line, of this episode can become clearer if we think of this narrative in terms of three "Acts":[10]

*Act I*: Homer decides not to go to church
In this first part of the narrative, the episode gives a series of contrasting scenes which emphasis how enjoyable Homer's morning is and how unenjoyable church is proving for Marge and the children (e.g., Homer has a hot shower whilst, in the next scene, we see Marge and the kids shivering because the church heating has broken; Homer wins a radio phone-in competition then, in the next scene, the people in the church realize that the door has frozen shut whilst they have been in the service). The conclusion of this series of contrasting scenes of Homer and Marge's morning comes with Marge and the children arriving home, frozen and relieved their ordeal is over, and Homer announcing that he has decided never to go to church again.

*Act II*: People try to persuade Homer to go back to church but he refuses
This second act begins with Homer's dream in which God confronts him about his decision not to go to church and in which he persuades God that it isn't necessary for him to go. The scenes in this act then generally focus on a series of attempts by different people to persuade Homer, unsuccessfully, to return to church. Lisa accuses him of blasphemy. Reverend Lovejoy quotes scripture at him. The Flanders stalk Homer, singing a chorus at him to persuade him that church can be fun. Finally, Marge appeals to him to think about how important it is to make sure that their children are brought up properly, and about the tension his decision places on their marriage. Homer refuses all of these attempts at persuasion in different ways (e.g., telling Lisa he will recant on his death-bed if he is wrong, and escaping the Flanders in a spoof car chase). In this act, a smaller number of other scenes emphasize the benefits that Homer gets from his new approach to his religious life (e.g., getting time off work for spurious religious holidays that he invents whilst in the bar). This act is therefore structured in a way that emphasizes Homer's confidence in his decision to reject organized religion, and the benefits he derives from this decision. This confidence is demonstrated in the final line of this Act when Homer declares: "Everyone in the world is stupid except me."

*Act III*: Homer is saved from the fire, realizes the religiously motivated care that others have for him and decides to go back to church
The scenes in this final act focus on the drama of Homer's rescue from his house. Firstly, Apu, the local Hindu shop-keeper sounds the alert when he sees the house on fire and comes with the fire-engine to put out the fire. Then born-again Christian Ned Flanders breaks into the house and drags Homer to safety from it. We then see Krusty, the Jewish clown, rescuing the Simpsons' cat as it clings (painfully) to his face. The "moral" of the story, towards which the narrative has been building, is then presented as Homer sits in the burnt remains

of his kitchen with his friends and neighbors. Homer decides there must be a point to his experience, and initially decides that the point is that God is vengeful. Reverend Lovejoy tells him this isn't the point, though, and that God didn't cause the fire but instead was working through the hearts of the friends and neighbors who saved him whether these neighbors were "Christian, Jew, or miscellaneous." Homer recognizes that his friends have indeed shown genuine concern for him, and regrets mocking their faith. He decides to go back to church again. The program does not allow this to be any kind of pious reconversion, though, for although Homer does return to church as promised, we finally see him there asleep, with his snoring drowning out the sermon.

Thinking about this episode in terms of these three acts, we can see that the story is structured to focus on certain key themes and issues:

- a contrast between experiences of spending time in church and spending time outside of church, and an illustration of why deciding not to go to church may lead to more immediately enjoyable experiences (Act I);
- a range of reasons that people might put forward for why people should attend church, and how these could be rejected (Act II);
- the value of religious faith in making people more outward-looking and concerned for their neighbor (Act III).

The way in which this narrative explores these themes is to use characters as means of expressing different perspectives on life and organized religion. In semiotic terms, the meaning of the narrative is therefore established partly through the system of similarities and differences between the characters in the story. Homer, for example, represents qualities such as self-centeredness, hedonism, laziness, lust, misanthropy, and stupidity. By contrast, Marge represents qualities of concern for others, religious devotion, and commitment to duty. The ironically named Reverend Lovejoy, however, particularly represents qualities such as morbidity (he preaches on "the Lamentations of Jeremiah – the long version"), suspicion, and condemnation. Through the relationships between these (and other) characters, the narrative therefore sets up certain contrasts and tensions, e.g.:

- duty (Marge) vs. self-interest (Homer);
- concern for others (Marge) vs. misanthropy (Homer);
- humane religious devotion (Marge) vs. condemnatory religious devotion (Revd Lovejoy);
- sympathy for organized religion (Marge, Revd Lovejoy) vs. antipathy towards organized religion (Homer);
- morbidity (Revd Lovejoy) vs. hedonism (Homer).

The differences between these characters therefore generate different answers to the question of whether and why people should be involved in organized religion. From the self-centered, hedonistic, and misanthropic position represented by Homer there is no good reason to attend church, because church is boring and the time spent there could be used for more pleasurable activities. From the perspective of Revd Lovejoy, church attendance is a religious requirement that might provide us with some chance of avoiding the punishment that otherwise awaits us in hell. From Marge's perspective, church attendance is a duty that one owes to God and to others, and helps people to live good and moral lives. The oppositions and tensions between these characters therefore provide us with different positions for viewing the narrative's central concern.

It would be far too simplistic to think that the narrative portrays any one of these character positions as inherently "good" or "evil." The ironic tone of *The Simpsons*, after all, means that any position can be cut down to size or be shown to have its flaws by a well-placed joke. Nevertheless, the narrative of this episode does imply certain preferences between these opposing positions. This preference can be seen in the fact that the "happy" ending of the narrative (a characteristic feature of the comedy genre) entails some changes in key characters' positions. The characters in this narrative are not therefore fixed signs, whose meaning never changes throughout the narrative. Rather the capacity for the meanings and qualities associated with characters to change during the narrative is an integral part of the dramatic process.

Two significant changes are demonstrated by Revd Lovejoy and Homer. Revd Lovejoy, through most of the episode, represents a morbid and punitive form of religious faith. In the end, though, he voices a more humane and tolerant version of religion when he observes that God's action in the world is demonstrated through those who saved Homer's life. Similarly Homer's position also shifts. As he recognizes his arrogance towards others, he is grateful that they were more concerned for him than he was for them. He repents of his misanthropic attitude (a typical occurrence in the program – we know his misanthropy will be back when we watch the show next week), and as part of his more open attitude to others he agrees to go back to church. The "happy" nature of these character shifts suggests that the narrative is encouraging a certain view of the world, in which people show some concern for others and do not lapse into religious intolerance or selfish hedonism.

So far, then, this analysis of the "text" of this episode of *The Simpsons* suggests that the narrative is fundamentally concerned with the question of whether and why people should be involved in organized religion. Furthermore the narrative tends towards a view that organized religion is a good thing in so far as it makes people more humane and concerned for those around them.

In what sense is this story significant for a wider audience, though? Is it simply concerned with specific events in the lives of fictional, animated characters which have no relevance beyond the mythical city limits of Springfield? It is possible to see the story as having wider implications if we see the leading characters and contexts of *The Simpsons* as metonyms that represent wider communities and social structures. The Simpsons family, for example, can be viewed as a metonym for typical American family life, with its inherent tensions and ambiguities. The Flanders serve as a metonym for highly devout, born-again Christian spirituality that represents a significant part of American religious life (see Roof, 1999, pp.182ff.). Reverend Lovejoy and his First Church of Springfield functions as a metonym for institutional religion in America, and the wider community of Springfield can be seen as a metonym for small town American life. If we accept this metonymic interpretation of "Homer the Heretic" then its narrative can be interpreted as dealing not only with the particular lives of the characters, but with more general questions about the nature and function of organized religion in the life of American society.

A further level of analysis can be added to our discussion if we think of "Homer the Heretic" in terms of cultural discourses. The interpretation of this narrative, so far, has suggested that it encourages thinking about religion in terms of its practical benefits for human welfare and social life. Thinking about religion in this kind of way is not unique to this episode of *The Simpsons*. Indeed it forms part of a wider cultural discourse of "civil religion" that has been a significant cultural tradition since the founding of the American Republic.

The notion of civil religion did not originate in America. Writing in eighteenth-century France, the philosopher Jean-Jacques Rousseau commented that:

> it matters very much that each citizen should have a religion. That will make him love his duty; but the dogmas of that religion concern the State and its members only so far as they have reference to morality and to the duties which he [sic] who professes them is bound to do to others. Each man may have, over and above [this shared civil religion] what opinions he pleases . . . provided [he is a] good citizen in this life . . . The dogmas of civil religion ought to be few, simple and exactly worded, without explanation or commentary. The existence of a mighty, intelligent and beneficent Divinity, possessed of foresight and providence, the life to come, the happiness of the just, the punishment of the wicked, the sanctity of the social contract and its laws: these are its positive

dogmas. Its negative dogmas I confine to one, intolerance, which is a part of the cults we have rejected. (cited from Woodhead and Heelas, 2000, p.239).

Whilst such a concept of civil religion may not have been identified quite so directly by the founding fathers of America, the assumption that a generalized set of religious beliefs contributed to the common good was nevertheless important to them (see Bellah, 1985, p.223).[11] Whilst these generalized religious beliefs may have been loosely drawn from Christianity, these beliefs were broad enough to include a wide range of religious beliefs. "God" was the foundation of this civil religion, but the more exclusive figure of "Christ" does not play a significant role within it. As Robert Bellah notes, when Alexis De Toqueville visited America in the 1830s, he observed that American civil religion supported "the mores that make democracy possible . . . hedging in self-interest with a proper concern for others" and restrained "'that excessive and exclusive taste for well-being' so common among Americans" (ibid., p.223).

This notion of a generalized religion supporting the common good is essentially the notion of religion which is articulated in Reverend Lovejoy's speech about how God has prompted Homer's faithful neighbors to save his life. We can perhaps see this even more clearly in the way in which God is represented in Homer's dreams, as a giant human figure, with long white hair and beard, framed by glowing light and whose face is obscured. This image of God is close enough to popular Western images of God to be meaningful, but is also sufficiently inclusive as to permit a range of different religious beliefs. There is nothing, for example, in this image of God that indicates that he is specifically the God of Christianity. Rather he is, as Rousseau put it, the "mighty, intelligent and beneficent Divinity, possessed of foresight and providence." Similarly the vision of heaven in Homer's dream – a place amongst the clouds in which George Washington beats Jimmy Hendrix at air hockey – provides reassurance of "the life to come" and "the happiness of the just."

A textual analysis of "Homer the Heretic," drawing on narrative, semiotic, and discursive approaches, therefore suggests that this narrative is primarily concerned with the role and value of organized religion in American society. Furthermore, through the narrative, we see a particular way of thinking about religion emerging that emphasizes its value in promoting human welfare and concern for others. This view is itself part of a wider cultural discourse of "civil religion" within America that encourages an inclusive set of religious beliefs and practices that promote the common good. Despite it's role as a short piece of televised entertainment, "Homer the Heretic" can also be understood as a discussion of the role of organized religion in contemporary American culture and a reflection of a particular American discursive tradition in relation to this area of life.

Whilst "Homer the Heretic" can broadly be read as supporting a notion of American civil religion, a measure of caution still needs to be taken on this. The tone of *The Simpsons* is fundamentally ironic, arguably reflecting the awareness of its audience that no perspective or lifestyle choice is without its limitations or ambiguities in the contemporary world (see Dalton et al., 2001, for a useful discussion on this point). This episode is, for example, equal-handed in its comic treatment of different religious attitudes. Thus Ned Flanders' prayer that God direct Homer "safe and true" to the mattress on the ground as he pushes him out of the burning upstairs bedroom is rewarded by Homer landing on the mattress, doing a spectacular back-flip and smashing back into the house through the front window. Similarly Homer's observation that God didn't save Ned Flanders' house from burning, even though "he's a regular Charlie Church," is followed by a rain cloud miraculously putting out the Flanders' fire and then by a rainbow hovering over the miraculously repaired roof. "D'oh!," responds Homer.

Thus, whilst the program broadly seems to support a notion of civil religion, even this position is not embraced without some qualification. Religion may be useful in promoting the common good, the program concludes, but Reverend Lovejoy's sermons are still dull enough to put you to sleep.

## a theological reflection on "homer the heretic" and civil religion

If we think about "Homer the Heretic" as a popular cultural text that broadly supports a discursive tradition of American civil religion then theological reflection on this text will need to acknowledge that such a view of religion is not without controversy. A leading critic of such a view of religion is Stanley Hauerwas, one of the most influential American theologians of recent years. Hauerwas argues that the notion that religion exists primarily to support decent liberal democratic society leads to an impoverished view of what it means to be a committed follower of a particular faith tradition. In one of his sermons, for example, Hauerwas critiques what he sees as the vacuous inclusivity of the Methodist Church in America, saying:

> If you are unsure whether or not Jesus is the second person of the Trinity you can be a Methodist. If you think God is just as likely to be absent as present in the Eucharist you can be a Methodist. If you think that Christian participation

in war raises no moral questions you can be a Methodist . . . But you cannot be a Methodist if you think it proper to exclude anyone else on any of the above grounds.

Such an inclusive church would seem to be one well fitted for success. Yet it is dying. I suspect it is so because people fail to see why they should belong to a church built on being inclusive, since any volunteer service agency will do just as well. Moreover, such agencies are usually better run. (Hauerwas, 1995, p.40)

Hauerwas goes on to argue that notions of an inclusive Church based on general notions of tolerance drawn from a liberal society fail to recognize the proper theological ground on which Christian acceptance of others is based. He comments:

The unity of which Paul speaks, that between Jews and Greeks, is made possible through the common confession that Jesus is Lord, who has saved us by being raised from the dead. That unity is not based on the acceptance of everyone as they are because we want to be inclusive, but rather comes from the fire of Christ's cross, through which we are transformed by being given distinctive service in God's kingdom. (ibid., p.40)

Hauerwas' central objection to notions of civil religion, therefore, rest on his argument that seeing religion merely as a prop for liberal democratic society is to neglect any distinctive vision or ethical claims that arise out of that religious tradition. Religion becomes the mouthpiece for liberal democratic values, rather than being able to speak with its own authentic theological voice. Rather than being able to offer a whole vision of life, this kind of civil religion relegates religious belief to the sphere of the private preferences and conscience of the individual, from which it is not expected to make any serious or distinctive contribution to the moral and political life of wider society (see ibid., p.199ff.). Not only does civil religion render religious faith a privatized and essentially meaningless phenomenon, but liberal readings of religion also lead to a distortion of religious traditions. Hauerwas argues that to see the Gospels, for example, as simply endorsing liberal values such as justice or the Golden Rule is to rid them of any distinctive content. Indeed, if the Bible simply reinforces values that we can already talk about without reference to the Bible, then why even bother reading the Bible at all (Hauerwas, 1981, p.58)?[12] Hauerwas is therefore keen to avoid thinking ways of thinking about religious tradition in terms of values or principles that can easily be detached from that tradition. As he puts it, "Jesus did not have a social ethic, but . . . his story is a social ethic" (ibid., p.37).[13]

Rather than seeing faithful religious life as simply equating to being a good citizen of liberal democratic society, Hauerwas sees it in a Christian context as requiring a commitment to be part of the Church which bears certain normative stories about God's saving actions in the world. Again, this Church, if it is to be true to itself, does not exist simply as another institutional support for liberal democracy but as a "community pledged constantly to work out and test the implications of the story of God, as known through Israel and Jesus Christ, for its common life as well as the life of the world" (Hauerwas, 1983, pp.132f.). Being a Christian, for Hauerwas, does not then simply equate to being sympathetic to liberal values such as justice and tolerance, but involves a commitment to seeing one's life as radically challenged and transformed by the distinctive life and vision of the Christian Church as the redeemed people of God.

Hauerwas' theology is therefore fundamentally opposed to the kind of notion of a civil religion that we noted earlier in the work of Jean-Jacques Rousseau. Whilst Reverend Lovejoy's speech at the end of "Homer the Heretic" may appear to some viewers a heart-warming appeal for a generous, liberal religious ethos, from Hauerwas' perspective it involves an insidious corrosion of the heart of what it means to be distinctively Christian. Indeed it could be seen as a persuasive and heart-warming end to the program by Western audiences precisely because it reinforces the contemporary cultural hegemony around liberal democratic values (see Hardt and Negri, 2000). "Homer the Heretic," from Hauerwas' perspective, is therefore a text that we should approach with a heavy measure of theological skepticism.

Part of Hauerwas' popularity as a contemporary theologian has precisely been because he has been able to articulate a vision of religious life which has its own character and integrity rather than simply being determined by the values of contemporary liberal democracy. Hauerwas' approach may sound aggressively neoconservative and, as such, appealing to the contemporary Christian Right in America.[14] In reality, though, his thought is heavily influenced by Anabaptist ecclesiology and ethics which leads him to place a much stronger emphasis on nonviolence and rejection of secular political influence than is often associated with contemporary popular American neoconservative theology (see Hauerwas, 1995, pp.65ff.; Hauerwas and Huebner, 1999). Hauerwas (2000, p.10) is also keen to avoid being seen as a "sectarian, fideist tribalist," committed to religious fundamentalism or a withdrawal from engaging with wider society. Yet despite these more conciliatory parts of his thought, Hauerwas' polemic against equating religious conviction with the values and institutions of liberal democracy does contain its own dangers.

There are certain elements of Hauerwas' analysis of civil religion which can be seen as genuinely helpful. To reduce religious traditions simply to the role of mouth-pieces for liberal democratic values and institutions is indeed to limit their potential for offering a distinctive vision for existence. Even Jeffrey Stout, one of the leading contemporary philosophical exponents of the Western democratic tradition, is inclined to agree that contemporary American civil religion is "incoherent and alienating" to many committed religious believers, and "a travesty of true faith" (2004, p.1). Whilst Hauerwas' desire to separate religion and democracy may be reasonable enough in terms of maintaining the integrity of religious traditions, his treatment of liberal democracy in this process is far more problematic. In Hauerwas' rhetoric, liberal democracy exists primarily as a threat and trap to the distinctive life and identity of the Christian Church. His desire that the Church should simply be allowed to be the Church indicates a positive view of Christian community, but implies a deeper suspicion towards wider social and political institutions. Whilst it would be wrong to characterize Hauerwas as a fundamentalist, his antiliberal rhetoric places him closer to Christian and Muslim fundamentalists who reject the validity of liberal democracy as a basis for society (see, e.g., Keppel, 1994). Whilst we may not ultimately be attracted by Reverend Lovejoy's reduction of religious faith to a liberal civil religion, does Hauerwas' position offer a satisfactory alternative for the relationship between religion and society that does not risk sliding into a religious withdrawal from democratic practices and institutions? At a time when democracy is already threatened by such diverse forces as the influence of global business interests on the political process, political corruption, aggressive religious fundamentalism, and politically biased media, does Hauerwas' view of liberal democracy encourage people to care enough about democratic society to fight to maintain it?

Hauerwas may be right to want to separate religious communities and tradition from the practices and institutions of liberal democracy. But given the range of pressures that already limit the ability of contemporary democracies to function well, it is unhelpful for theologians to depict liberal democracy as something essentially to be regarded with suspicion. What is needed are ways of thinking about the relationship between religion and democracy that allows religious communities to maintain their own distinctive view of the world as well as a commitment to nurturing the wider democratic practices and structures of their society. In this context Jeffrey Stout (ibid.) makes a strong case for a pragmatic view of democratic society as an on-going project based around values which aspire to promote human well-being, such as freedom, respect, justice, and mutual responsibility. Stout does not agree that religious traditions should be coerced into a single theory of the nature of society and well-being – indeed his pragmatic approach rejects the need for there to be any such overarching theory of democracy or society. Furthermore, whilst the democratic values just listed remain important for guiding the project of democracy, the meaning of these values is itself open to definition through democratic conversation. Stout advocates an approach in which members of society continue to talk and relate together in ways that reflect democratic values, and in which it is open for each person to offer their own account (whether religious or secular) of how life is to be understood and lived. To think of democratic society in this way is to see it as an unfolding conversation based on certain guiding values that make that conversation possible and meaningful. Stout's approach offers an alternative to the civil religion of Reverend Lovejoy or the religious isolationism suggested by Hauerwas' theological rhetoric. This alternative is one in which religious communities are freed to offer their own distinctive visions of life, but in which these different visions are brought into the realm of open democratic debate in which societies can attempt to work out what it means to live well in our times. Whether Stout's vision of the possibility of a renewed commitment to democratic values and processes can be realized remains an open question, but it is undoubtedly one of the most pressing social questions of our age.

## conclusion

In this chapter, then, we have explored a range of methods that can help us in interpreting the meanings of texts without any reference to the mind, personality or intentions of the author. As we noted earlier, the way in which texts are experienced and interpreted is fundamentally shaped by our own particular social contexts, but even if we recognize the impossibility of establishing a single, universal meaning for the text we are studying it is still possible for us to think in terms of better or worse, more or less satisfactory interpretations.[15] By using the methods we have discussed in this chapter, it is possible for us to become clearer about how the particular structure and content of a given text leads it to generate certain kinds of meanings rather than others. Whether we regard auteur criticism as a useful or fundamentally misguided approach, these text-based methods of study offer a valuable means for trying to understand texts on their own terms rather than simply assuming that our immediate response to the text is the only possible interpretation.

Through this chapter we have seen how approaches such as semiotics, narrative analysis, and Foucauldian discourse analysis can help us to "read" popular cultural texts such as "Homer the Heretic." Studying authors and texts will be useful methods of studying popular culture if we want to use popular cultural "texts" as the basis for theological reflection and missiological critique. What these methods cannot do so well, though, is to clarify the meanings and significance of popular culture in people's everyday lives. Whilst the approaches to textual criticism that we have discussed here can help us to think about the form and content of "Homer the Heretic" in a more structured and rigorous way, these methods cannot tell us how actual audiences who watch this episode interpret it or what significance *The Simpsons* has in their lives. To gain a clearer picture of the meaning and significance of popular culture in everyday life we need to turn to another method of study, ethnography, and this will be the focus of the next chapter.

Chapter 8

# an ethnographic approach to studying popular culture: the religious significance of club culture

## introduction

In the previous two chapters, we have looked at two particular ways of inter-preting popular cultural texts – namely, by examining the "author" of the text and then by studying the text itself in terms of its content and structures. Whilst these methods can generate valuable insights into forms of popular culture that we may be studying, approaches that simply focus on the meaning of popular cultural texts will give us only an incomplete understanding of the role that cultural resources play in everyday life.

In earlier chapters, we have seen how writers such as Michel de Certeau, John Fiske, and Paul Gilroy have argued that the way in which people make use of popular cultural resources (whether films, fashion, music, TV pro-grams, or even public spaces) is not constrained simply by the meanings that the designers of those resources may have intended for them. Rather the "authorized" meanings of these resources can be creatively subverted by people as they get used in ways not intended or envisaged by their creators. We have also seen, though, that this more optimistic emphasis on people's freedom and creativity in making use of popular culture is also challenged by those (such as Adorno and Marcuse) who tend to see popular culture more as a system that constrains and limits those who live within it.[1] This debate about the creative or constraining nature of the relationship between the indi-vidual and wider culture remains a central issue in contemporary social and cultural theory, with a growing number of writers exploring how individual autonomy and cultural constraint can both be understood as important aspects of everyday life (see, e.g., Moores, 1993, pp.138ff.).

If we accept, however, that individuals have some creative freedom in the ways in which they make use of cultural resources, then it is problematic to assume that the "meaning" that an author or a cultural critic identifies in a particular piece of popular culture is necessarily the same meaning that other users or audiences will find in it. To give one example, in his book *Virtual Faith*, Tom Beaudoin (1998) argues for the existence of a particular kind of "Generation X" spirituality, partly through analyzing the content of certain music videos. Thus, through his reading of the video for the REM single "Losing My Religion," Beaudoin suggests that there is a longing amongst members of "Generation X" for a Jesus who is liberated from the certainties of the institutional Church and who becomes a more vulnerable and ambiguous figure with whom they can identify. In many respects, this is a stimulating interpretation of that music video. I have found it an interesting experiment, though, to show some of my classes this video and then to show them Beaudoin's interpretation of it. A common response from my students is that they would never have interpreted the video exactly in the way that Beaudoin does, and many of them do not even identify what Beaudoin interprets as the Christ-figure in the video to be Jesus. We could speculate on how satisfactory a reading Beaudoin offers of this video, but the more direct observation to be made at this point is that the "meaning" of a particular piece of popular culture may be interpreted in quite different ways depending on people's particular interests, experiences, and contexts.[2]

One important way in which this process has been thought about within cultural studies is through reference to Stuart Hall's (1990) concept of "encoding" and "decoding." In a discussion of the work of the media, Hall noted that TV producers, writers, journalists, and presenters seek to "encode" a particular set of meanings or interpretations into their programs. The media audience is not therefore presented with "raw" facts, but with a particular selection and ordering of material that offers a particular "narrative" that makes sense of it in a specific way. This can be seen as true even in "reality" TV shows such as "Big Brother" or "Pop Idol" in which the audience is shown edited clips of interactions between contestants that reinforce certain interpretations of their characteristics and relationships. Indeed a TV program will appear more coherent if its creators and presenters have been successful in "encoding" a particular interpretation of their material within it.

Although particular meanings may have been encoded into popular cultural texts, this does not necessarily mean that their users or audiences will interpret them in line with these "encoded" messages. For when the audience or user "decodes" the text, Hall suggested that there is a range of different ways in which they may relate to the original "encoded" message. Some parts of the audience may, in fact, interpret the text wholly in line with its encoded message. For example, in this instance, a person reading a newspaper article critical of asylum seekers would fully accept the negative characterizations of asylum seekers within it. An alternative approach to "decoding" would be for someone to adopt a "negotiated code," in which they might broadly accept the encoded meanings but make some adjustments to it. Thus, for example, another person might read the same article on asylum seekers and broadly accept the criticisms made of them, whilst thinking that these criticisms did not necessarily apply to the specific asylum seekers that they knew through contacts at their local church. A third approach, Hall suggested, would be an "oppositional" approach to decoding which would involve a radical challenge or rejection of the encoded meanings. Such an oppositional approach would take the newspaper article on asylum seekers and, rather than accepting its perspective, critique the racist or xenophobic stereotypes that the article was perpetuating. The prior experience, knowledge, and commitments of the reader would doubtless have an influence on the way in which they would decode this article, but it could not be assumed that the meanings encoded within it by the journalist would necessarily be accepted uncritically by their readers.

This basic principle of the encoding and decoding of popular cultural texts raises important questions for those wanting to explore the meaning and significance that popular culture holds for people in everyday settings. If we simply study the meanings that are "encoded" in popular culture (either intentionally by their creators or through our analysis of the meanings inherent in the content and structure of the text), then we neglect the possibility that different meanings may be created as these are "decoded" in everyday settings. This is an important point for different types of study in religion and popular culture. If, for example, we wish to explore whether popular culture serves religious functions in contemporary society, then it is inadequate to base this on theoretical arguments. We might assume that a sport such as baseball may have a religious significance for fans, but unless we actually study the experiences, attitudes, and practices of baseball fans in real life settings, we will not be able to establish how valid our assumptions really are. Similarly, from a missiological perspective, it is inadequate to make inferences about the values and beliefs of Western culture simply through studying popular cultural "texts." A fuller insight into significant beliefs, values, and practices of contemporary society can only be achieved by exploring how popular cultural resources are used and experienced in everyday settings.

If we are interested in the role and meanings that popular culture has for people in everyday life then we will need to use methods of study that help us to examine these "real world" attitudes, experiences, and practices rather than just focusing on the popular cultural "text" itself. This emphasis on studying the role and meanings of popular culture in everyday life has thus led to a "turn to ethnography" in cultural and media studies. As a research method, ethnography has a much longer history within the discipline of anthropology (and to a lesser degree sociology), but it is only within the past twenty years or so that it has become more widely used within cultural and media studies. This has led to the emergence of a growing number of "audience reception" studies that seek to explore how people relate to media technology and content in everyday settings (see, e.g., Morley, 1980; Liebes and Katz, 1993; Gray, 1992; Buckingham, 1993; Brooker and Jermyn, 2003). In addition to this, other work has been undertaken that explores the meaning that people attribute to other popular cultural practices and resources such as shopping (Miller, 1998), *Star Trek* fandom (Porter and McLaren, 1999), or as we shall see later in this chapter, clubbing (Malbon, 1998).

As a method of research, ethnography is a qualitative approach that seeks to make interpretations of human attitudes, experiences, and practices through different approaches to collecting and analyzing data (see Gray, 2003, for a useful discussion of how to undertake such research). Main sources of data that ethnographers typically work with are notes that they create from observing particular events or interactions between people, formal or informal interviews with people, or texts and other resources that shed light on the particular culture or context that they are studying. This cannot be understood as "objective" or "scientific" research as the data that the researcher collects is inevitably shaped by their personality, their interests, and the nature and quality of their relationships with their research participants. Furthermore, the process of making sense of the data that is collected is necessarily an interpretative one, in which the researcher seeks to develop the most plausible reading(s) of their data, whilst acknowledging that others may wish to interpret the same data with somewhat different emphases. Given the degree of personal involvement in the research process, it is therefore important for the ethnographic researcher to maintain a reflexive attitude to their work. It is also important for the researcher to be able to reflect on how their particular approach to this subject and to their participants may have shaped the data they have received, as well as how any hunches or biases they have may be distorting their interpretation of the data.

The aim of this chapter is to provide an example of how an ethnographic approach can be used as part of a study in theology and popular culture. In the remaining parts of this chapter, I will therefore give an overview of an ethnographic research project that I have been involved in that explores the potential religious functions of club culture. Initially this will involve a description of the rationale, aims and methods of this study, before a summary of the main findings is provided. A dialogue will then be developed between some of these main findings and wider theological resources, that will help us to think critically about club culture as a means of experiencing transcendence.

## exploring the religious functions of club culture

As we noted earlier in chapter 2, one line of enquiry that has been developed within the literature on religion and popular culture is whether particular forms of popular culture serve religious functions within contemporary society. Such studies adopt a functionalist view of religion, exploring whether a particular instance of popular culture serves communal, existential/hermeneutical, or transcendent functions typically associated with religion.

Whilst there is evidence of a growing number of such studies amongst writers in North America, this kind of research has a particular significance in the context of Britain and, more generally, Western Europe. The most recent national survey of church attendance in England indicated that church attendance fell by around one million between 1989 to 1998 (Brierley, 1999, 2000).[3] By 1998, only 7.5% of the population in England attended church on a regular basis, and the ageing demographics of church congregations suggests that this number will fall further until it reaches some kind of plateau. The significance of such statistics continues to be debated. One interpretation is that Britain is now primarily a secular or post-Christian society, in which people have little meaningful involvement with Christian institutions or beliefs (see, e.g., Bruce, 2002). An alternative view is that whilst church involvement is now clearly a minority activity, there is still a diffuse spirituality in wider British society that has at least some loose connections with Christian orthodoxy (see, e.g., Davie, 1994). However one interprets these statistics, though, the fact that no more than 12–13% of the British population are involved in regular worship or observance in any of the major religions raises the question of what alternative resources may be serving religious functions in contemporary Britain. As the novelist Douglas Coupland comments:

But then I must remind myself we are living creatures – we have religious impulses – we *must* – and yet into what cracks do these impulses flow in a world without religion? It is something I think about every day. Sometimes I think it is the only thing I should be thinking about. (1994, p.273)

The aim of this research project was to explore the phenomenon of club culture in Britain and to ask in what ways, if any, it can be interpreted as serving religious functions for those who participate in it. Initially I will explain some of the associations between club culture and religious discourse, practice, and experience that justify such a study, before setting out the main methods used in the study. I will then go on to present and reflect on the main findings that arose out of it.

Firstly, though, it is necessary to give a brief definition of what I mean by the term "club culture" in a British context. By club culture, I mean a network of dance venues and events, products (such as CDs, magazines, dance-wear fashion), people (e.g., DJs, promoters and clubbers), and supporting media that have emerged since the late 1980s in Britain and which are organized around particular forms of electronic music.[4] Whilst the term "rave culture" is still used by some British commentators, or by writers about club scenes in other parts of the world (e.g., Silcott, 2000), it is far less common for people actively involved in British club culture to refer to it in terms of "rave." For British clubbers, the term "rave" typically refers to large unlicensed outdoor dance events that took place between 1987 to 1993. The introduction of the Criminal Justice Act by the Conservative Government in 1994 made such events illegal and drove the "rave" scene into more regulated club nights in town or cities (see Collin, 1997). Major outdoor dance events are now generally only offered by large commercial organizations who observe proper licensing and health and safety requirements.

Club culture has been a major part of British youth culture since the late 1980s. It has become a thriving commercial scene including not only small club nights, but also major companies such as Cream and the Ministry of Sound who offer not only club nights, but who also produce their own dance CDs and magazines, and who even offer their own travel agencies to enable people to attend clubbing venues outside of Britain. In this context it is important to note that British club culture is not confined geographically to Britain, but also runs a number of important club nights on the Mediterranean island of Ibiza which provide a focus for holidays for many thousands of young British adults each year.

Having given some background to what I mean by "British club culture," it will be helpful to explain why it may be relevant to think of it in terms of its religious significance. There are a number of different sources which make connections between club culture and religion.

Firstly, this club scene is characterized by the widespread use of illegal recreational drugs, primarily Ecstasy (or MDMA), Cannabis, and Amphetamines, and to a lesser extent, Cocaine, Ketamine, LSD, and GHB (see Parker et al., 1998; Hammersley et al., 2002).[5] Writers such as Timothy Leary (1998) and Alexander Shulgin (1997) have explored the use of such drugs as a means for developing religious experience, and have suggested that contemporary club culture can be seen in part as a continuation of the psychedelic movement's interest in pursuing altered states of consciousness. The British writer, Nicholas Saunders, who did much to publicize positive and negative effects of Ecstasy, also had a strong interest in the religious and spiritual aspects of the use of this drug and wrote about the emergence of a "rave spirituality" (see Saunders et al., 2000; also www.ecstasy.org , 2003). It is worth noting at this point, though, that the primary effects of Ecstasy are different to hallucinogens such as LSD. Ecstasy primarily effects users through flooding the brain with the neuro-transmitters Serotonin and Dopamine, which can cause users to experience heightened levels of energy and physical sensitivity, as well as a strong sense of well-being and feeling of emotional connection with others (see, e.g., Thomas, 2002). Whilst Ecstasy is thus unlikely to produce visionary experiences associated with hallucinogenic drugs, the typical effects of Ecstasy use nevertheless have a significant impact on the way in which people experience the clubbing night out, as we shall see shortly.

Secondly, it is not uncommon for DJ's, club promoters or other commentators to use religious discourse when referring to the club scene. Some club nights are given names with religious allusions (in my own home city, "God's Kitchen," and "House of God" are two examples of this) and it is also not unusual for club flyers to use religious iconography. In 1998, the London-based club the Ministry of Sound offered to provide sponsorship for the "Spirit Zone" of the London Millennium Dome, with the club's chief executive justifying this offer with the claim that "we're disillusioned with religion: television, the internet and the Ministry of Sound have replaced it" (Lynch, 2002, p.74). The use of this religious discourse often has an ironic flavor to it, and we may wish to be skeptical of club promoters who use such language to talk up businesses in which they have a commercial interest. Nevertheless the use of this discourse also often implies the claim that club culture fulfils functions for a new generation of young adults that may traditionally have been associated with religious groups and institutions.

Thirdly, a number of writers have argued that aspects of club culture resemble certain forms of religion or can be seen as a means to religious experience. Nicholas Saunders (Saunders et al. 2000, p.168) and Simon Reynolds (1998, pp.407ff.) have both claimed that clubbing can be seen as a trance-based ritual in which participants share a common ecstatic state and celebrate a sense of unity with the clubbing crowd. The use of rhythmic drum beats, and consciousness-altering substances, in a dark, disorienting setting, also leads them to draw specific analogies between clubbing and earlier pagan or Dionysian rituals. The British sociologists of religion, Paul Heelas and Linda Woodhead (2002), have also suggested that club culture can be seen as a "secondary institution" (reflecting Peter Berger et al.'s (1973) use of the term) which provides a social network that values individual experience and the development of the self. Such secondary institutions are, they suggest, increasingly significant as loose communities of value and belief in the context of Western society in which growing numbers of people disengage from primary institutions such as traditional religious organizations. Writers have also suggested connections between clubbing and religious or transformative experience. For example, Hakim Bey's (2003) notion of the "Temporary Autonomous Zone" (TAZ) has been applied to club culture. Bey described the TAZ as a temporary and transformative release from social control, an experience of uprising that does not lead to the subsequent repressions usually associated with revolution. This notion has been applied to clubbing in the sense that the experience of dancing can itself become a moment of pure immediacy and escape from social constraints that transforms the person as they re-engage with the day-to-day world (see, e.g., Fusion Anomaly, 2003).[6] Similarly Ben Malbon (1998), who has conducted the most substantial published ethnography of the British club scene to date, suggests that clubbers undergo "oceanic experiences" whilst dancing in which they feel part of a unity greater than themselves.[7] Whilst Malbon suggests that these experiences may partly be associated with the use of recreational drugs such as Ecstasy, he also comments that these experiences do not seem to be wholly dependent upon the use of these drugs and are also reported by people not using them.

Fourthly, in clubbers' own narratives about their experiences it is not uncommon to find references to clubbing as a source of powerful and transformative experiences. As one clubber has commented:

I had my first E experience when I was twenty-five, just a couple of years ago. It has led to many personal and spiritual experiences which have changed my life for the better. . . . I can remember that first time watching people bonding on and off the dance floor, watching friends and strangers embrace, and I felt amazed and elated, and thought how right it seemed. A stranger caught my smile, and instead of stonewalling me, he smiled right back, and at that moment I felt my natural love for others bubble up as I lost my barriers of fear. I found that night that I was able to tell my friends how much I loved and valued them, and I could make connections with many other people because I had lost my usual mistrust of strangers. (Harrison, 1998, p.26).

Accounts of these transformative experiences amongst clubbers commonly point to experiences both of a transformed sense of self (cf. Rietveld, 1998 on clubbing and the deconstruction of self) and greater freedom and intimacy in relationships with others.

This wide range of connections between club culture and religion suggest that there are serious grounds for exploring whether club culture does serve religious functions for those who participate in it. The literature which suggests connections between club culture and religion tends, however, (with the exception of Malbon's work) to either be theoretical or based simply on anecdotal evidence. The aim of the study to be presented here is to begin to develop a clearer body of empirical data on the significance that clubbing can have for young British adults and thus to help us to think about the religious functions that clubbing may serve in people's lives.

The empirical part of this study was conducted over a two-year period by myself and a post-graduate student, Emily Badger. Whilst observation of club nights formed part of this project, the main data for this study came from interviews with a total of 37 people who attend, or had recently attended, clubs on a regular basis and who regarded clubbing as an important part of their lives. For this study, the decision to interview people away from the clubs reflected the fact that people were reluctant to give much time to a research interview whilst enjoying a night out and that interviewing participants in clubs whilst they were using recreational drugs would produce data of limited use.

We contacted people for this study by a range of different methods including advertising at a local college and on an internet discussion board for a particular club night, as well as using personal contacts. We found that participants often suggested other people who would be interested in taking part in this study, and we were able to develop further interviews through these contacts – an approach known as "snowball" sampling. A total of 37 participants took part in the study, of whom 24 were male and 13 were female. The age range of participants was between 16–32, with the vast majority aged between 16–23. All of the participants in this research project were white, which is a reflection of the lack of ethnic diversity in the type of club that we were studying. This lack of diversity is striking given that we were conducting this project in a city which has a substantial number of black and Asian inhabitants. The mix of age and gender is also broadly typical of the groups who attend these clubs.

The aim of the research interviews was to encourage participants to talk about what role clubbing played in their lives and to explore what significance clubbing had for them. In an initial series of pilot interviews, involving 11 of the 37 participants, people were also asked if they believed clubbing had any "religious" or "spiritual" significance for them, or whether these terms could be meaningfully applied to club culture more generally.

This initial series of pilot interviews clarified two important issues that guided the design of the subsequent interviews. Firstly, it became clear that participants' attitudes and the way in which they made sense of their experiences partly reflected the type of club nights that they attended. In particular, it was found that participants' experiences, attitudes, and reflections were likely to differ depending partly on the type of music played at the club they attended and even more significantly on the types of recreational drugs that were primarily used at that club. A person attending a club playing mainly R "n" B music, in which alcohol was the most commonly used drug, would for example tend to offer somewhat different accounts of their motivations for going clubbing to someone who attended a techno club night in which Ecstasy was more commonly consumed.[8] This initial finding illustrated the dangers of thinking about club culture as a single, homogenous entity, where as in reality it is a complex network of different and more specific club cultures (see Thornton, 1995). It also led to the decision, in this project, to focus on interviewing participants who attended particular styles of club night (house, hard house, techno) in which alcohol consumption played a less significant role than the consumption of Ecstasy and other illegal recreational drugs. Whilst this more specific focus for the project means that the findings can clearly not be generalizable across all forms of "night-clubbing" activity, it is important to note that house and techno club nights remain a very important element within the wider British club scene as well as having a significant presence in major cities in America.

A second significant finding from the pilot phase of the project was that, with only one exception, participants did not explicitly think about their clubbing experiences using terms like "religious" or "spiritual."[9] Indeed many participants were skeptical of seeing clubbing in religious terms, with some suggesting such views were naïve or the result of having taken a few too many drugs. This initial finding led to any explicit reference to religion or spirituality being dropped from subsequent interviews.

In the remaining interviews, we continued to ask participants to talk about what significance clubbing had in their lives and how they made sense of their clubbing experiences. In addition to this we divided these remaining interviews into two sets. One set (15 participants) was made up of people who were beginning to disengage from the club scene. They were also asked what had brought them into clubbing originally, what led them to go clubbing less often, and whether their view of clubbing had changed over time. The results from these particular questions will be written up elsewhere. The second set (11 participants) were additionally asked a question that explored whether they had "mystical" experiences in the context of clubbing nights out, and we shall return to this issue shortly.

Having conducted the interviews, we then analyzed the data to try to identify core themes that ran through the interviews. To do this we adopted a modified form of grounded theory analysis (see, e.g., Strauss and Corbin, 1990; Maykut and Morehouse, 1994) in which we initially broke the interviews down into more specific "units of meaning" or short quotations that made specific points. After generating these units of meaning for all of the interviews, we then grouped these units into categories which highlighted particular themes and issues. Whilst participants clearly differed in the specific ways in which they narrated their experiences, and talked about the meaning that clubbing had for them, it was also possible to identify a number of common themes that were present across the majority of the interviews. As we shall now see, a number of these themes were relevant to communal, hermeneutical, and transcendent functions of religion.

It became clear, for example, that the social and communal elements of clubbing experiences were often very important for participants. Indeed participants frequently talked about the clubs that they attended in terms of extended families or communities of friends. For some this clubbing community had proved invaluable, as one interviewee commented:

> I've had about two years up until a few months ago where everything was really fucked up. Most people would probably have killed themselves, but I just carried on really. I found all these people [at these club nights] . . . despite all the problems I've had with my family, they're like a totally different family . . . Another thing is, at the end of the week if everything's gone bad, you know you can go clubbing and you've got all your friends to talk to. (Nick, 17)

The clubbing community thus provided participants with a social network that they perceived to be generally welcoming and friendly, and within which they developed close friendships[10] that were important sources of support and intimacy.[11] This clubbing "family" was also, for many participants, characterized by certain shared values such as accepting others, tolerating diversity, and feeling free to express oneself in authentic ways. The strength of commitment to these values amongst many participants was indicated when they spoke of people who attended club nights, but who did not fit into the clubbing community because they failed to share these values. Two of the common types of people who were described in this context were "beer boys" and "try hards." "Beer boys," for example, were young male clubbers who drank alcohol rather than using drugs such as Ecstasy. Their alcohol use was seen as often associated with aggressive behavior on their part, and they were also seen as being more likely to be intolerant or judgmental of others (e.g., being homophobic). Similarly "try hards" were described as people who followed the latest trends in dance music, fashion, and drug use, but who lacked sufficient autonomy to develop their own tastes.[12] The difference between "true" clubbers, in contrast to beer boys and try hards was therefore not simply a matter of taste in fashion or drug use, but of more fundamental attitudes. As another interviewee commented:

> The whole thing with it is that with our scene we're not afraid to be who we want to be . . . we don't care what anyone really thinks of us, we will be who we want to be, but everyone else [beer boys, try hards] . . . in a way they just do what everyone else tells them to do . . . If you could put it into pictures: we're on free range and they're all locked up in the chicken coup. (Tom, 24)

Whilst this description of the "true" clubbing community as an inclusive and welcoming extended family may sound somewhat idealized, there was also evidence of participants being able to reflect more critically on the nature of this community. In particular, some participants raised the issue of whether the warmth and acceptance of the clubbing community is simply a consequence of clubbers being "loved up" on Ecstasy.[13] Many of the participants could recognize times whilst using Ecstasy when they had met new people and felt a deep sense of connection with them, only for this to wear off as they began to come down from the drug's effects. This led some participants to question whether the warmth of the clubbing community was as genuine as it might first appear, or whether it was simply part of a physiological response to Ecstasy use. Indeed it was often those who had been involved in clubbing for longer periods of time, and whose prolonged use of Ecstasy meant that they experienced less of the positive emotional effects of the drug, who were more likely to raise this issue.[14] At the same time, other participants recognized that part of the warmth of the clubbing community was drug induced, yet commented that genuine support and intimacy could still be found within it. As one commented:

Obviously pills make you think that you love everybody and that everything's wicked and that you're friends with everybody. But if you can do a come down with people and not have one act of paranoia and feel comfortable with them, then you know you have found true friends, in a way, because it's not the drugs. (Jessica, 20)

It was clear from these research participants that the social and communal aspects of clubbing were an important part of their experience. This "clubbing community" was seen as characterized by certain shared values such as acceptance, tolerance, personal autonomy, and authenticity. Whilst the degree of warmth and acceptance in this community was seen critically by some as an effect of Ecstasy use, the majority of participants still recognized that clubbing provided them with an opportunity to form deeper and more intimate relationships with some other people.

In addition to these social and communal aspects of club culture, it became clear that the participants tended to make use of a broadly similar hermeneutical framework through which they made sense of their clubbing experiences. This framework can be described as a "therapeutic discourse" in which participants reflected on their experiences in terms of their implications for their psychological well-being and their on-going personal development. For example, one interviewee commented:

[Because of clubbing] I'm a lot more open with people. It gives you a certain openness with people. You can talk about anything and I've got a lot more confidence in myself. I was really shy and quiet before. Everyone goes on about how drugs are a positive influence and a lot of clubbers will say to try it because it has a positive influence. (Mike, 21)

Similarly, another told me:

[Clubbing] makes you more confident – it makes you accept people. I mean I used to look at people and think what is she wearing and why is he wearing that, and now I don't care. I was ignorant I admit . . . I would say that for the few years it lasts it's wonderful, and it lasts forever because once you get your confidence up you can do anything. (Andy, 17)

Many of the participants spoke about how the accepting, tolerant ethos of their club nights provided a space in which people were allowed to be themselves and to become more confident. One commented that people who may have been bullied at school, or who may have found it hard to find a peer group for themselves, had found in clubbing a place where they could retain their individuality but still be accepted by those around them. Another interviewee observed that, in his experience, many of the people who were attracted to the kind of club nights that he went to were struggling with some kind of emotional difficulty and sought some kind of help through their clubbing relationships.

Even participants who did not talk about clubbing as a means of dealing with specific personal difficulties, still spoke about their clubbing experiences in terms of their wider self-development. One participant, Hannah, for example, spoke about how her experiences of using drugs such as Ecstasy and Amphetamines had heightened her awareness of her sexuality and sharpened her awareness of different kinds of physical experience. Many other participants spoke about how clubbing had made them more "well-rounded" as people. Whilst they were not always able to be very explicit about what "well-rounded" meant in this context, it nevertheless carried connotations for them of being more open-minded, tolerant, and better able to deal with people different to themselves.

When reflecting on the significance of clubbing in their lives, participants thus tended to interpret their experiences through a therapeutic discourse that emphasized psychological healing and personal development. This discourse can be seen as closely tied to what social theorists such as Anthony Giddens (1991), Kenneth Gergen (1991), and Zygmunt Bauman (2001) have referred to as the "reflexive project of the self," which is characteristic of late modern culture. Participants therefore made sense of clubbing through a wider cultural discourse, in which clubbing was seen as generally making a positive contribution to their sense of selfhood and to the way in which they would approach relationships with others in the future. Participation in club culture was therefore associated with a particular hermeneutical framework ("therapeutic discourse") through which participants interpreted their clubbing experiences and their lives more generally.

Finally, some of the interviews generated interesting findings in relation to clubbing as a means of encountering transcendence or the numinous. A subgroup of the sample (11 participants) were shown four short statements that summarized William James' (1902) four criteria for a mystical experience in the form of the following question:

"When clubbing/dancing, have you ever had particular experiences?"

- that you find it hard to put into words;
- that felt meaningful to you, or that influenced how you feel about the rest of your life;
- that may have lasted for only a short period of time;
- in which you felt passive, or caught up in something?

As noted earlier, the pilot phase of the study indicated that participants did not generally find the explicit use of terms such as "religious" or "spiritual" meaningful. Whilst William James' model of mystical experience can be criticized for offering an overly psychological and individual understanding of mysticism, I chose to use it here as an alternative way of stimulating participants to talk about experiences that could be construed in religious terms. Although the small number of participants who were asked this question obviously raises issues of generalizability, three interesting issues worth noting arose out of their responses.

Firstly, seven of the eleven participants who were presented with this question immediately associated with the four statements. Sometimes this was indicated by knowing smiles or laughs, or in one case, when someone commented that "what you've got written down there is exactly why I go clubbing." Those who did not identify with the four statements tended to go through them in order and reflected on whether they had experienced any of these at any point whilst clubbing. By contrast, those who identified with the statements tended to react immediately to them as a summary of a kind of experience that they recognized.

Secondly, when the participants who identified with these four criteria began to talk about their experiences, their narratives took very different forms. One person spoke about a time when the crowd in which he was dancing seemed to be powerfully engaged in a shared experience that led to a group hug on the dance floor involving fifty people. By contrast, another participant told a story of how his profound experience was one of peace and separation from what was going on around him, in which for a period of time he was alone and caught up in the music. Another spoke of an intense moment of connection with her boyfriend on the dance floor –" feeling that every cell of my body was a part of every cell of his." Others, however, went on to tell stories that seemed to have little direct relationship to oceanic or mystical experiences. Examples of these included having a DJ borrow one of the participant's records and the dance floor going mad when the particular track was played, or of another DJ allowing one of the participants to choose a record as it was his birthday. The experiences that were narrated by participants thus took widely different forms, but also shared the common theme of moments of intense joy and bliss.

Thirdly, when the participants told these stories, none of them made use of a religious or transcendence discourse to understand them. There was no sense for any of the participants that in these moments of intense bliss they were engaging with any significant spiritual source either within or beyond themselves. Equally, none of the participants reported any sense of "metaphysical revelation" in relation to these experiences, by which the experience transformed their understanding of life. Thus, whilst the several of the participants were inspired by James' criteria of mystical experience to tell stories of experiences that they clearly valued greatly, these experiences did not appear to be fully mystical in the sense that James himself intended.

The conclusions arising out of this particular piece of research are necessarily tentative. We have noted that club culture is not a homogenous social movement, but consists of a range of different subgenres and related networks. It cannot therefore be assumed that the findings of this current project – which relate primarily to house, techno and hard house clubs in which Ecstasy is commonly used – necessarily apply to club nights based on other types of music or primarily on the consumption of alcohol. Similarly the fact that the interviews present us with clubbers' self-reports provide an interesting perspective on what significance they perceive clubbing to have in their lives, as well as the discourses they use to make sense of their clubbing experiences. But to gain a fuller picture of the functions that clubbing serves for this sample, we would also need to draw on detailed observations of how people actually relate to each other in clubs and understand more about their attitudes, relationships and experiences outside of the clubbing night out.

Nevertheless, despite the limitations of this data there is reasonable evidence that club culture did perform religious functions in some sense for the majority of the participants in this study. For example, club culture did offer participants an important experience of being bound into a community with a broadly shared ethos. Although some participants were wary of having too idealized an understanding of the clubbing community, most participants saw it as an important social network in which they felt accepted and free to explore their identities. As a loose community, it provided a structure in which they could develop closer relationships with new people or with existing friends. Within the clubbing community there was also clearly a sense of a shared ethos of tolerance, expressivity, and authenticity, as well as suspicion towards those less committed to these values. Furthermore, for the vast majority of participants their experiences of clubbing were bound up with a "therapeutic discourse" that shaped the way in which they interpreted their clubbing experiences and thought about the significance of clubbing to their lives more generally. This therapeutic discourse thus offered an important hermeneutical framework through which participants understood their lives. Whilst this style of discourse is far from unique to club culture – and can be seen as reinforced in other parts of popular culture as diverse as the counseling movement, popular film, and lifestyle TV programs and magazines – participation in clubbing nevertheless provided an important opportunity for people to practice this discourse in relation to their lives. Finally, at least for some participants, there was a sense that clubbing gave them a chance to connect with something vital and joyful in life. Whether these can be thought of as experiences of "transcendence," however, is something that we will return to in the last part of this chapter.

From this summary of the ways in which club culture appears to meet communal, hermeneutical, and existential functions for participants, it is possible to concur with Heelas and Woodhead's suggestion that club culture be understood as a "secondary institution." Secondary institutions can be characterized in the following way:

> Compared with primary institutions, secondary ones are relatively detraditionalized. Whether by being grounded in a faith-inspired past or in rules or regulations worked out by the exercise of reason, the traditionalized primary institution provides an *order of things* to be obeyed . . . By contrast, secondary institutions are considerably less regulative and authoritative and therefore provide much greater freedom for people to exercise autonomy. Much greater value is accorded to the experiential rather than the deferential, with participants encouraged to express themselves, explore their feelings, grow individually and in relation to one another. (Heelas and Woodhead, 2002, p.53)

Club culture can therefore be seen as one of many secondary institutions in contemporary Western culture which provide an experiential framework through which people are able to extend their project of the self and develop their relationships with others. The particular age-range of the majority of clubbers (typically 16–23) further suggests that, as a secondary institution, club culture has a particular role in helping young people negotiate the transition from adolescence to early adulthood.

If club culture does serve religious functions for some people in Western society, this raises normative questions of whether it does so in ways that are healthy and constructive. It is to these questions that we shall now briefly turn.

## clubbing, relationship, and transcendence

There are many aspects of the beliefs, values, and practices associated with club culture that could provide a useful focus for theological reflection and dialogue. We could, for example, think about the understanding of community and friendship that exists within this sample of clubbers and reflect on the degree to which it does offer a genuinely redemptive resource. We might also want to explore values such as authenticity, autonomy, and self-expression that seem so important in this club culture, both to think about the Western cultural roots of these values and how we might evaluate the strengths and limitations of these values as a basis for our lives. The role of recreational drug use in this setting also raises interesting questions about what represents "genuine" experiences of intimacy, joy, and unity. Within the confines of this chapter, though, I wish to focus briefly on the issue of transcendence as it relates to the reported experiences of some of the members of this sample.

As we noted earlier, some of the participants in this study immediately warmed to William James' criteria of a mystical experience, and associated these criteria with experiences that they had on clubbing nights out. As we also noted, though, the narratives that these participants told did not fit neatly into recognizable accounts of mystical experience, but represented a more diverse collection of stories of moments of pure bliss.

From a theological perspective, it is particularly striking that these participants did not make use of any kind of "transcendence" discourse to interpret these experiences. There was no sense, for them, that they were connecting with any ultimate or absolute source either within or beyond themselves, and these stories of bliss related simply to experiences within their own psyches or in their immediate relations with those around them. Whilst the ecstatic or oceanic states that these participants reported may appear to be like religious or mystical experiences, there are some significant differences between their experiences and other theological understandings of encounters with transcendence.

The emergence of modernity in Western culture has had the effect of challenging traditional religious systems of belief and authority. One of the consequences of this amongst some modern theologians has been a growing interest in the personal and experiential basis of religious faith, as opposed to attempts to defend such faith on the basis of formal theological arguments or doctrines. Friedrich Schleiermacher (1821/1969), for example, argued that religious faith arose out of a basic experience of "absolute dependence," in which a person recognizes that the life and world that they inhabit and act within is something that is fundamentally given to them (see Clements, 1991). This experience is different to that of "relative dependence," in which a person understands that there is a world beyond them that is able to act upon them, and which they are able to act in and influence to some extent as well. "Absolute dependence" is thus not simply the recognition that I am not entirely in control of my life and its circumstances, but the recognition that the basic fact of existence is something utterly given to me and beyond my control.

Schleiermacher's emphasis on the importance of a sense of relationship to the absolute as a basis for religious faith has been taken up in different and, arguably in some respects, contrasting ways by subsequent writers. Rudolf Otto (1923), for example, wrote about the basis of religious experience as an encounter with the "numinous," a transcendent object which we perceive as beyond us and before which we are utterly aware of our createdness and finitude. Paul Tillich (1952) spoke about the religious life in terms of a relationship with the "ground of being" on which our existence rests and through which we are fundamentally acceptable and accepted. Emmanuel Levinas wrote about the importance of perceiving life in terms of relation to the Other, who is already beyond any direct comprehension but who challenges us to live in ethical relationship with those around us (see Peperzak et al., 1996).

What is striking about these different theological and philosophical perspectives is that each emphasize the importance of a sense of relationship to that which is absolutely and ultimately beyond us. None of these writers conceptualize God in simplistic terms as a personal other who can be understood in terms comparable to other human relationships. Indeed, for each of them, the emphasis is placed more strongly on the incomprehensibility of that absolute source. Within this mystical emphasis, however, the sense of the importance of relationship remains strong. This absolute may be found only where "concepts fail" (Otto, 1923, p.xxii), or be seen as the "God above God" (Tillich, 1952), that which transcends any possible notion of the divine. But despite the impossibility of finally naming or conceptualizing this Other, these writers still understand a sense of relationship to the Other as a basic element of authentic and healthy human existence.

Interestingly, it is precisely this sense of relationship to an absolute source that appears lacking amongst the participants in this study. As one of my participants, Paul, commented:

> I wouldn't describe [clubbing] as a religious experience. There've been times when I might start to think that maybe I was experiencing something more, but . . . I don't think I'd like to call it spiritual . . . I think it's more a case of unlocking things inside you, inside of you rather than outside of you . . . There have been times when I've come off the dance floor and sort of thought to myself, "Is this the way to find meaning and stuff?" But then always the next day I'll wake up and think, "No, I was just having a really, really good time." And I don't think there's really anything more to it. (Paul, 23)

Whilst Paul clearly demonstrates a reflective approach to his clubbing experiences, it is evident that he understands these ultimately as intra-psychic events which are significant moments of personal experience, but which do not imply any connection with something beyond himself. My participants would therefore interpret their moments of joy and bliss in clubbing in terms of their self-development or their relationships with those immediately around them. But they do not discuss the possibility that their clubbing experiences are deepening their sense of connection with the absolute in life, or that these experiences make them more aware of the fact that existence is ultimately given to us rather than created by us.

Some important questions follow on from this. Is it possible that these participants do not talk about a sense of connection with the absolute in life because they genuinely do not experience this or because they lack a discourse that would enable them to describe their experiences in this way? Participants such as Paul appeared to believe that to think of their experiences as "religious" would necessarily imply a sense of connection with a personal God who is "up there" or "out there" somewhere. They seemed to have no discursive or conceptual resources that would help them to speak about transcendence or the absolute in a way other than through talking simplistically about a personal God in whom they had no strong belief. Does this necessarily mean that their experiences of clubbing did not involve any sense of relationship to the absolute, the Other, or the ground of being, though? Or does this reflect more on the relative poverty of contemporary popular discourses of transcendence?[15]

A related question concerns the effects of this lack of experience or discourse of transcendence. If these participants do not understand themselves, even in moments of profound connection and ecstasy, to be connecting with what it absolute or ultimate in life, then what are the spiritual or moral consequences of this? I would suggest that it implies a limit to the kinds of transformative vision that can arise out of these kinds of experience. It is clear that the vast majority of participants in this study valued the way in which clubbing had given them opportunities for self-development or greater intimacy with other people. The boundaries of this transformation generally seemed to end, however, at the limits of the self and the friendship networks that individuals had in the clubs. The value of such transformative experiences should not be denigrated, and rather than representing a scene of mindless hedonism this study suggests that club culture can, for some people, be an important space for personal and social development. What is lacking, however, is a deeper sense of transformation in which people in the club scene are challenged and helped to ask deeper questions about the meaning of their lives, the nature of the world in which they live, or their relationship to the absolute reference point of existence. More specifically, it is notable that the mainstream club culture that I was exploring has few formal connections with wider political or spiritual movements that think critically about issues such as globalization, fair trade, human rights, or wider questions about life's meaning.

Arguably, this lack of a wider transformative vision in this club scene could be seen as partly connected to the lack of a useful discourse of transcendence for those who take part in it. If people can only interpret moments of profound joy or connection in clubs through a therapeutic discourse that views these experiences in terms of personal and relational development, then it becomes harder for such experiences to become the basis of more profound religious or moral visions of life. Through a discourse of transcendence, it might be possible for some people in the club scene to see how their experiences offer a moment of connection or insight with the ground of reality that could then prompt them to ask more radical questions of their lives and their communities. Whilst this remains a speculative suggestion, it does again raise the question of what it might mean to develop popular discourses of transcendence that could enable people to reflect more broadly on the significance of their lives.

## conclusion

The discussion presented in this chapter is an attempt to demonstrate the role of ethnographic methods in providing material for theological reflection on contemporary popular culture, as well as an initial discussion of religious and theological aspects of club culture. This study is an explorative piece of work that invites further empirical studies of club cultures as well as more substantial theological reflection of the material that arises out of such studies.

One of the most important observations to arise out this chapter, however, concerns the significance of empirical research into popular cultural practices. Whilst theoretical arguments about the religious significance of club culture may, at first sight, appear convincing, it remains important to explore what significance club culture actually has for those who take part in it. Whilst this kind of empirical work can be demanding in terms of time and resources, it remains a vital element in understanding and critiquing contemporary popular culture. For without such work, we risk developing theological analyses that are well argued theoretically, but do not properly reflect the attitudes, experiences, and practices of people in the real world settings that we claim to be able to speak about. Taken together, auteur, text-based, and ethnographic approaches to studying popular culture represent an important range of methods that can enable us to interpret popular culture in more complex ways, and thus to develop theological critiques that are better informed and more convincing.

# Chapter 9

# taking steps towards a theological aesthetics of popular culture

The essence of popular cultural practice is making judgments and assessing differences.

(Frith, 1996)

## introduction

Throughout the course of this book we have looked at some of the core issues, themes, and methods in the academic study of popular culture. More specifically, we have considered why those working within theology and religious studies have studied popular culture, and what specific contribution these disciplines might make to this field. I have suggested, in particular, that theology's distinctive contribution to the study of popular culture arises out of the fact that theology is a *normative* discipline. It is concerned with questions about the nature of truth, what constitutes a meaningful view of life, what it means to live good and fulfilling lives and to build just and peaceable communities. Furthermore theology involves exploring these questions in relation to the possibility of an absolute reference point to life which might inform how we think about truth, meaning, goodness, and justice.

In drawing this book to a close, I want to return to this issue of the distinctive place of theology in the academic study of popular culture and to develop another way of talking about this form of theological study. More specifically I want to present the kind of study that I am advocating in terms of the development and practice of a *theological aesthetics of popular culture*. To explain what I mean by this phrase we will need initially in this chapter to think more about the meaning of the term "aesthetics" and to consider why the notion of an "aesthetics of popular culture" has often been ignored or rejected in academic circles. By exploring these issues, we will then be able to consider what it means to develop a theological aesthetics of popular culture, as well as some of the elements that might define such an aesthetics.

## what is "aesthetics"?

One of the complexities of talking generally about aesthetics is the fact that this word can be used by scholars in somewhat different ways. It may be used, at a more everyday level, to think about aesthetics as referring to the idea of taste or style. So when we talk about this or that person's "aesthetic," we might be referring to their particular style in fashion or their taste in music. In some ways this use of the term "aesthetic" is helpful for our discussion here as it implies a process of making judgments or discriminating between what forms of culture one likes or dislikes, or thinks is better or worse in some sense. This sense of aesthetics being tied to making evaluative judgments is important, and we will return to this point shortly.

In academic contexts, the study of aesthetics tends to embrace a wide range of different issues and concerns (see de Bolla, 2001, pp.5ff.). In the context of the study of the history of art, aesthetics can involve an interest in the style, techniques, and ideas of a particular artist. In philosophy, the word "aesthetics" sometimes denotes the philosophical study of art, including questions such as how we understand the defining qualities of what makes something art and the nature of the experience of being in the presence of art. More generally, aesthetics is also talked about in terms of the philosophy of beauty, and the relationship of our understanding of beauty (in the contexts of art, design, or the "natural" world) to our understanding of truth and goodness.

The study of theology and aesthetics, or "theological aesthetics," is also not a neatly defined discipline. For some writers, "aesthetics" play a central role in how we understand and do theology. Hans Urs von Balthasar (1982), for example, understands theological aesthetics as being broadly concerned with the study of beauty in relation to God. Von Balthasar argues that our specific experiences of beauty have a sacramental function in alerting us not only to the beauty of the object we experience, but in pointing us beyond this object to the truth and goodness of God which is the ultimate source of all beauty (ibid., p.118). Von Balthasar therefore conceives of theological aesthetics as involving two essential tasks, namely understanding how we perceive the beauty of God's self-revelation in the world and understanding how God reveals divine truth and beauty to us and enables us to participate in it. As the study of divine revelation and the human experience of, and response to, this revelation, von Balthasar therefore sees theological aesthetics as concerned with understanding central issues at the heart of Christian belief.

A more specific understanding of theological aesthetics is to see it (like some philosophical approaches to aesthetics) as the theological study of the nature and significance of art. This might, for example, include questions such as what defines "religious" art (Wolterstorff, 2004), how art can inform our understanding of the nature and limitations of theological language (Dillenberger, 1986) or how theological concepts such as the Incarnation relate to the artistic imagination (Hart, 2000).

This brief survey of the different uses of the term "aesthetics" demonstrates that there is no clear commonly agreed agenda about what the study of aesthetics specifically involves. One concern that underlies several (though not all) of these different types of study is an interest in making evaluative judgments about particular phenomena.

This might involve asking whether an object can properly be understood as art or not (see, e.g., Freeland, 2001), or whether a piece of art is good art or not. Or it might involve asking whether a particular object is truly beautiful or whether, in theological terms, a particular object reveals something of the truth and beauty of God. The basic observation I want to make at this point, though, is that aesthetics is often concerned with making evaluative judgments. Is this better than that? Is this beautiful or not? Is it well-designed or is it an example of exceptional technical skill or creativity? Is it profound or trivial? Is it morally and spiritually uplifting, or a waste of time? This process of aesthetic evaluation is arguably an integral part of how we approach our everyday life. Yet the notion of an aesthetics of popular culture (i.e., some kind of theory or basis on which we can base of evaluative judgments of popular culture) has tended to be rejected or ignored in academic circles. In the next part of the chapter, we will think briefly about why this has been the case.

## the struggle to develop an aesthetics of popular culture

To use the terms "aesthetics" and "popular culture" in the same breath is still a relatively rare occurrence in academic circles. There are three particular reasons why the notion of an aesthetics of popular culture has been ignored or rejected by academic writers.

Firstly, the association of "aesthetics" with art has meant that aesthetics has tended to be seen as a form of study that is concerned primarily with "high" culture. The discipline of philosophical aesthetics has often implicitly or explicitly reinforced the distinction between "high" and "low/mass/popular" culture that we noted back in chapter 1. The underlying assumption here is that "high" culture demonstrates exemplary aesthetic qualities, where as "popular" culture is merely debased, low-brow entertainment devoid of any aesthetic value.[1] As Richard Shusterman points out (2000, p.169), this assumption seems so compelling amongst many cultural critics that it has become a point of consensus even between right-wing reactionary critics such as Allan Bloom and Marxist critics such as Theodore Adorno.

Secondly, questions of aesthetic judgment have tended to be overlooked by those cultural critics who have a far more positive understanding of the place of popular culture in society. As Simon Frith observes (1996, p.14), the recent tradition of British and American popular culture studies has tended to focus on the constructive social and political effects of popular culture. In these approaches, popular culture tends either to be seen as a means of resisting dominant cultural ideologies and structures (in the British tradition) or as a means of preserving diversity in the context of a pluralist society (in the American tradition). Partly in reaction to the denigration of popular culture by other academics and cultural critics, this growing discipline of popular culture studies has tended to adopt a positive, even celebratory, tone to its discussions. A good example of this is John Fiske's (1989) account of popular culture as the place in which people express their freedom and autonomy in the face of wider social and cultural structures over which they have little direct control. Whilst the desire to defend the value of popular culture may be understandable, one of the consequences of this approach has been the tendency to neglect aesthetic questions of whether some forms of popular culture are actually better in some sense than others. The broad debate about whether "popular culture" as a whole has any merits or not has therefore tended to polarize critics and supporters of popular culture into positions where it becomes harder to think of the possibility of there being good *and* bad, better *and* worse forms of popular culture.

A third reason why questions of aesthetics have tended to be neglected in relation to popular culture concerns the ideological skepticism that many social and cultural critics feel towards notions of "taste" and "aesthetic judgment." The eighteenth-century philosopher David Hume is a good example of someone who believed that it was possible for people with the right kind of education and quality of mind to be able to develop genuinely good taste in their appreciation of art. In Hume's view, such taste was not simply the expression of an individual's personal preferences, but could provide a true assessment of the aesthetic value and quality of a particular piece of art (Freeland, 2001, p.9f.). This notion of pure, good taste has been regarded with greater ideological suspicion, however, by more recent scholarship. In his major study of the social functions of taste, Pierre Bourdieu (1984) argued that taste is not a neutral or "purely" aesthetic sense of judgment, but an important marker of social status and identity. The ability to demonstrate certain kinds of taste thus provides an important role in establishing a person's place within wider social and class structures.[2] Taste therefore becomes a way of clarifying one's status within wider society, and the "cultural capital" that a person acquires through their particular social background and education will influence the kind of activities and groups that they can participate in.[3] Bourdieu's work has been highly influential in recent sociology and cultural studies. One of the effects of this for popular culture studies is that when questions of taste have been explored, they tend to be thought about in terms of how that taste reflects particular cultural discourses or serves to define a person's identity, place and opportunities in wider society (see, e.g., Thornton, 1995; Frith, 1996, pp.36ff.). Whilst this emphasis provides an important corrective to the notion that taste is purely about issues of aesthetic discrimination, it has also tended to obscure the notion that it may still be important to make aesthetic judgments about the culture that we inhabit.

Simon Frith (1996, 1998) is one of the leading writers to have suggested that the neglect of questions of aesthetics relating to popular culture represents a serious deficit in current academic work on popular culture. Frith argues that the process of making evaluative judgments about popular culture is an integral part of what it means for us to be involved in cultural practices. If, following the definition proposed at the start of this book, we think of popular culture as the environment, resources, and practices of everyday life then it is clear that making judgments about these environments, resources, and practices is a part of day-to-day living. Each day of our lives we form conscious or less conscious judgments about what forms of popular culture we find attractive, interesting, worthwhile, stimulating, enjoyable and inspiring. In forming these judgments about the environment, resources and practices of everyday life, we are practicing an aesthetic of popular culture even though we may not be conscious that we are doing so, nor entirely aware of the grounds on which we base these aesthetic judgments. Clearly these judgments play an important role in establishing our sense of identity in the world (Frith, 1996, p.18), but they do not simply involve questions of identity but wider questions about what we believe is genuinely good, enjoyable, and worthwhile.

Frith has argued that the neglect of aesthetics in popular culture studies has led to a divide between the academic classroom and the outside world

(1998, p.571). The study of popular culture in the classroom tends to focus on analyzing how a particular piece of popular culture relates to wider social and cultural structures and processes. On leaving the classroom, though, conversation is more likely to turn quickly to one's feelings about, say, the particular film or piece of music that was studied and whether one actually liked it or not. If the academic study of popular culture is to make a useful contribution to how we think about our everyday judgments and responses to contemporary culture then it needs to bridge this gap and address far more explicitly how we can develop an aesthetics of popular culture. In the final part of this chapter we will now look at how writers like Simon Frith and Richard Shusterman, who are pioneering figures in this area, might begin to help us understand what it means to practice a theological aesthetics of popular culture.

## steps towards a theological aesthetics of popular culture

The process of developing an aesthetic of popular culture is a complex one for a number of different reasons.

Firstly, there can be a reluctance even amongst those who enjoy different forms of popular culture to developing an aesthetic language to make sense of what makes popular culture good and bad. For many people, popular culture is enjoyable simply because it is enjoyable, and to try to analyze this enjoyment in more detail can provoke bemused, inarticulate, or exasperated responses (see, e.g., Frith, 1996, p.74).

Secondly, the notion of developing aesthetic criteria for evaluating popular culture can be regarded with suspicion on the grounds that responses to popular culture are so subjective that it is unlikely we can ever have a discussion on this issue that goes beyond the statement of personal preferences. In response to this, however, it could be argued that aesthetic experiences are by their very nature subjective, but that this does not mean they cannot provide us with any insights into an object's real qualities. Indeed it is only possible for us to perceive the qualities of an art-work or piece of music precisely through the media of our subjective thoughts, feelings, and physical sensations (De Bolla, 2001, p.18).

Thirdly, given the breadth of forms that popular culture takes it is open to question as to whether it is possible to frame a set of aesthetic criteria that can be used to evaluate all forms of popular culture. Is it feasible, for example, to have a common set of aesthetic criteria by which we could judge dance, interior design, film, and sport? I will shortly suggest a range of criteria that might be used to evaluate popular culture, but it is important to recognize that the relevance of particular criteria will differ depending on what it is we are judging, and that particular forms of popular culture may require specific criteria.

Fourthly, to talk about an aesthetics of popular culture could be seen as hopelessly simplistic if it encourages the idea that there is a single, ideal form to which all popular culture should aspire. Such a notion is unrealistic, though. As Simon Frith (1996, p.276) points out, different forms of popular music exist within an on-going field of tensions between "authenticity and artifice, sentimentality and realism, the spiritual and the sensual, the serious and the fun." There is no single correct way for popular music to resolve these different tensions, and any aesthetics of popular culture will need to be sufficiently flexible to judge different cultural texts and practices on their own terms and in their own specific context.

The process of developing an aesthetics of popular culture will not therefore be a straightforward one, but I would like here to suggest some of the key elements that it may involve. Following Richard Shusterman (2000, p.195), I would want to begin with the assumption in John Dewey's (1934) pragmatist aesthetics that the central principle of aesthetic judgment should be the extent to which an object meets the needs, or enhances the experience, of the "live creature." In other words, aesthetics should seek to evaluate objects and practices on the basis of their effects for human experience, relationships, and communities. We might ask, therefore, if engaging with particular forms of popular culture lead us to "a refreshed attitude toward the circumstances and exigencies of ordinary experience" or gives us an enhanced experience of life (ibid., pp.9, 19). Similarly we might also ask whether a form of popular culture is catalytic in the sense of provoking constructive experiences, attitudes and practices that spill over into other parts of our lives or whether it simply promotes an enervating passivity in us (ibid., p.10). Such an approach to aesthetics is radically different to those that focus on esoteric or disinterested accounts of beauty. To build aesthetic judgments on the basis of effects for human experience and relationships is a more consistent approach, though, to the kind of contextual theological project that I have been advocating in this book.

On the basis of this central pragmatist principle, it is possible to identify a range of more specific criteria that might help us to form aesthetic judgments of particular examples of popular culture:

1    Does the popular cultural text or practice demonstrate an impressive level of *technical skill*? Does it involve a level of competence or performance skill

that is difficult to achieve and thus an admirable symbol of human achievement?

2   Does it exemplify *originality, imagination, or creativity*?[4] If it is a cultural text, does it go beyond or make imaginative use of standard conventions within its genre, or introduce us to something we have not previously seen, heard or thought about in the same way (ibid., p.189)? Or if it is a performance or practice, is it in some way innovative or going beyond existing structures and experiences?

3   Does it offer a satisfying *reflection of human experience*, and/or provide a means for empathizing with a range of different experiences (see, e.g., Frith, 1996, pp.49f.)? Does it make us more aware of the nature and texture of a particular experience? Does it successfully evoke a particular mood? Is it coherent, believable, and "true to life," whilst at the same time retaining the capacity to surprise and provoke us?

4   Does it offer a valuable *vision of the meaning of our lives*? Does it have a particular "moral"? Do we experience ourselves as being, in some sense, "addressed" or challenged by it? Does this meaning have some kind of catalytic effect that changes other parts of our lives?

5   Does it provide us with *genuinely pleasurable experiences*, whether emotional, sensual, or intellectual?[5]

6   Does it encourage *constructive relationships* between people or make certain *useful and enjoyable forms of social interaction* possible?

7   Does it make possible a *sense of encounter with "God," the transcendent, or the numinous*?

8   Does it successfully *serve the functions* for which it has been created? For example, does a piece of dance music actually make people from a certain social group want to get on their feet and dance? If it is a household appliance, does it work effectively?

9   Is it *authentic*? This may apply particular in relation to performance where we may want to know if a particular performance is a genuine expression of a person's physical, technical, and emotional capabilities (see, e.g., recurrent doping scandals in world sport).

These criteria are merely provisional and open for further discussion. It may be that others might be added. For example, the durability of a particular literary work or piece of music has often been seen as a sign of its aesthetic quality. Whether it is right to give such weight to durability, and whether this criteria could be usefully applied to popular culture which tends by its very nature to be ephemeral, remains open to question though (see Shusterman, 2000, p.180). Another important issue to think about is the relationship between popular culture and imaginative and sensual escapism. Are all forms of escapism constructive, and if not, how can we judge better or worse forms of escapism?[6]

Having a range of different aesthetic criteria for evaluating popular culture is important, though. Whilst these cannot be treated simplistically as a check-list that all good popular culture should demonstrate in equal measure, it is also clear that forms of popular culture that meet only one of the above criteria are likely to be severely limited in value. A session musician might, for example, pick up an electric guitar and demonstrate a high level of technical competence in playing lead riffs that he has learnt with different bands. But if this performance is devoid of any other originality or emotional stimulus, we are likely to find it quite empty (Frith, 1996, p.58). As noted above each of these criteria is likely to be more relevant for some forms of popular culture than for others. Questions of technical skill, imagination, and functionality might be highly relevant in the design of kitchen implements, for example, but questions of existential meaning or encounter with transcendence are likely to be much less so.

How then do these basic principles and criteria for an aesthetics of popular culture relate to what it means to begin to develop a specifically theological aesthetics of popular culture?

First of all, I would suggest that the criteria that I have listed above provide a broad outline of the different dimensions of what it means to be fully human. These criteria suggest that popular culture can play an important role in providing us with meaningful visions of existence and understandings of human experience, opportunities for enjoying and practicing skills, imagination, and creativity, the means of experiencing cerebral, sensual, and emotional pleasure, resources for developing relationships and communities, and a way of encountering transcendence. These criteria highlight the intellectual, physical, emotional, and spiritual dimensions of our existence, as well as the individual, relational, social, and transpersonal contexts within which human life is lived.

Whilst these criteria may help us to see the different aspects of what it means to be human, they invite further discussion about what it means to live each of these different elements of human life in truthful, good, authentic, and fulfilling ways. A theological aesthetics of popular culture will attempt to explore these questions through reference to our understandings of the absolute reference point in life. This will mean asking whether the visions of existence offered through popular culture are truthful or meaningful. It will involve asking whether popular culture provides insights into human experience in ways that are honest, challenging, and redemptive. It will mean reflecting on the role that skills, imagination, and creativity play as part of a good and fulfilled existence, and in relation to our place in the wider natural order. It should lead us to ask what forms of pleasure are healthy and constructive and what forms of pleasure are not. It will require us to ask about the nature of healthy human relationships and what it means to build just and peaceable communities. And it will ultimately lead us to think about how popular culture might contribute to our relationship and encounter with the absolute reference point of life.

What I have offered here is no more than an initial set of notes for the on-going development of a theological aesthetics of popular culture. As yet this is not a project that has been seriously undertaken within the wider literature in theology, religion, and popular culture. But my hope is that even the incomplete account I have given here may provide some encouragement for others to take up this challenge of thinking of how a theological aesthetics might inform a more conscious and critical reflection on the environments, resources, and practices of everyday life.

Within Western culture, an increasing emphasis has been placed on the importance of life in the here and now as religious institutions experience the effects of detraditionalization and "spiritualities of life" flourish (Woodhead & Heelas, 2000). Yet curiously, despite the emphasis our culture places on the importance of fulfillment through everyday life, we appear to have little by way of critical resources to help us think about what is genuinely positive or what is genuinely harmful in our day-to-day lives. The vacuum left by the willingness of the academic community to engage with such questions is increasingly filled by popular psychology and lifestyle TV shows that provide people with practical advice, but little critical distance from which to take a broader view of life. This book has tried to show how the disciplines of theology and religious studies might engage more directly with the question of how to think critically about our everyday lives.

In concluding this book, I want to emphasize this on-going need for the theological and cultural criticism of the everyday and for imaginative and constructive interventions in contemporary culture. Whilst I do not fully share Adorno's pessimism about the nature of contemporary culture, I find his analysis more compelling than those who adopt a more celebratory approach to popular culture. Like Simon Frith (1996, p.20) I find myself drawn to the idea of the "unpopular popular" within culture which arises out the belief that "the 'difficult' appeals through the traces it carries of another world in which it would be 'easy.'" And like him, I sympathize with the idea that the "utopian impulse, the *negation* of everyday life, the aesthetic impulse that Adorno recognized in high art, must be part of low art too" (ibid., p.20). Here's to the musicians, poets and artists, the visionaries, critics, prophets and prophetesses who will make that happen.

# notes

## preface

1   In the spirit of Adorno's notion of a dialectical approach to cultural criticism (discussed later in chapter 4), it may still be helpful to attempt wider surveys of popular culture (e.g., Detweiler and Taylor, 2003) even if only to clarify where such surveys need to be strengthened conceptually and methodologically.

## chapter 1

1   Partly as a reaction against the political disengagement that certain forms of post-modernism seemed to promote (see Callinicos, 2003, pp.11–13).
2   Major theorists of language in the twentieth-century, such as Saussure, Derrida and Wittgenstein, would argue that language does not function in a nomenclaturist way by simply labeling objects that we already see in the external world, but rather the meaning of words is shaped by the language system in which the words are used and the lived contexts of the communities that use them. It is more in keeping with these theoretical understandings of language to understand terms such as "religion" or "popular culture" as examples of academic discourse that construct the world in particular ways in order to make certain kinds of research and debate possible (see, e.g., King, 1999).
3   Another level of complexity in attempting to define popular culture is that some of the key writers discussed in this section do not use the term popular culture at all. Indeed it is very unusual for the precise term "popular culture" to appear in academic writing before the early 1960s, which obviously post-dates the work of writers such as Arnold, Leavis, and Greenberg. Nevertheless, the use of the term "mass culture" by F.R. Leavis or "kitsch" by Clement Greenberg can reasonably be interpreted as pointing towards the same kinds of practices and products of everyday life that later writers have pointed to through using the term "popular culture".

4   The writing of the West's first major art historian, Giorgio Vasari (1550/1987), can be understood precisely as an early attempt to construct a certain kind of understanding of *high culture*, based around a particular narrative of the relationship between classical artists and sixteenth-century Florentine artists.

5   Another way in which some writers have constructed "popular culture" as a threatening, alien presence is precisely to characterize it as something "foreign" that has originated from another part of the world (see Storey, 1998, p.5).

6   This original version of the game which pre-existed the Football Association regulations of the mid nineteenth century was generally contested between the populations of two villages on a "pitch" spanning several miles between the villages. A violent affair, this game would often lead to participants suffering broken limbs, and there were occasional fatalities (see Easton et al., 1988).

7   The internet database, Sociological Abstracts, gives the following number of books and articles containing the key words "popular culture" in the decades since 1960: 1960–70, 22 publications; 1970–80, 110 publications; 1980–90, 573 publications; 1990–2003, 2,508 publications.

8   A further, quite feasible, explanation for the exponential growth of interest in popular culture in the late twentieth century concerns the growth of what Pierre Bourdieu refers to as the "new petite bourgeoisie" (see Bourdieu, 1984, pp.354ff.). Bourdieu argues that this emerging social group has a strong interest in certain forms of popular entertainment as well as increasing access to university education (and certainly access to Higher Education increased significantly in Britain from the 1960s onwards). In this context, he suggests, it is unsurprising that the new petite bourgeoisie have wanted to focus academic attention on forms of popular culture and popular entertainment that might previously have been considered outside the scope of proper academic enquiry.

## chapter 2

1   There are, clearly, other ways in which a typology of literature on theology, religion and popular culture could be drawn up. Jeffrey Mahan (2000, p.295), for example, distinguishes between the different audiences that people in this field are writing for (i.e., those with an academic interest in the description and analysis of contemporary culture, those with an academic interest in methodological questions concerning the study of contemporary culture, those with an religious interest in what it means to engage appropriately in contemporary culture, and those with an interest in social and cultural reform). This is a useful supplementary model to the typology that I set out here. John Lyden's (2003) distinction between theological, ideological and functionalist approaches

is also helpful, though essentially subsumed within the framework that I offer here.

2   Whilst those involved in approaches (i) and (ii) tend to be involved in religious, media or cultural studies, and those involved in approaches (iii) and (iv) are more likely to be theologians, these neat distinctions do not always hold up in practice. Stating these as four distinct approaches also risks obscuring the fact that a given writer may within the same book, or even within the same article, adopt more than one of these approaches. In such cases, though, whilst a writer may use more than one of these approaches, there are most likely to have a primary interest in only one of them. For example Beaudoin (1998) demonstrates an interest in representations of God in popular culture, the religious functions of popular culture, and theological reflection on popular culture, but his primary interest is in a missiology of Western culture.

3   The lack of impact that theology and religious studies has made to the wider field of cultural studies both reflects weaknesses in some theological and religious work in this area, as well as some guiding assumptions within cultural studies. Some of the work on popular culture done by theologians and religious scholars over the past ten years has shown an insufficient awareness of basic concepts and debates in cultural studies (e.g., Beaudoin, 1998). As a consequence, this work is unlikely to be taken seriously by other cultural scholars. At the same time, cultural studies has tended to adopt an unnecessarily secular set of assumptions about the unimportance of theological and religious analyses of contemporary culture. As theologians and scholars of religion develop greater methodological sophistication in their work, it is to be hoped that they will have greater success in challenging these secular assumptions and making a useful contribution to this wider field.

4   I do not wish to claim that the whole of the literature on theology, religion, and popular culture fits neatly into these four categories. I would suggest, though, that any religious or theological literature that does not fit into these categories tends either to be simply banal (engaging in popular cultural study for no clear purpose) or that it tends to be generic cultural studies that just happens to be conducted by someone working in a Department of Theology or Religious Studies. The main exception to this is a small, but growing literature from a religious or theological perspective on the ethics of involvement in particular forms of popular culture. Examples of this include discussions of media ethics (see Mitchell and Marriage, 2003, pp.285ff.) and sport ethics (see, e.g., Hoffman, 1992). Whilst raising interesting issues, this type of literature remains relatively small and is focused primarily at practitioners in various forms of popular culture. Because of its more specific audience, I have chosen not to include as a major category for discussion here.

5   On this issue, see also Beckford, 1998, pp.96ff.

6   Morgan's study is interesting in that it challenges Walter Benjamin's (1938/1968) classic notion that the mass production of an image reduced its "aura," and

thus its capacity to serve as a medium for significant transcendent or religious experience.

7  This assumption reflects a particular position within "media effects" debates that we will consider in more detail in chapter 4.

8  "[Faith refers] to the spiritual state, or existential condition, constituted by a person's present response to the ultimate divine Reality. This ranges from the negative response of a self-enclosed consciousness which is blind to the divine presence, whether beyond us or in the depths of our own being, to a positive openness to the Divine which gradually transforms us and which is called salvation or liberation or enlightenment. This transformation is essentially the same within the different religious contexts within which it occurs: I would define it formally as the transformation of human existence from self-centredness to Reality-centeredness. This is the event or process of vital significance which one can see to be occurring in individuals all over the world, taking different forms within the contexts of the different perceptions of the Ultimate made available by the various religious traditions." (Hick, 1990, p.162).

9  This kind of theological and religious study was also encouraged by books such as Harvey Cox's (1965) *The Secular City*, which encouraged theologians to move on from traditional religious debates and develop theologies that were relevant for the new structures and practices of secular society.

10  From a functionalist point of view, it is possible to see how the cultural significance of electronic media and consumer culture that we will go on to discuss in chapter 3 could be understood in terms of meeting communal, existential, and hermeneutical functions of religion.

11  Whilst Lelwica and Graybeal are critical of the harmful effects of these values and beliefs of dieting, Graybeal offers an interesting discussion of whether in spite of these harmful effects, women may actually develop some important virtues and characteristics even through their negative experiences of dieting.

12  Lyden's (2003, pp.137ff.) recognition, for example, of the importance of ethnographic research into the ways in which audiences experience and 'make use' of films is a helpful pointer forward for this area of study. Mitchell (2003, pp.337ff) also makes a similar point about the importance of the emerging emphasis on audience reception studies in the field of religion and the media.

13  For a further discussion and critique of this understanding of 'Generation X', see Lynch, 2002, pp.15ff.

14  Bridger and Neal, for example, both write from relatively conservative Christian perspectives, and Mark Pinsky, a Jewish writer, has produced a text that is primarily aimed at a conservative religious audience.

15  For other examples of this kind of study see Miles, 1996; Stone, 2000; Beckford, 2001, pp.98ff.

# Chapter 3

1   It is important to recognize here that the experience of electronic technology both within Western culture, and globally, has also been significantly influenced since the end of the Second World War by the innovations and products of major Japanese corporations (see, e.g., du Gay et al, 1997).

2   See du Gay et al, 1997, pp.91f., for similar claims by cultural critics of the deleterious social effects of the Sony Walkman.

3   There are other things that we could note about electronic media such as the ways in which they change our sense of space (e.g., we no longer need to be in the same physical space as someone to have a conversation with them and can watch live events happening outside of our immediate location). Similarly, electronic media also change our experience of time: global communication can now work at the speed of fiber optic cables and satellite transmissions, and past events can be viewed again on screen as if we were watching them live. For more detailed discussion of this, see Thompson, 1999.

4   See, for example, the role of a limited number of blockbuster films in boosting global cinema audiences. It is important, however, to not to make to generalized statements about the global nature of media such as television, given that such media still have significant regional variations in different parts of the world, see, e.g., Sinclair et al., 1996.

5   A related example would be that of electronically-mediated entertainment becoming the focus for face-to-face interaction (e.g., watching a film with family or friends, or having a conversation with someone about the content of a television program, see, e.g., Storey, 1999, p.110).

6   There are particular economic reasons why the 1980s were significant in the development of consumer culture, notably the effects of a long period of governance by Republican and Conservative administrations in America and Britain who pursued a strong policy of economic liberalism, as well as the increased access of consumers to personal loans and other forms of credit.

7   Veblen's idea of "conspicuous consumption" is also useful for establishing a link between the cultural message conveyed by commodities and their social visibility. In other words, commodities convey a message to other people only if they see me associated with these commodities. This may explain why certain more visible commodities (e.g., our clothing, car, jewellery, Hi-Fi system) projects a lifestyle image more strongly than less visible commodities such as toothpaste or toilet cleaner. Thus, I project what kind of person I am by the clothes I wear, but much less so by the brand of toothpaste that I use.

8   With industrialization, however, came an increasing trend of the production of cheap, mass-produced imitations of luxury goods. For example, in Britain in the 1880's, there was a growth in the mass production of cheap "star diamond" jewellery in imitation of the style of jewellery worn by the Princess of Wales at that

time. Such mass production has the paradoxical effect of both emphasizing the desirability of the original item, whilst undermining its exclusiveness through its mass imitation. I am grateful to Dr Francesca Carnevali for the historical information on this point.

9    The role of "taste' in defining one" social status and affiliations has been explored in detail in the work of Pierre Bourdieu.

10    Baudrillard was not the first writer to offer a structuralist analysis of commodities, though. Roland Barthes had offered an important critique of contemporary Capitalist society using this kind of structuralist theory in his book *Mythologies* (1957/2000).

11    This might seem a rather obvious point, but its significance becomes clearer if we recognize that human languages describe and divide up the world in different ways. For example, whilst there are only a handful of English words that describe different types of snow, there are more than thirty such words in the Inuit language (see Hall, 1997). The meaning of Inuit words for "snow' are therefore much more subtle than in English, because there are so many different ways of referring to snow in Inuit. The meaning of an individual word is therefore clearly influenced by the particular range of other words in the language system of which it is a part.

12    See also: "[O]utside the field of its denotation, the object becomes substitutable in a more or less unlimited way within the field of connotations, where it assumes sign-value. Thus the washing machine *serves* as an appliance and *acts* as an element of prestige, comfort, etc. It is strictly this latter field which is the field of consumption. All other kinds of objects may be substituted here for the washing machine as signifying element. In the logic of signs, as in that of symbols, objects are no longer linked in any sense to a *definite* function or need. Precisely because they are responding here to something quite different, which is either the social logic or the logic of desire, for which they function as a shifting and unconscious field of signification." (Baudrillard, 1998, pp.76ff.).

13    The process of developing and maintaining "brand" identity is now made more complex in the marketplace as retailers seek to promote customers loyalty to the "brand" of their particular range of shops, rather than the "brands" produced by particular manufacturers (Corstjens and Corstjens, 1995).

## Chapter 4

1    As such, Adorno's notion of the culture industry can therefore be seen as a critical vision of a "Taylorized" cultural system in which human beings are reduced to component parts of a greater system geared to economic profit.

2    Adorno's concern with the capitalist system was shared by Herbert Marcuse, another leading member of the Frankfurt School. In his introduction to Marcuse's *One Dimensional Man*, Douglas Kellner comments that Marcuse

"slices through the ideological celebrations of capitalism and sharply criticizes the dehumanization and alienation in its opulence and affluence, the slavery in its labor system, the ideology and indoctrination in its culture, the fetishism in its consumerism, and the danger and insanity in its military-industrial complex" (Marcuse, 2002, p.xxx).

3   This process of the "fetishism of the commodity" is, in Marxist theory, an extension of the shift from the "use-value" to the "exchange-value" of the product. For when commodities acquire the abstract cultural meanings associated with "exchange-value", it becomes easier for them to function as part of a wider cultural system of deception than if products are simply thought of in terms of their direct "use-value".

4   These concepts also share common ground with Marcuse's (1991) notion that contemporary capitalism generates "false needs" and that the attempt to satisfy such needs merely leads to greater compliance with the capitalist system. For similar critiques of consumer culture see Haug, 1986; Bauman, 2000.

5   Twitchell (1999), however, notes the irony of the commercial success of books that critique consumer culture and offer ideas about how to move away from consumption-based lifestyles.

6   Gilroy also notes how such local practices are encouraged by recording artists, e.g. by including versions of songs without vocals on the B-side of disks to enable MC's or rappers to perform over them. Gilroy (1993) gives another specific example of black resistance to the commodification of popular music in the case of the Funkedelic/Parliament, a group of musicians who signed to different record labels using different band names, thus demonstrating the arbitrariness of the popular music industry.

7   This process is partly facilitated through "trend-spotting" agencies who send people out on to the streets to spot what cutting edge fashions are being developed by ordinary people (see, e.g., Klein, 2001).

8   For further examples of the appropriation of radical cultural practices and symbols by the culture industry, see Frank, 1997, on the incorporation of 1960s counter-culture into American advertising during that decade, and Rushkoff, 1999, pp.10ff., on the incorporation of underground methods of "mutant media" by marketing and advertising agencies in the 1990s.

9   Bourdieu shares this pessimism. "It requires blind faith in ordinary individuals" (undeniable but limited) capacity for "resistance" to assume, along with a certain "postmodern cultural criticism," that television viewers' active cynicism (exemplified by channel surfing) can do much to counter the cynicism of its producers, whose mindset, working conditions, and goals – reaching the biggest public with that "extra something" that "sells" – make them more and more like advertising people. Facility with the games of cultural criticism – their "I know that you know that I know" – is not universal. Nor is the ability to spin out elaborate "readings" of the "ironic and metatextual" messages cynically manipulated by television producers and ad people. Anyone who thinks this has simply surrendered to a

populist version of one of the most perverse forms of academic pedantry."
(Bourdieu, 1998, pp.8f.)

10 Postman's critique can therefore be seen as part of a wider debate on the role of the media in shaping public life, for example, in encouraging or discouraging active participation and sense of citizenship in democratic societies (see Dahlgren, 1995).

11 Other examples of this in relation to "serious" issues would include talk-shows which take human interest stories and seek to evoke an emotional response in relation to these or (in the case of shows like Jerry Springer) turn them into more obviously facile entertainment.

12 Interestingly, Postman (1986, p.167) suggested that one response to the crisis posed by television was for TV programs themselves to be more reflexive and ironic about how they turn serious issues into entertainment. This approach has indeed been taken up by a number of satirical TV programs, including, most notably in Britain, the spoof news-program *Brass Eye* which was eventually withdrawn after controversy surrounding on episode focusing on pedophilia.

13 One specific example of this is the greater availability of email and the internet in the work-place which means that workers engage in entertainment-based activities such as sending joke emails or surfing the net during work hours.

14 For a more positive evaluation of the skills needed to engage with contemporary electronic media, see Rushkoff, 1996.

15 In the movie length *South Park: Bigger, Longer and Uncut* the directors make a clear attempt to highlight the absurdity of a culture which is far more concerned about bad language in films and TV programs than about the damage caused, for example, by armed conflict conducted by its governments.

16 This emphasis has its roots in the Marxist critique of ideology which has subsequently been taken up within feminist and black cultural theories (see, e.g., Beckford, 1998; Storey, 2001).

17 From the conservative side, George Bush Sr suggested that "America should be more like *The Waltons*, and less like *The Simpsons*" (Pinsky, 2001), and vice-presidential candidate Dan Quayle criticized the soap opera *Murphy Brown* for its liberal sexual morality (Castells, 1996). Interestingly, both *The Simpsons* and *Murphy Brown* included these comments in subsequent episodes to make counter-criticisms and jibes at these politicians.

18 For a more substantial analysis of the social and cultural context of these deaths, see Beckford, 2004.

19 There was never actually any evidence that James Bulger's killers had ever watched *Child Play III* (Petley, 1997), but the repeated connection between this film and the toddler's murder in the popular press meant that this association has persisted in the public memory of the case. This is a useful example of how the rhetoric of "common sense" can hide an underlying weakness in evidence. For Marilyn Manson's response to the often wild allegations about the effects of his music, see Manson, 1998).

20   In addition to the criticisms of this research listed below, it is also worth noting that many of these studies have assumed a behaviorist model of human action which claims that actions are simply direct responses to specific stimuli (i.e., the stimulus of violent media content thus produces the response of violent behavior). This behavioral model now enjoys less support within academic psychology as it is seen as providing too simplistic an account of human motivation and action. It has now been largely displaced by cognitive models that emphasize the significance of the individual's interpretation of their environment for their behavior.

21   For more detailed discussions of these issues see, e.g., Frith, 1998; Dyer, 2002.

22   Buchanan (2000) makes the very interesting point that de Certeau's belief in the human capacity for resistance reflected his theological commitment to a notion of transcendence; for however powerful or all-encompassing a sociocultural system might appear to be, the notion of transcendence implies that there is always a space which it can never fully colonies or control.

## chapter 5

1   This distinction does not always work neatly in terms of the work of individual scholars. Pete Ward (1996, 1999), for example, has written on the use of popular culture within Evangelical Christianity, yet works primarily as a theologian. Martin and Ostwalt's (1995) book on religion and film includes contributions from people working within religious studies departments who offer theological analyses of film. Furthermore, Anthony Pinn (1995, 2000, 2003) has undertaken work that fits clearly within the interests and methods of religious studies, and at other times has undertaken work that is more directly theological.

2   Truth/meaning and goodness/practice are included as dyads in this way to give some recognition to the complexities of these terms. Whilst some theologians would still assert the possibility of gaining some objective or final truth about God or existence through reason or revelation, other writers would emphasize the interpretative nature of our theologies. Some theologians will therefore see "truth" as a realistic goal of theology, whilst others will think more in terms of helpful and meaningful human interpretations of the Divine. Similarly a concern with "goodness" has been the traditional focus of theological ethics, but the emergence of theologies of liberation, "practice," or "praxis" has become an important concept in emphasizing how theological concepts can have important implications for relationships and social structures beyond the specific moral acts of individuals and communities.

3   Some forms of postmodern theology see themselves as engaging with the task of making sense of a decentered universe in which there is no intelligible absolute reference point. I would suggest that such forms of theology still fit within my

definition precisely because they are still attempting to address how we construct our values and beliefs in relation to the question of the presence or absence of such an absolute reference point.

4  One of the challenges for people who do not have any religious commitments and who engage in theological reflection concerns their ability to identify resources that help them speak about the absolute reference point of life ("Theos"). Atheists, paradoxically, may find this easier than agnostics in that the atheist rejection of God as a personal being opens up the possibility of finding absolute reference points in other places (e.g. in pleasure, choice, or moral responsibility). An agnosticism, formed out of the tolerance of diversity of religious belief within liberal democratic societies, can be much less articulate about how we can think about the absolute reference point of life.

5  Whilst it is possible to speak in terms of "Buddhist theology," "Hindu theology," "Muslim theology," or "Sikh theology," Western theology remains primarily associated with the Jewish and Christian traditions. For those with particular religious commitments (e.g. to the Christian faith), it may be more helpful to revise my definition of theology along the following lines: "Theology is the process of seeking normative answers in relation to the Christian tradition to questions of truth/meaning, goodness/practice, evil, suffering, redemption and beauty in specific contexts."

6  As Paul Tillich (1959. p.47f.) put it: "There is no sacred language which has fallen from a supernatural heaven and been put between the covers of a book. But there is human language, based on man's [sic] encounter with reality, changing through the millennia, used for the needs of daily life, for expression and communication, for literature and poetry, and used also for the expression and communication of our ultimate concern. In each of these cases the language is different. Religious language is ordinary language, changed under the power of what it expresses, the ultimate of being and meaning. The expression of it can be narrative (mythological, legendary, historical), or it can be prophetic, poetic, liturgical. It becomes holy for those to whom it expresses their ultimate concern from generation to generation. But there is no holy language in itself, as translations, retranslations, and revisions show."

7  Although Niebuhr himself was aware of our partial and limited ability to understand the ultimate truth of Christ, one of the unfortunate effects of his distinction between "Christ" and "culture" is the implication that Christ can be understood outside of specific cultural assumptions or that the Church is in any way able to stand outside of "culture." This view is contradicted by the growing recognition within contemporary theology that theological reflection is itself a form of cultural activity (see Tanner, 1997, pp.63ff.).

8  For more context on Niebuhr's work, see Johnson, 1996.

9  This approach is comparable to the *anthropological* model of contextual theology identified by Bevans (1992). This approach places a high value on the notion

of divine activity within human culture beyond the boundaries of the Christian Church. It is well illustrated by Warren's plea for "a deep humility, by which we remember that God has not left himself without a witness in any nation at any time . . . Our first task in approaching another people, another culture, another religion, is to take off our shoes, for the place we are approaching is holy. Else we may find ourselves treading on men's [sic] dreams. More serious still, we may forget that God was here before our arrival." (cited in ibid., p.49).

10　This form of theology of culture typically reflects what Bevan (1992, p.16) refers to as a "creation-centered" theological orientation which places a strong emphasis on the possibility of receiving revelation in the context of day-to-day life.

11　Lyden (2003, pp.17ff.) adopts a different view to mine, suggesting that the "Christ and Culture in Paradox" model gives more emphasis to a dialogue between theology and culture than "Christ the Transformer of Culture." Lyden argues that the latter is more concerned with the redemptive appropriation of cultural forms rather than a critical dialogue between faith and culture. Whilst Lyden is correct that the transformation model is partly concerned with cultural appropriation, I would still argue that this model adopts a more constructive view of dialogue with culture precisely because it has a more optimistic view of the possibility of redeeming culture. By contrast, the more Lutheran "Christ and Culture in Paradox" tends to view faith and cultural practice as autonomous spheres between which substantial dialogue is not possible (see Niebuhr, 1951, pp.176f.).

12　Another limitation of Niebuhr's typology is that the positions of "Christ against Culture" and "The Christ of Culture" are somewhat extreme and few contemporary cultural theologians would associate themselves with these approaches. Indeed it is possible that some of those writers whom Niebuhr associates with these extreme positions, would not characterize their views in this way themselves (see Lyden, 2003, p.14).

13　In one sense, the applications approach can be seen as "Barthian" in the sense that it rests on a basic belief in the disjuncture between truth as revealed by God and the wider beliefs and values of contemporary culture. In practice, though, Barth's theology of culture was somewhat more complex than this, and in some respects fits within the "Christ and Culture in Paradox" model as well as "Christ the Transformer of Culture" (see Parma, 1983).

14　A fundamental motivation in Tillich's theology was his concern that Christian symbols should be able to speak in meaningful and constructive ways to contemporary culture. As he put it, "we are faced with a desperate task, in some respects: to try to reinterpret Christian symbols so that they may become powerful again" (Brown, 1965, p.96).

15　Browning's notion of horizons in this context is informed by the hermeneutical theory of Hans Georg Gadamer (1989).

16　On the role of virtue in the practice of theology study (in this case, hermeneutics), see Fowl and Jones, 1991.

## chapter 6

1   There is clearly an issue question about whether we attempt to hold this network of methods together on the basis of some overarching theory or whether we simply use them more pragmatically to see what different insights they can generate for us. Wood (1992) is a good example of the former, in which genre and auteur criticism are incorporated in an approach that is basically ideological. My own neopragmatic philosophical assumptions incline me towards the latter approach, however (see Lynch, 1999).

2   For more detailed discussions of these approaches, see, e.g., Nicholls, 1976, 1985; Mast et al., 1992; Hill & Gibson, 2000; Dick, 2002. It is worth noting that all of these references are to books exploring methods of analysing film. In general methodological discussions in popular culture studies are most advanced in the field of film studies, because this area has received more sustained academic attention than other aspects of popular culture. Arguably this is because the analysis of film bears a close resemblance to literary criticism, and has therefore been seen as a more credible focus for academic activity.

3   This kind of psychological interpretation is encouraged by the film itself through the lengthy explanation of Norman Bates' character and actions by the psychiatrist in the closing scenes.

4   For a more detailed introduction to concepts of ideology, see Storey, 2001.

5   Reflecting the nature of the film industry of that time, auteur critics of the 1950s and 1960s typically focused on the work of male directors, thus reflecting a longer historical trend in Western culture of critics giving more attention to the work of male artists than female artists.

6   Whilst some suggest that this new, more cautious interest in the auteur marks a shift away from naïve, neoromantic views of the individual creative artist evident in earlier auteur criticism, it could be argued that earlier auteur critics were themselves aware of these wider historical and cultural factors. As Andrew Sarris (1976, p.247) has put it, 'the purity of personal [artistic] expression is a myth of the textbooks'.

7   Indeed in its first week of release *The Eminem Show* not only topped the album chart, but sold more copies than the next 24 albums in the chart put together.

8   As a musical style, rap is characterised by the use of spoken vocals (which often use poetic devices such as rhyme and scanning) over a stylised, repetitive beat. Rap music also typically makes use of loops sampled from other music tracks to build up the musical background over which the rapper gives their vocal performance. Rap music forms part of the wider hip hop culture that emerged out of poor black urban communities in the 1970s and 1980s, which was also characterised by particular forms of dancing, fashion, and visual arts (see Pinn, 2003).

9   Eminem himself is sensitive to the issue of his racial identity as a rapper. Whilst being defensive about his right to perform rap, he is also realistic that as a white

performer he is able to achieve greater levels of commercial success than if he were black (see, e.g., "White America" on *The Eminem Show*). His status as a white rapper, though, has remained a focus for controversy and appears to underlie the on-going feud between Eminem and the leading hip hop magazine, *The Source*.

10    The biographical information in the following chapters is taken from Huxley, 2000, Bossa, 2003, and Hasted, 2003. Of these, Nick Hasted's recent biography provides the most substantial and well-researched data.

11    Until relatively recently, Eminem presented himself as being three years younger than he actually was (Hasted, 2003, p.18). Again this raises interesting issues, from an auteur approach, in terms of how an understanding of an artist can be shaped by the way in which they are marketed. Presumably the decision to present Eminem to the world as three years younger than he actually is partially reflects the concern that he should not appear 'too old' for his teenage fan-base.

12    Marshall ultimately felt vindicated by the court's eventual decision to award her only $1700 damages after costs.

13    This is described, with some artistic reworking, in the track 'Brain Damage' on *The Slim Shady LP*.

14    Marshall regularly spent his teenage years sleeping at other peoples' houses. On one occasion, he had given money to a friend to arrange the rental of a new apartment, but when he tried to move in he discovered that this friend had simply stolen this money. He reports that he had no option but to break in back at the apartment he had just left and to live there for a while despite the fact that it had no heating or lighting.

15    In the track 'Brain Damage' on *The Slim Shady LP*, Eminem fantasises his school principal joining in a physical attack on him.

16    In this context, it is worth noting that Eminem's lyrics on his first album *Infinite* were less violent, and the more explicit levels of violence in his music can be seen in part as an attempt to appeal more to the white audience that is attracted to this and as part of attempts to market him as a "shock rapper," (see Halsted, 2003, pp.60, 72).

17    For example, in the track 'Guilty Conscience' on *The Slim Shady LP*, Slim Shady acts as the 'devil's voice' encouraging people to rob, rape, and kill unfaithful partners, counter-balanced by the voice of conscience played by Dr Dre.

18    Though it seems, from his latest album *The Eminem Show*, that the use of the Slim Shady persona in the past has now given him enough confidence to voice his own anger and feelings of revenge towards his mother and Kim as Eminem (see, e.g., the tracks 'Cleaning out my closet' and 'Hailie's Song').

19    It is not uncommon on Eminem's albums to have images on one track slightly undercut or put in a new context by the following track. On *The Marshall Mathers LP*, the indiscriminate rage of 'Kill You' is modified by the representation of Eminem as the sane, caring figure in 'Stan'. Similarly on *The Eminem Show*, the tough gangsta image of Eminem on the track 'Soldier' is undercut by the following track, 'Sayin' goodbye to Hollywood' which presents him as a

vulnerable person who needs to retreat from public scrutiny to preserve his sanity.

20    This assertion, whilst sounding like traditional Christian piety, is informed by Ford's reading of contemporary philosophers such as Levinas and Ricoeur. From Levinas, for example, Ford takes the idea that I am confronted by the call of the "Other" on my life through the face of the other person that I encounter.

21    See the lyrics of 'Sing for the Moment' on *The Eminem Show*.

22    Even on *The Eminem Show*, which is less overtly misogynistic than *The Marshall Mathers LP*, we still find a track like 'Drips' which portray women simply as seductive carriers of sexually transmitted diseases.

23    A comparison could be drawn, for example, between the ways in which Tupac and Eminem deal with their mothers in their music. Whilst both Tupac and Eminem are clear in their work about the shortcomings of their upbringings, Tupac's work shows a constructive willingness to both attempt to understand his mother and hold her accountable for her actions in a way that is absent in Eminem's lyrics (see, e.g., Dyson, 2001, pp.21ff.).

24    Someone present at a seminar at which I presented this part of the chapter as a paper commented how, from the perspective of his experience in inner city ministry, Eminem served as a positive role model of a father who was prepared to stay with and support his child.

## chapter 7

1    There is a growing literature on specific issues associated with interpreting material, visual, and auditory culture. For example, on material culture see Tilley, 1990; Dant, 1999; on visual culture, see Heywood and Sandywell, 1999; Evans and Hall, 1999; on auditory culture/musicology, see Begbie, 2000; Bull and Back, 2003.

2    Although the theoretical emphasis on text over author has found important expression in late twentieth-century poststructuralist criticism, it is not an idea that originates with poststructuralism and can be traced in earlier critical movements such as formalism (see Burke, 1992, pp.11ff.).

3    Writers in this style of textual criticism criticism have coined the phrase, the "intentional fallacy," to refer to the mistaken belief that we are able to infer the intentions and motivations of the author from the content of the text.

4    For more detailed reading on this, readers may wish to consult Stam et al (1992), Bignell (2002), and Thwaites et al. (2002).

5    For a discussion of the complementary influence of the work of the American pragmatist philosopher C.S. Peirce on semiotics see Jensen (1995).

6    In this context, Barthes also argued importantly that these arbitrary cultural meanings often had an ideological function in obscuring the real social relationships

associated with these objects. Thus Barthes suggested that to understand drinking red wine primarily as a symbol of patriotism tended to obscure the fact that this wine may have been produced in Algeria on land taken from smaller landowners and by people who derived little economic or cultural benefit from this industry.

7   The narrative concepts that we will note here would still be criticized by some post-modern literary critics as making too strong an assumption about common narrative structures and conventions. Nevertheless, I would argue that they still have practical value in helping us to think about the structure of individual narratives that we wish to study whilst not falling into the more restrictive structuralist theories of narrative offered by Propp and Frye.

8   For further helpful summaries of Foucault's understanding of discourse, see, e.g., Kendall and Wickham, 1999, pp.34–56; Mills, 2003, pp.53–66; also Merquior, 1991; Barker, 1998.

9   The screenplay for this episode can be found at www.snpp.com/episodes/9F01.html.

10  These 'Acts' are suggested not only by the way in which the narrative is structured, but also through the presence of fade outs at certain points in the episode (in which the screen goes completely blank between two particular scenes) which partly allow for advert breaks, but which also suggest significant breaks in the narrative.

11  For a discussion of different understandings of American civil religion (e.g., prophetic, liberal, and conservative versions), and of the different forms and functions of civil religion in different cultural contexts, see Parsons, 2002.

12  Hauerwas is therefore deeply suspicious of attempts to read and make use of Scripture outside of the context of the specific life, vision and authority of the Church, and is highly critical of attempts to reduce the text of Scripture to a mouth-piece for contemporary liberal values (see Hauerwas, 1993).

13  For a further critique on the effects of liberal theology on Christian ethics, see Hauerwas, 1992, pp.23–50.

14  His neoconservative leanings are certainly indicated, for example, in his sympathy for the theology of Karl Barth; see Hauerwas, 2001.

15  Again, what counts as a more or less satisfactory interpretation of a text will, to some extent, be shaped by the assumptions and preunderstandings of our cultural context, but there is also a sense in which the structure and content of a particular text does place certain constraints on the range of interpretations we can possibly make of it.

# chapter 8

1   In the context of film studies, this more pessimistic understanding of the capacity of culture to shape human thought and action was reflected in the work of

*Screen* magazine whose contributors often sought to explore how particular films placed their audiences into certain "subject positions" that limited their range of responses, (see Moores, 1993, pp.12–6; Turner, 2003, pp.85–9).

2   Jacqueline Bobo has done interesting work in this context, of comparing the way many black cultural critics responded negatively to Steven Spielberg's film *The Color Purple* with the way in which black audiences interpreted and experienced the film in more positive ways. Whilst members of these audiences were often aware of the problems inherent, for example, in the film's representation of black men or its romanticization of its content, they were still able to find constructive images of redemption and survival within it. As Bobo comments, these positive interpretations of the film do not mean that the film itself is without flaws, but it does demonstrate the capacity of audiences to "read against" the limitations of a popular cultural text and make constructive use of it for themselves.

3   This statistic is particularly remarkable given that the Church of England had declared the 1990s to be a "decade of evangelism" in which church growth was a significant priority for it.

4   Initially this network drew on the styles of "house" music from Chicago and "techno" from Detroit, with British musicians and producers creating their own versions of this music in significant quantities by the late 1980s. Subsequently there has been considerable differentiation in the types of electronic music used in British club culture with major genres now including jungle, drum and bass, hip-hop, and R&B, as well as a range of sub-genres of house and techno such as trance, hard house, funky house, and gabba techno (see Collin, 1997).

5   The use of such recreational drugs is an integral part of the types of club and dance music that I was studying here. Researchers have sometimes written about the house music scene in a way that gives little mention to the recreational drug use associated with it – presumably in an attempt to protect any identifiable research participants (see, e.g., Bennett, 2000). However, it is not possible to get an accurate picture of this scene without understanding the physiological effects of the drugs being used and the influence of this on the ethos of these types of club.

6   Bey's work tends not to be well-known in mainstream British club culture, however, and tends to be referred to more commonly in parts of the British club scene such as the "conscious partying" network that has stronger connections with global movements interested in the relationship between rave and spirituality.

7   Malbon's work here is itself informed by studies of religious and mystical experience undertaken by Laski and Lewis.

8   One example of this relates to clubbing and sexual experiences. It was more common for people to attend alcohol-based clubs with the expectation of meeting potential sexual partners, where as Ecstasy-based clubs tend to be oriented less around "pulling" sexual partners.

9   The only person in the pilot phase who interpreted their experiences in religious terms was someone who had strong Evangelical commitments and who saw clubs

as places in which there was an on-going battle between good and bad spiritual forces.

10   Some of these friendships would be developed with people who were met for the first time through attending club nights, though it was also common for people to attend these nights with existing groups of friends and to find some of these existing friendships deepened through experiences in the club.

11   Many of the club nights that participants attended were predominantly white (a fact reflected in the sample for this study). It is striking that they tended to regard their clubs as genuinely inclusive places when the very substantial ethnic minority groups in the local area were almost completely under-represented in those clubs.

12   One specific contrast that was made in this context was between "try hards" who would make sure that they had the right fashionable clothing labels to wear when they went out, and more authentic clubbers who made their own clothes which often integrated the logo of their favorite club night.

13   One of the physiological effects of Ecstasy (MDMA) is the release, and delayed re-absorption, of serotonin within the brain. Effects of being flooded with serotonin in this way can include a sense of deep well-being and a feeling of greater empathic connection with others.

14   Prolonged or excessive use of Ecstasy will, over time, lead to serotonin depletion to the brain. Such depletion means that the Ecstasy user might still experience greater energy levels through using the drug, but would be much less likely to experience the same degree of well-being or connection with others. Clubbers in the early stages of Ecstasy use can thus be seen as having a "honeymoon period" in which they experience the emotional effects of the drug far more powerfully. The diminishing emotional returns of prolonged Ecstasy use can lead to decreasing levels of enjoyment in going to clubs, and over time this can lead people to disengage with the club scene. Certainly, in the sample for this research project, the participants who were attending clubs much less frequently than they used to often cited the diminishing effects of Ecstasy use (and related factors) as a reason for this.

15   The notion that people continue to have significant mystical or broadly religious experiences, but lack a language with which to describe or make sense of these, is also suggested by Hunt's (2003) study of the "spirituality of those who don't go to church".

## chapter 9

1   Frith (1996, pp.17f.) and Shusterman (2000, pp.169ff.) both reject the notion that aesthetic questions, or criteria on which aesthetic judgments are based, necessarily only apply to "high" art. Indeed both observe that there are no reasonable grounds why aesthetic judgments can only be formed in relation to "high" rather

than "popular" culture. As Frith puts it, "the fact that the objects of judgment are different doesn't mean that the processes of judgment are" (ibid., p.17).

2 Bourdieu's research indicated, for example, that knowledge of the work of film actors tends to be spread fairly evenly across social and cultural groups. By contrast, appreciation of the work of specific film-directors tends to be more common amongst people who have undertaken higher education (Bourdieu, 1984, pp.27f.). From a sociological perspective, this means that the ability to talk about the work of particular film directors tends to function as a social marker that one comes from a more educated social class. Popular media, such as tabloid newspapers or popular magazines, therefore tend to focus on the latest work of particular actors, or on news about their personal lives. More "serious" specialist film publications, aimed more at an educated middle-class audience, will tend to pay more attention to the ideas and work of particular directors.

3 Both Frith (1996, pp.9f.) and Shusterman (2000, p.172) argue that Bourdieu's work reinforces the assumption that "high" culture is intrinsically superior in aesthetic terms to "popular" culture. Whilst the ability to appreciate "high" culture may indeed have an important function as a marker of social identity and status, Bourdieu sees the appreciation of "high" culture as a significant form of cultural capital precisely because such appreciation involves a greater level of education and aesthetic judgment. Whilst an aesthetic judgment is therefore evident in Bourdieu's work, it is therefore one that further excludes the possibility of developing an aesthetics of popular culture. As Simon Frith (ibid.) comments, the kind of aesthetic discrimination that Bourdieu associates with "high" culture is also practiced by those who make conscious and critical judgments about the quality of different forms of popular culture.

4 Valuing originality, imagination, and creativity as signs of aesthetic quality can be seen as in keeping with Romantic and Marxist cultural traditions which are critical of standardized cultural products (see Frith, 1996, p.69). The "commonsense" valuing of originality in the context of popular music is demonstrated by the fact that cover bands who play other people's songs tend to be seen as less significant that bands who write their own original material (ibid., p.57).

5 Frith (1996, p.266) notes Schopenhauer's belief that "both our experience of the body and our experience of music possess a depth, an immediacy, and an intensity which cannot be obtained in other ways".

6 For a key discussion of the role of popular culture as a means of imaginative escapism, see Radway's (1987) seminal discussion of women's engagement with popular romance novels.

# bibliography

Adorno, T. (1991) *The Culture Industry: Selected Essays on Mass Culture*. London: Routledge.

Anderson, R. (1995) *Consumer Culture and TV Programming*. Boulder: Westview Press.

Andrew, D. (2000) "The unauthorized auteur today," in (eds.) R. Stam and T. Miller, *Film and Theory: An Anthology*, Oxford: Blackwells, pp.20–30.

Anijar, K. (2001) "Selena – prophet, profit, princess," in (eds.) E. Mazur K. McCarthy, *God in the Details: American Religion in Popular Culture*, New York: Routledge, pp.83–102.

Arnold, M. (1889) *Culture and Anarchy: An Essay in Political and Social Criticism*. London: Smith, Elder, and Co.

Axtell, J. (1999) "The first consumer revolution," in (ed.) L. Glickman, Consumer Society in American History: A Reader. Ithaca: Cornell University Press, pp.85–99.

Barker, C. (1999) *Television, Globalization and Cultural Identities*. Buckingham: Open University Press.

Barker, M. (2001) "The Newson report: a case study in 'common sense,'" in (eds.) M. Barker and J. Petley, *Ill Effects: The Media/Violence Debate*, London: Routledge, pp.27–46.

Barker, M. and Petley, J. (2001) "Introduction: from bad research to good – a guide for the perplexed," in (eds.) M. Barker and J. Petley, *Ill Effects: The Media/Violence Debate*, London: Routledge, pp.1–26.

Barker, P. (1998) *Michel Foucault: An Introduction*. Edinburgh: Edinburgh University Press.

Barthes, R. (1957/2000) *Mythologies*. London: Vintage.

Barthes, R. (1977) *Music, Image, Text*. London: Fontana.

Bartholomew, C. and Moritz, T. (eds.) (2000) *Christ and Consumerism: Critical Reflections on the Spirit of our Age*. Carlisle: Paternoster Press.

Baudrillard, J. (1970) *The Consumer Society*. London: Sage.

Baugh, L. (1997) *Imaging the Divine: Jesus and Christ-Figures in Film*. Kansas: Sheed and Ward.

Bauman, Z. (2000) *Liquid Modernity*. Cambridge: Polity.

Beaudoin, T. (1998) *Virtual Faith: The Irreverent Spiritual Quest of Generation X*. Chichester: Jossey-Bass.

Beckford, R. (1998) *Jesus is Dread: Black Theology and Black Culture in Britain*. London: DLT.

Beckford, R. (2001) *God of the Rahtid: Redeeming Rage*. London: DLT.

Beckford, R. (2004) *God and the Gangs*. London: DLT.

Begbie, J. (2000) *Theology, Music and Time*. Cambridge: Cambridge University Press.

Bellah, R. (1985) *Habits of the Heart: Individualism and Commitment in American Life*. Berkeley, CA: University of California Press.

Benjamin, W. (1968) *Illuminations*. New York: Shocken.

Bennett, A. (2000) *Popular Music and Youth Culture: Music, Identity and Place*. Basingstoke: Macmillan.

Berg, M. (1994) *The Age of Manufactures, 1700–1820*. (2$^{nd}$ edition). London: Routledge.

Berger, P., Berger, B. and Kellner, H. (1973) *The Homeless Mind: Modernization and Consciousness*. Harmondsworth: Penguin.

Bergeson, A. and Greeley, A. (2000) *God in the Movies*. New Brunswick: Transaction Publishers.

Bevans, S. (1992) *Models of Contextual Theology*. Maryknoll, NY: Orbis.

Bey, H. (2003) "The temporary autonomous zone," downloaded from *http://www.t0.or.at/hakimbey/taz/taz.htm* on 17/10/2003.

Bhattacharrya, G., Gabriel, J. and Small, S. (2002) *Race and Power: Global Racism in the Twenty-First Century*. London: Routledge.

Bignell, J. (2002) *Media Semiotics: An Introduction*. (2$^{nd}$ edition). Manchester: Manchester University Press.

Bosch, D. (1995) *Believing in the Future: Toward a Missiology of Western Culture*. Valley Forge, PN: Trinity Press International.

Bobo, J. (2002) "Watching *The Color Purple*: two interviews," in (ed.) G. Turner, *The Film Cultures Reader*, London: Routledge, pp.444–68.

Bourdieu, P. (1984) *Distinction: A Social Critique of the Judgment of Taste*. London: Routledge and Kegan Paul.

Bourdieu, P. (1998) *On Television and Journalism*. London: Pluto.

Bozza, A. (2003) *Whatever You Say I am: The Life and Times of Eminem*. London: Bantam.

Bridger, F. (2002) *A Charmed Life: The Spirituality of Potterworld*. London: Image.

Brierley, P. (1999) *UK Christian Handbook Religious Trends 2000/2001*. London: HarperCollins.

Brierley, P. (2000) *The Tide is Running Out: What the English Church Attendance Survey Reveals*. London: Christian Research.

Briggs, A. and Burke, P. (2002) *A Social History of the Media: From Gutenberg to the Internet*. Cambridge: Polity.

Brooker, W. and Jermyn, D. (eds.) (2003) *The Audience Studies Reader*. London: Routledge.

Brown, D. (1965) *Ultimate Concern: Tillich in Dialogue*. London: SCM.

Browning, D. (1991) *A Fundamental Practical Theology*. Minneapolis: Fortress.

Bruce, S. (2002) *God is Dead: Secularization in the West*. Oxford: Blackwell.

Bruner, J. (1986) *Actual Minds, Possible Worlds*. Cambridge, MA: Harvard University Press.

Buchanan, I. (2000) *Michele de Certeau: Cultural Theorist*. London: Sage.

Buckingham, D. (1993) *Reading Audiences: Young People and the Media*. Manchester: Manchester University Press.

Buckingham, D. (2001) "Electronic child abuse? Rethinking the media" effect on children," in (eds.) M. Barker and J. Petley, *Ill Effects: The Media/Violence Debate*, London: Routledge, pp.63–77.

Bull, M. and Back, L. (eds.) (2003) *The Auditory Culture Reader*. Oxford: Berg.

Bulman, R. (1981) *A Blueprint for Humanity: Paul Tillich's Theology of Culture*. Lewisburg: Bucknell University Press.

Burke, S. (1992) *The Death and Return of the Author: Criticism and Subjectivity in Barthes, Foucault and Derrida*. Edinburgh: Edinburgh University Press.

Burr, V. (1995) *An Introduction to Social Constructionism*. London: Routledge.

Callinicos, A. (2003) *An Anti-Capitalist Manifesto*. Cambridge: Polity.

Campbell, C. (1987) The Romantic Ethic and the Spirit of Modern Consumerism. Oxford: Blackwell.

Campbell, H. (2003) "Approaches to religious research in computer-mediated communication," in (eds.) J. Mitchell and S. Marriage, *Mediating Religion: Conversations in Media, Religion and Culture*, London: T&T Clark, pp.213–28.

Carnevali, F. (2003) "Golden opportunities: jewellery making in Birmingham between mass production and speciality," *Enterprise and Society*, no.2, vol.4, pp.272–98.

Carter, C. and Weaver, C.K. (2003) *Violence and the Media*. Buckingham: Open University Press.

Castells, M. (1996) *The Rise of the Network Society*. Oxford: Blackwell.

Caughie, J. (ed.) (1981) *Theories of Authorship*. London: BFI.

Cauty, J. and Drummond, B. (1998) *The Manual: How to Have a Number One Hit The Easy Way*. London: Ellipsis.

Chaney, D. (1993) *Fictions of Collective Life: Public Drama in Late Modern Culture*. London: Routledge.

Chaney, D. (2002) *Cultural Change and Everyday Life*. London: Palgrave.

Chopp, R. and Taylor, M. (eds.) (1994) *Reconstructing Christian Theology*. Minneapolis: Fortress.

Clapp, R. (2000) *Border Crossings: Christian Trespasses on Popular Culture and Public Affairs*. Grand Rapids: Brazos.

Clements, K. (ed.) (1991) *Friedrich Schleiermacher: Pioneer of Modern Theology*. Minneapolis: Augsburg.

Collin, M. (1997) *Altered State*. London: Serpent's Tail.

Cone, J. (1970) *A Black Theology of Liberation*. Philadelphia: Lippincott.

Cooper, J. and Skrade, C. (eds.) (1970) *Celluloid and Symbols*. Philadelphia: Fortress.

Corstjens, J. and Corstjens, M. (1995) *Store Wars: The Battle for Mindspace and Shelf-space*. Chichester: John Wiley.

Coupland, D. (1994) *Life After God*. London: Simon and Schuster.

Coupland, D. (1992) *Generation X*. London: Abacus.

Cox, H. (1965) *The Secular City: Urbanization and Secularization in Theological Perspective*. London: SCM.

Creed, B. (2000) "Film and psychoanalysis," in (eds.) J. Hill and P. Church Gibson, *Film Studies: Critical Approaches*, Oxford: Oxford University Press, pp.75–88.

Crossick, G. and Jaumain, S. (1999) *Cathedrals of Consumption: The European Department Store 1850–1939*. Aldershot: Ashgate.

Currie, M. (1998) *Postmodern Narrative Theory*. Basingstoke: Palgrave.

Dahlgren, P. (1995) *Television and the Public Sphere: Citizenship, Democracy and the Media*. London: Sage.

Dalton, L., Mazur, E. and Siems, M. (2001) "Homer the Heretic and Charlie Church: parody, piety and pluralism in *The Simpsons*," in (eds.) E. Mazur and K. McCarthy, *God in the Details: American Religion in Popular Culture*, New York: Routledge, pp.231–248.

Dant, T. (1999) *Material Culture in the Social World*. Buckingham: Open University Press.

Davie, G. (1994) *Religion in Britain Since 1945: Believing without Belonging*. Oxford: Blackwell.

Davie, G. (2002) *Europe – the Exceptional Case: Parameters of Faith in the Modern World*. London: DLT.

Dayan, D. and Katz, E. (1992) *Media Events: The Live Broadcasting of History*. Cambridge, MA.: Harvard University Press.

Deacy, C. (2001) *Screen Christologies: Redemption and the Medium of Film*. Cardiff: University of Wales Press.

De Bolla, P. (2001) *Art Matters*. Cambridge, MA.: Harvard University Press.

De Certeau, M. (1984) *The Practice of Everyday Life*. Berkeley: University of California Press.

Detweiler, C. and Taylor, B. (2003) *A Matrix of Meanings: Finding God in Popular Culture*. Grand Rapids: Baker Academic.

Dewey, J. (1934) *Art as Experience*. New York: Minton, Balch and Co.

Dick, B. (2002) *Anatomy of Film* (4th edition). Bedford/St Martins: Boston.

Dillenberger, J. (1986) *A Theology of Artistic Sensibilities*. London: SCM Press.

Di Maggio, P. (1998) "Cultural entrepeneurship in nineteenth-century Boston: the creation of an organizational base for high culture in America," in (ed.) J. Storey, Cultural Theory and Popular Culture: A Reader, Harlow: Prentice-Hall, pp.454–75.

Dorfman, A. and Mattelart, A. (1991) *How to Read Donald Duck: Imperialist Ideology in the Disney Comic*. New York: International General.

Dowd, M. (2002) "The boomer's crooner," *New York Times*, Sunday November 24, 2002.

Drane, J. (2000) *The McDonaldization of the Church*. London: DLT.

Du Gay, P., Hall, S., Janes, L., Mackay, H. and Negus, K. (1997) *Doing Cultural Studies: The Story of the Sony Walkman*. Milton Keynes: Open University Press.

Durkheim, E. (1915) *The Elementary Forms of Religious Life*. London: George Allen and Unwin.

Dyer, R. (2002) *Only Entertainment*. (2nd edition). London: Routledge.

Dyson, M. (2001) *Holler if You Hear Me: Searching for Tupac Shakur*. London: Plexus.

Easton, S., Howkins, A., Laing, S., Merricks, L. and Walker, H. (1988) *Disorder and Discpline: Popular Culture from 1550 to the Present*. Aldershot: Temple Smith.

Eco, U. (1981) *The Role of the Reader: Explorations in the Semiotics of Texts*. London: Hutchinson.

Edwards, T. (2000) *Contradictions of Consumption: Concepts, Practices and Politics in Consumer Culture*. Buckingham: Open University Press.

Eminem (2002) *Angry Blonde*. New York: Regan.

Evans, C. and Herzog, W. (2002) "Introduction," in (eds.) C. Evans and W. Herzog, *The Faith of Fifty Million: Baseball, Religion and American Culture*, Louisville: Westminster John Knox, pp.1–10.

Evans, J. and Hall, S. (eds.) (1999) *Visual Culture: The Reader*. London: Sage.

Evans, M., Moutinho, L. and Van Raaij, W. (1996) *Applied Consumer Behaviour*. Harlow: Addison-Wesley.

Ewen, S. (1988) *All Consuming Images: The Politics of Style in Contemporary Culture*. New York: Basic Books.

Featherstone, M. (1991) *Consumer Culture and Postmodernism*. London: Sage.

Ferré, J. (2003) "The media of popular piety," in (eds.) J. Mitchell and S. Marriage, *Mediating Religion: Conversations in Media, Religion and Culture*, London: T&T Clark, pp.83–92.

Fish, S. (1980) *Is There a Text in This Class? The Authority of Interpretive Communities*. Cambridge, MA.: Harvard University Press.

Fiske, J. (1989) *Understanding Popular Culture*. London: Unwin Hyman.

Forbes, B. (2000) "Introduction: findings religion in unexpected places," in (eds.) B. Forbes and J. Mahan, *Religion and Popular Culture in America*, Berkeley: University of California Press, pp.1–20.

Forbes, B. and Mahan, J. (eds.) (2000) *Religion and Popular Culture in America*. Berkeley: University of California Press.

Ford, D. (1999a) *Self and Salvation: Being Transformed*. Cambridge: Cambridge University Press.

Ford, D. (1999b) *Theology: A Very Short Introduction*. Oxford: Oxford University Press.

Ford, D. (ed.) (2004) *The Modern Theologians* (3rd edition). Oxford: Blackwell.

Fowl, S. and Jones, L.G. (1991) *Reading in Communion: Scripture and Ethics in Christian Life*. London: SPCK.

Frank, T. (1997) *The Conquest of Cool: Business Culture, Counterculture, and the Rise of Hip Consumerism.* Chicago: Chicago University Press.

Freeland, C. (2001) *But is it Art?* Oxford: Oxford University Press.

French, S. (1996) *The Terminator (BFI Modern Classics).* London: British Film Institute.

Freud, S. (1910) *Leonardo da Vinci and a Memory of His Childhood.* London: Penguin.

Frith, S. (1996) *Performing Rites: On the Value of Popular Music.* Oxford: Blackwell.

Frith, S. (1998) "The Good, the Bad, and the Indifferent: Defending popular culture from the populists," in (ed.) J. Storey, *Cultural Theory and Popular Culture*, Harlow: Prentice-Hall, pp.570–586.

Frye, N. (1971) *Anatomy of Criticism: Four Essays.* Princeton, NJ: Princeton University Press.

Fusion Anomaly (2003) "Temporary Autonomous Zones" downloaded from http://fusionanomaly.net/taz.html on 17/10/2003.

Gadamer, H-G. (1989) *Truth and Method.* 2$^{nd}$ edition. London: Sheed and Ward.

Gardiner, M. (2000) *Critiques of Everday Life.* London: Routledge.

Garratt, S. (1998) *Adventures in Wonderland: A Decade of Club Culture.* London: Headline.

Gauntlett, D. (2001) "The worrying influence of 'media effects' studies," in (eds.) M. Barker and J. Petley, *Ill Effects: The Media/Violence Debate*, London: Routledge, pp.47–62.

Geertz, C. (1973) *The Interpretation of Cultures: Selected Essays.* New York: Basic Books.

Gergen, K. (1991) *The Saturated Self.* New York: Basic Books.

George, N. (2000) *Hip Hop America.* London: Penguin.

Gibson, A. (1999) *Postmodernity, Ethics and the Novel: From Leavis to Levinas.* London: Routledge.

Giddens, A. (1991) *Modernity and Self-Identity.* Polity: Cambridge.

Gillespie, M. (1995) *Television, Ethnicity and Cultural Change.* London: Routledge.

Gilroy, P. (1993) *Small Acts: Thoughts on the Politics of Black Cultures.* London: Serpent's Tail.

Giroux, H. (1994) *Disturbing Pleasures: Learning Popular Culture.* London: Routledge.

Glickman, L. (ed.) (1999) *Consumer Society in American History: A Reader.* Ithaca: Cornell University Press.

Gray, A. (1992) *Video Playtime: The Gendering of a Leisure Technology.* London: Routledge.

Gray, A. (2003) *Research Practice for Cultural Studies.* London: Sage.

Grayson, K. (2000) "Why do we buy counterfeits?," in (ed.) J. Pavitt, Brand New, Lonond: V&A, p.98.

Green, L. (1987) *Let's Do Theology: A Pastoral Cycle Resource Book.* London: Mowbray.

Greenberg, C. (1939) "Avant-garde and kitsch," *Partisan Review*, VI, no.5, pp.34–49.

Greenberg, C. (1940) "Towards a newer Laocoon," *Partisan Review*, VII, no.4, pp.296–310.

Groome, T. (1987) "Theology on our feet: a revisionist pedagogy for healing the gap between Academia and Ecclesia," in (eds.) L. Mudge and J. Poling, *Formation and Reflection: The Promise of Practical Theology*, Philadelphia: Fortress Press, pp.55–78.

Godawa, B. (2002) *Hollywood Worldviews: Watching Films with Wisdom and Discernment*. Downers Grove, IL.: IVP.

Goethals, G. (1990) *The Electronic Golden Calf: Images, Religion and the Making of Meaning*. Cambridge, MA.: Cowley Publications.

Goldman, R. and Papson, S. (1998) *Nike Culture*. London: Sage.

Goodchild, P. (2002) *Capitalism and Religion: The Price of Piety*. London: Routledge.

Graham, E. (2002) Representations of the Post/Human. Manchester: Manchester University Press.

Graybeal, J. (2001) "*Cathy* on slenderness, suffering and soul," in (eds.) E. Mazur and K. McCarthy, *God in the Details: American Religion in Popular Culture*, New York: Routledge, 181–98.

Gregson, N. and Crewe, L. (2003) *Secondhand Cultures*. Oxford: Berg.

Gutierrez, G. (1973) A *Theology of Liberation: History, Politics and Salvation*. New York: Mary Knoll Press.

Hall, S. (1981) "Notes on deconstructing the 'popular,' " in (ed.) R. Samuel, *People's History and Socialist Theory*, London: RKP, pp.227–240.

Hall, S. (1990) "Encoding, Decoding," in (ed.) S. During (2002) *The Cultural Studies Reader*, London: Routledge, pp.507–17.

Hall, S. (1997) *Representation: Cultural Representations and Signifying Practices*. London: Sage.

Hall, S. and Jefferson, T. (1976) *Resistance through Rituals: Youth Subcultures in Post-War Britain*. London: Hutchison.

Hamilton, M. (1995) *The Sociology of Religion: Theoretical and Comparative Perspectives*. London: Routledge.

Hammersley, R., Khan, F. and Ditton, J. (2002) *Ecstasy and the Rise of the Chemical Generation*. London: Routledge.

Hardt, M. and Negri, A. (2000) *Empire*. Cambridge, MA.: Harvard University Press.

Harrison, M. (1998) *High Society: The Real Voices of Club Culture*. London: Piatkus.

Hart, T. (2000) "Through the arts: hearing, seeing and touching the truth" in (ed.) J. Begbie, *Beholding the Glory: Incarnation through the Arts*, London: DLT, pp.1–26.

Hasted, N. (2003) *The Dark Story of Eminem*. London: Omnibus.

Hauerwas, S. (1981) A *Community of Character: Towards a Constructive Social Ethics*. Notre Dame: University of Notre Dame Press.

Hauerwas, S. (1983) *The Peaceable Kingdom: A Primer in Christian Ethics*. London: SCM Press.

Hauerwas, S. (1992) *Against the Nations: War and Survival in a Liberal Society*. Notre Dame: University of Notre Dame.

Hauerwas, S. (1993) *Unleashing the Scripture: Freeing the Bible from Captivity to America*. Nashville: Abingdon.

Hauerwas, S. (1995) *In Good Company: The Church as Polis*. Notre Dame: University of Notre Dame Press.

Hauerwas, S. (2000) *A Better Hope: Resources for a Church Confronting Capitalism, Democracy and Postmodernity*. Grand Rapids: Brazos.

Hauerwas, S. (2001) *With the Grain of the Universe*. London: SCM Press.

Hauerwas, S. and Huebner, C. (1999) "History, theory and Anabaptism: a conversation on theology after John Howard Yoder," in (eds.) S. Hauerwas, C. Huebner, H.Huebner and M. Nation, *The Wisdom of the Cross: Essays in Honor of John Howard Yoder*, Grand Rapids: Eerdmans, pp.391–408.

Haug, W. (1986) *Critique of Commodity Aesthetics: Appearance, Sexuality and Advertising in Capitalist Society*. Cambridge: Polity.

Hebdige, D. (1979) *Subculture: The Meaning of Style*. London: Methuen.

Heelas, P. and Woodhead, L. (2002) "Homeless minds today?" in (ed.) L. Woodhead, *Peter Berger and the Study of Religion*, London: Routledge, pp.43–72.

Herrmann, J. (2003) "From popular to arthouse: an analysis of love and nature as religious motifs in recent cinema," in (eds.) J. Mitchell and S. Marriage, *Mediating Religion: Conversations in Media, Religion and Culture*, London: T&T Clark, pp.189–200.

Heywood, I. and Sandyqood, B. (eds.) (1999) *Interpreting Visual Culture: Explorations in the Hermeneutics of the Visual*. London: Routledge.

Hick, J. (1990) *A John Hick Reader*. (edited by Paul Badham). Basingstoke: MacMillan.

Highmore, B. (2002) *Everyday Life and Cultural Theory: An Introduction*. London: Routledge.

Hill, J. and Church Gibson, P. (eds.) (2000) *Film Studies: Critical Approaches*. Oxford: Oxford University Press.

Hiltner, S. (1958) *A Preface to Pastoral Theology*. New York: Abingdon.

Hodgson, P. (1994) *Winds of the Spirit: A Constructive Christian Theology*. London: SCM.

Hoffman, S. (ed.) (1992) *Sport and Religion*. Champaign, Ill.: Human Kinetics Books.

Holland, S. (2001) "Our ladies of the airwaves: Judge Judy, Dr Laura and the new public confessional," in (eds.) E. Mazur K. McCarthy, *God in the Details: American Religion in Popular Culture*, New York: Routledge, pp.217–30.

hooks, b. (1981) *Ain't I a Woman: Black Women and Feminism*. Boston, MA: South End Press.

hooks, b. (1994) *Outlaw Culture: Resisting Representations*. London: Routledge.

hooks, b. (1996) *Reel to Real: Sex, Race and Class at the Movies*. London: Routledge.

Hoover, S. (2000) "The cross at Willow Creek: seeker religion and the contemporary marketplace," in (eds.) B. Forbes and J. Mahan, *Religion and Popular Culture in America*, Berkeley: University of California Press, pp.145–60.

Hoover, S. (2003) "Religion, media and identity: theory and method in audience research on religion and media," in (eds.) J. Mitchell and S. Marriage, *Mediating Religion: Conversations in Media, Religion and Culture*, London: T&T Clark, pp.9–20.

Hunermann, P. (2001) "Evangelization of Europe? Observations on a Church in peril," in (ed.) R. Schreiter, *Mission in the Third Millenium*, Maryknoll, NY: Orbis, pp.57–80.

Hunsberger, G. (1998) *Bearing the Witness of the Spirit: Lesslie Newbigin's Theology of Cultural Plurality*. Grand Rapids: Eerdmans.

Hunt, K. (2003) "Understanding the spirituality of people who do not go to church," in (eds.) G. Davie, P. Heelas and L. Woodhead, *Predicting Religion: Christian, Secular and Alternative Futures*, Aldershot: Ashgate, pp.159–69.

Hunt, S. (2001) *Anyone for Alpha? Evangelism in a Post-Christian Society*. London: DLT.

Hurley, N. (1970) *Theology Through Film*. New York: Harper and Row.

Huxley, A. (1932) *Brave New World*. London: Chatto and Windus.

Huxley, M. (2000) *Eminem: Crossing the Line*. London: Plexus.

Iwamura, J. (2000) "The oriental monk in American popular culture," in (eds.) B. Forbes and J. Mahan, *Religion and Popular Culture in America*, Berkeley: University of California Press, pp.25–43.

Jacobs, M. (1992) *Sigmund Freud*. London: Sage.

James, W. (1902) *The Varieties of Religious Experience*. London: Longmans.

Jasper, D. (1997) "On systematizing the unsystematic: a response," in (eds.) C. Marsh and G. Ortiz, *Explorations in Theology and Film*, Oxford: Blackwells, pp.235–44.

Jenkins, H. (1992) *Textual Poachers: Television Fans and Participatory Culture*. New York: Routledge.

Jensen, K. (1995) *The Social Semiotics of Mass Communication*. London: Sage.

Jewett, R. (1993) *St Paul at the Movies: The Apostle's Dialogue with American Culture*. Louisville: Westminster John Knox.

Jewett, R. (1999) *St Paul Returns to the Movies: Triumph Over Shame*. Grand Rapids: Eerdmans.

Jewett, R. (2000) "The disguise of vengeance in *Pale Rider*," in (eds.) B. Forbes and J. Mahan, *Religion and Popular Culture in America*, Berkeley: University of California Press, pp.243–57.

Jindra, M. (2000) "It's about faith in our future: *Star Trek* fandom as cultural religion," in (eds.) B. Forbes and J. Mahan, *Religion and Popular Culture in America*, Berkeley: Unversity of California Press, pp.165–79.

Johnson, W. (ed.) (1996) *H. Richard Niebuhr: Theology, History and Culture*. New Haven: Yale University Press.

Johnston, R. (2000) *Reel Spirituality*. Grand Rapids, MI: Baker.

Kamitsuka, D. (1999) *Theology and Contemporary Culture: Liberation, Postliberal and Revisionary Perspectives*. Cambridge: Cambridge University Press.

Kendall, G. and Wickham, G. (1999) *Using Foucault's Methods*. London: Sage.

Keppel, G. (1994) *The Revenge of God*. Cambridge: Polity.

King, R. (1999) *Orientalism and Religion: Postcolonial Theory, India and "The Mystic East."* London: Routledge.

Klass, M. (1995) *Ordered Universes: Approaches to the Anthropology of Religion*. Boulder: Westview.

Klein, N. (2001) *No Logo*. London: Flamingo.

Kreitzer, L. (1993) *The New Testament in Fiction and Film: On Reversing the Hermeneutical Flow*. Sheffield: Sheffield Academic Press.

Kreitzer, L. (1994) *The Old Testament in Fiction and Film: On Reversing the Hermeneutical Flow*. Sheffield: Sheffield Academic Press.

Kreitzer, L. (2002) *Gospel Images in Fiction and Film: On Reversing the Hermeneutical Flow*. London: Continuum.

Kuenzli, R. (ed.) (1996) *Dada and Surrealist Film*. Cambridge, MA: MIT Press.

Kupfer, J. (1999) *Visions of Virtue in Popular Film*. Boulder, CA.: Westview.

Lartey, E. (2000) "Practical theology as a theological form," in (eds.) J. Woodward and S. Pattison, *The Blackwell Reader in Pastoral and Practical Theology*, Oxford: Blackwell, pp.128–34.

Laski, M. (1961) *Ecstasy: A Study of Some Secular and Religious Experiences*. London: Cresset Press.

Leary, T. (1998) *The Politics of Ecstasy*. Berkeley: Ronin.

Leavis, F.R. (1930) *Mass Civilization and Minority Culture*. Cambridge: Minority Press.

Lee, M. (ed.) (2000) *The Consumer Society Reader*. Oxford: Blackwell.

Lelwica, M. (2000) "Losing their way to salvation: women, weight loss, and the salvation myth of culture lite," in (eds.) B. Forbes and J. Mahan, *Religion and Popular Culture in America*, Berkeley: University of California Press, pp.180–200.

Levine, L. (1988) *Highbrow/Lowbrow: The Emergence of Cultural Hierarchy in America*. Cambridge, MA: Harvard University Press.

Levine, L. (1993) *The Unpredictable Past: Explorations in American Cultural History*. New York: Oxford University Press.

Levine, L. (1996) *The Opening of the American Mind: Canons, Culture and History*. Boston: Beacon.

Liebes, T. and Katz, E. (1993) *The Export of Meaning: Cross-Cultural Readings of "Dallas."* (2nd edition). Cambridge: Polity.

Linderman, A. and Lovheim, M. (2003) "Internet, religion and the attribution of social trust," in (eds.) J. Mitchell and S. Marriage, *Mediating Religion: Conversations in Media, Religion and Culture*, London: T&T Clark, pp.229–40.

Lingenfelter, S. (1992) *Transforming Culture: A Challenge for Christian Mission*. Grand Rapids: Baker Books.

Lothe, J. (2000) *Narrative in Fiction and Film*. Oxford: Oxford University Press.

Lury, C. (1996) *Consumer Culture*. Cambridge: Polity.

Luzbetak, L. (1993) *The Church and Cultures: New Perspectives in Missiological Anthropology*. Maryknoll, NY: Orbis.

Lyden, J. (2003) *Film as Religion: Myths, Morals and Rituals*. New York: New York University Press.

Lynch, G. (1999) "A pragmatic approach to clinical counseling in context," in (ed.) J. Lees, *Clinical Counselling in Context: An Introduction*, London: Routledge, pp.20–33.

Lynch, G. (2002) *After Religion: "Generation X" and the Search for Meaning*. London: DLT.

Lyon, D. (1994) *Postmodernity*. Buckingham: Open University Press.

Lyon, D. (2000) *Jesus in Disneyland: Religion in Postmodern Times*. Cambridge: Polity.

MacIntyre, A. (1981) *After Virtue: A Study in Moral Theory*. London: Duckworth.

(eds.) Mackay, H. and O'Sullivan, T. (1999) *The Media Reader: Continuity and Transformation*. London: Sage.

Mahan, J. (2000) "Conclusion: establishing a dialogue about religion and popular culture," in (eds.) Forbes, B. and Mahan, J. Religion and Popular Culture in America, Berkeley: University of California Press, pp.292–300.

Malone, P. (1997) "Edward Scissorhands: Christology from an urban fairy-tale," in (eds.) C. Marsh and G. Ortiz, *Explorations in Theology and Film*, Oxford: Blackwells, pp.73–86.

Marcuse, H. (2002) *One Dimensional-Man*. London: Routledge.

Marsh, C. and Ortiz, G. (eds.) (1997) *Explorations in Theology and Film*. Oxford: Blackwell.

Martin, J. and Ostwalt, C. (1995) *Screening the Sacred: Religion, Myth and Ideology in Popular Film*. Boulder: Westview.

May, J. (ed.) (1992) *Image and Likeness: Religious Visions in American Film Classics*. New York: Paulist Press.

Maykut, P. and Morehouse, R. (1994) *Beginning Qualitative Research: A Philosophic and Practical Guide*. London: Falmer.

Mazur, E. and McCarthy, K. (eds.) (2001) *God in the Details: American Religion in Popular Culture*. New York: Routledge.

Malbon, B. (1998) *Clubbing: Dancing, Ecstasy and Vitality*. London: Routledge.

Maltby, R. (ed.) (1989) *Passing Parade: A History of Popular Culture in the Twentieth Century*. Oxford: Oxford University Press.

Manson, M. (1998) *The Long Hard Road Out of Hell*. London: Plexus.

Mast, G., Cohen, M. and Braudy, L. (eds.) (1992) *Film Theory and Criticism* (4th edition). New York: Oxford University Press.

McBride, J. (2001) "Symptomatic expression of male neuroses: collective effervescence, male gender performance and the ritual of football," in (eds.) E. Mazur and K. McCarthy, *God in the Details: American Religion in Popular Culture*, New York: Routledge, pp.123–38.

McCarthy, K. (2001) "Deliver me from nowhere: Bruce Springsteen and the myth of the American promised land," in (eds.) E. Mazur K. McCarthy, *God in the Details: American Religion in Popular Culture*, New York: Routledge, pp.23–46.

McDonald, D. (1957) "A theory of mass culture," in (eds.) B. Rosenberg and D. White, *Mass Culture: The Popular Arts in America*. London: Collier-MacMillan, pp. 59–73.

McLaren, B. (2002) *More Ready Than You Realize: Evangelism as Dance in the Post-modern Matrix*. Grand Rapids: Zondervan.

McLuhan, M. and Powers, B. (1989) *The Global Village: Transformations of World Life and Media in the Twenty-First Century*. Oxford: Oxford University Press.

Medved, M. (1993) *Hollywood vs. America*. New York: HarperCollins.

Merquior, J. (1991) *Foucault*. London: Fontana.

Meyrowitz, J. (1999) "No sense of place: the impact of electronic media on social behavior," (eds.) H. Mackay and T. O'Sullivan, *The Media Reader: Continuity and Transformation*, London: Sage, pp.99–120.

Miles, M. (1996) *Seeing and Believing: Religion and Values in the Movies*. Boston, MA: Beacon.

Miller, D. (1998) *A Theory of Shopping*. Cambridge: Polity.

Mills, S. (2003) *Michel Foucault*. London: Routledge.

Misa, T. (1995) *A Nation of Steel: The Making of Modern America 1865–1925*. Baltimore: John Hopkins University Press.

Mitchell, J. (2003) "Emerging conversations in the study of media, religion and culture," in (eds.) Mitchell, J. and Marriage, S., Mediating Religion: Conversations in Media, Religion and Culture, London: T&T Clark, pp.337–50.

Mitchell, J. and Marriage, S. (eds.) (2003) *Mediating Religion: Conversations in Media, Religion and Culture*, London: T&T Clark.

Moore, L. (1994) *Selling God: American Religion in the Market-Place of Culture*. New York: Oxford University Press.

Moores, S. (1993) *Interpreting Audiences: The Ethnography of Media Consumption*. London: Sage.

Morgan, D. (2003) "Protestant visual piety and the aesthetics of American mass culture," in (eds.) J. Mitchell and S. Marriage, *Mediating Religion: Conversations in Media, Religion and Culture*, London: T&T Clark, pp.107–20.

Morley, D. (1980) *The Nationwide Audience: Structure and Decoding*. London: British Film Institute.

Morley, D. (2000) *Home Territories: Media, Mobility and Identity*. London: Routledge.

Motherwell, R. (ed.) (1989) *The Dada Painters and Poets: An Anthology*. Cambridge, MA: Harvard University Press.

Muggleton, D. (2001) *Inside Subculture: The Post-Modern Meaning of Style*. Oxford: Berg.

Mulhern, F. (2000) *Culture/Metaculture*. London: Routledge.

Mulvey, L. (1975) "Visual pleasure and narrative cinema," *Screen*, 16, vol.3, pp.6–18.

Murodck, G. (2001) "Reservoirs of dogma: an archaeology of popular anxieties," in (eds.) M. Barker and J. Petley, *Ill Effects: The Media/Violence Debate*, London: Routledge, pp.150–69.

Murdock, G. and McCron, R. (1997) "The television and delinquency debate," (eds.) T. O'Sullivan and Y. Jewkes, *The Media Studies Reader*, London: Arnold, pp.181–7.

Nava, M. (1992) *Changing Cultures: Feminism, Youth and Consumerism.* London: Sage.

Neal, C. (2002) *The Gospel According to Harry Potter: Spirituality in the Stories of the World's Favourite Seeker.* Louisville: Westminster John Knox.

Nelson, J. (1976) *Your God is Alive and Well and Appearing in Popular Culture.* Philadelphia: Westminster Press.

Newbigin, L. (1983) *The Other Side of 1984: Questions for the Churches.* Geneva: WCC.

Newbigin, L. (1986) *Foolishness to the Greeks: The Gospel and Western Culture.* London: SPCK.

Newton, A. (1995) *Narrative Ethics.* Cambridge, MA: Harvard University Press.

Nicholls, B. (ed.) (1976) *Movies and Methods (Volume 1).* Berkeley: University of California Press.

Nicholls, B. (ed.) (1985) *Movies and Methods (Volume 2).* Berkeley: University of California Press.

Niebuhr, H.R. (1951) *Christ and Culture.* New York: Harper and Row.

Nolan, S. (2003a) "Towards a new religious film criticism: using film to understand religious identity rather than locate cinematic analogue," in (eds.) J. Mitchell and S. Marriage, *Mediating Religion: Conversations in Media, Religion and Culture,* London: T&T Clark, pp.169–78.

Nolan, S. (2003b) "Film and religion: an annotated bibliography," in (eds.) J. Mitchell and S. Marriage, *Mediating Religion: Conversations in Media, Religion and Culture,* London: T&T Clark, pp.369–74.

(eds.) O'Sullivan, T. and Jewkes, Y. (1997) *The Media Studies Reader.* London: Arnold.

Ortiz, G. (2003) "The Catholic Church and its attitude to film as an arbiter of cultural meaning," in (eds.) Mitchell, J. and Marriage, S., Mediating Religion: Conversations in Media, Religion and Culture, pp.179–88.

Otto, R. (1923) *The Idea of the Holy.* London: Oxford University Press.

Parker, H., Aldridge, J. and Measham, F. (1998) *Illegal Leisure: The Normalization of Adolescent Recreational Drug Use.* London: Routledge.

Parker, I. (1994) "Discourse analysis," in (ed.) P. Banister, *Qualitative Methods in Psychology,* Buckingham: Open University Press, pp.92–107.

Parratt, J. (1995) *Reinventing Christianity: African Theology Today.* Grand Rapids, MI.: Eerdmans.

Parratt, J. (1996) *A Guide to Doing Theology.* London: SPCK.

Parma, R. (1983) *Karl Barth's Theology of Culture: The Freedom of Culture for the Praise of God.* Allison Park, PA: Pickwick.

Parsons, G. (2002) *Perspectives on Civil Religion.* Aldershot: Ashgate.

Pattison, S. and Lynch, G. (2004) "Pastoral and practical theology," in (ed.) D. Ford, *The Modern Theologians* (3rd edn), Oxford: Blackwell, in press.

Pavitt, J. (ed.) (2000) *Brand New.* London: V&A.

Peperzak, A., Critchley, S. and Bernasconi, R. (eds.) (1996) *Emmanuel Levinas: Basic Philosophical Writings.* Indianapolis: Indiana University Press.

Petley, J. (1997) "In defence of "video nasties"," in (eds.) T. O'Sullivan and Y. Jewkes, *The Media Studies Reader,* London: Arnold, pp.188–95.

Petley, J. (2001) "Us and them," in (eds.) M. Barker and J. Petley, *Ill Effects: The Media/Violence Debate,* London: Routledge, pp.170–85.

Pevsner, N. (1968) *The Sources of Modern Architecture and Design.* London: Thames and Hudson.

Phillips, P. (1996) "Genre, star and auteur: an approach to Hollywood cinema," in (ed.) J. Nelmes, *Introduction to Film Studies,* London: Routledge, pp.121–66.

Pinn, A. (1995) *Why Lord? Suffering and Evil in Black Theology.* New York: Continuum.

Pinn, A. (2000) "Rap music and its message: on interpreting the contact between religion and popular culture," in (eds.) B. Forbes and J. Mahan, *Religion and Popular Culture in America,* Berkeley: University of California Press, pp.258–75.

Pinn, A. (2003) *Noise and Spirit: The Religious and Spiritual Sensibilities of Rap Music.* New York: New York University.

Pinsky, M. (2001) *The Gospel According to The Simpsons.* Louisville: Westminster John Knox.

Poling, J. (1996) "Race, gender and class in practical theology," in *Contact: The Interdisciplinary Journal of Pastoral Studies,* 120, pp.1–7.

Porter, J. and McLaren, D. (1999) *Star Trek and Sacred Ground: Explorations of Star Trek, Religion and American Culture.* New York: State University of New York Press.

Postman, N. (1985) *Amusing Ourselves to Death.* London: Methuen.

Propp, V. (1968) *Morphology of the Folktale.* Austin: University of Texas Press.

Putnam, R. (2000) *Bowling Alone: The Collapse and Revival of American Community.* New York: Touchstone.

Radford Ruether, R. (1983) *Sexism and God-Talk: Towards a Feminist Theology.* London: SCM.

Radway, J. (1987) *Reading the Romance: Women, Patriarchy and Popular Literature.* London: Verso.

Ramji, R. (2003) "Representations of Islam in American news and film: becoming the "Other"," in (eds.) J. Mitchell and S. Marriage, *Mediating Religion: Conversations in Media, Religion and Culture,* London: T&T Clark, pp.65–72.

Reay, B. (ed.) (1985) *Popular Culture in Seventeenth-Century England.* London: Croon Helm.

Reay, B. (1998) *Popular Cultures in England 1550–1750.* London: Longman.

Reynolds, S. (1998) *Energy Flash: A Journey Through Rave Music and Dance Culture.* London: Picador.

Rheingold, H. (1999) "The virtual community: finding a connection in a computerised world," in (eds.) H. Mackay and T. O'Sullivan, *The Media Reader: Continuity and Transformation,* London: Sage, pp.273–286.

Riddell, M., Pierson, M. and Kirkpatrick, C. (2000) *The Prodigal Project: Journey into the Emerging Church*. London: SPCK.

Rietveld, H. (1998) This is Our House: House Music, Cultural Spaces and Technologies. Aldershot: Ashgate.

Ritzer, G. (1999) *Enchanting a Disenchanted World: Revolutionizing the Means of Consumption*. Thousand Oaks, CA: Pine Forge Press.

Romanowski, W. (1996) *Pop Culture Wars*. Downers Grove, Ill.: IVP.

Romanowski, W. (2000) "Evangelicals and popular music: the contemporary Christian music industry," in (eds.) B. Forbes and J. Mahan, *Religion and Popular Culture in America*, Berkeley: University of California Press, pp.105–24.

Romanowski, W. (2001) *Eyes Wide Open: Looking for God in Popular Culture*. Grand Rapids, MI.: Brazos.

Roof, W. (1999) *Spiritual Marketplace: Baby Boomers and the Re-Making of American Religion*. Princeton, NJ.: Princeton University Press.

Roof, W.C. (2001) "Blood in the barbecue? Food and faith in the American South," in (eds.) E. Mazur and K. McCarthy, *God in the Details: American Religion in Popular Culture*, New York: Routledge, pp.109–22.

Rosenberg, B. and White, D. (eds.) (1957) *Mass Culture: The Popular Arts in America*. London: Collier-MacMillan.

Rushkoff, D. (1996) *Playing the Future: What We Can Learn from the Digital Kids*. New York: Riverhead.

Rushkoff, D. (1999) *Coercion*. New York: Riverhead.

Rycenga, J. (2001) "Dropping in for the holidays: Christmas as commercial ritual at the Precious Moments chapel," in (eds.) E. Mazur and K. McCarthy, *God in the Details: American Religion in Popular Culture*, New York: Routledge, pp.139–54.

Sabbah, F. (1985) "The new media," in (ed.) M. Castells, High Technology, Space and Society. Beverley Hills, CA: Sage, pp.215–28.

Sarris, A. (1976) "Towards a theory of film history," in (ed.) B. Nicholls, *Movies and Methods (Volume 1)*, Berkeley: University of California Press, pp.237–50.

Sarris, A. (1992) "Notes on the auteur theory in 1962," in (eds.) G. Mast, M. Cohen and L. Braudy, *Film Theory and Criticism* (4th edition), New York: Oxford University Press, pp.585–88.

Sartre, J-P (1948) *Existentialism and Humanism*. London: Methuen.

Sarup, M. (1996) *Identity, Culture and the Postmodern World*. Edinburgh: Edinburgh University Press.

Saunders, N., Saunders, A. and Pauli, M. (2000) *In Search of the Ultimate High: Spiritual Experiences Through Psychoactives*. London: Rider.

Schleiermacher, F. (1821/1969) *On Religion: Addresses in Response to its Cultured Critics*. Richmond, VA: John Knox.

Schreiter, R. (1997) *The New Catholicity: Theology Between the Local and the Global*. Maryknoll, NY: Orbis.

Shulgin, A. and Shulgin, A. (1997) *TiHKAL: The Continuation*. Berkeley: Transform Press.

Shuker, R. (2001) *Understanding Popular Music* (2nd edition). London: Routledge.

Shusterman, R. (2000) *Pragmatist Aesthetics: Living Beauty, Rethinking Art.* 2nd edition. Lanham, MD: Rowman and Littlefield.

Silcott, M. (2000) *Rave America.* London: ECW Press.

Silk, M. (2003) "Islam and the American news media post September 11," in (eds.) J. Mitchell and S. Marriage, *Mediating Religion: Conversations in Media, Religion and Culture,* London: T&T Clark, pp.73–82.

Sinclair, J., Jacka, E. and Cunningham, S. (eds.) (1996) *New Patterns in Global Television.* Oxford: Oxford University Press.

Slater, D. (1997) *Consumer Culture and Modernity.* Cambridge: Polity.

Spence, D. (1982) *Narrative Truth and Historical Truth: Meaning and Interpretation in Psychoanalysis.* New York: W.W. Norton and Co.

Stam, R., Burgoyne, R. and Flitterman-Lewis, S. (1992) *New Vocabularies in Film Semiotics: Structuralism, Post-Structuralism and Beyond.* London: Routledge.

(eds.) Stam, R. and Miller, T. (2000) *Film and Theory: An Anthology.* Oxford: Blackwells.

Stern, R., Jefford, C. and Debona, G. (1999) *Savior on the Silver Screen.* New York: Paulist Press.

Stone, B. (2000) *Faith and Film: Theological Themes at the Cinema.* St Louis: Chalice Press.

Stone, H. and Duke, J. (1997) *How to Think Theologically.* Minneapolis: Fortress.

Storey, J. (1996) *Cultural Studies and the Study of Popular Culture: Theories and Methods.* Edinburgh: Edinburgh University Press.

Storey, J. (ed.) (1998) *Cultural Theory and Popular Culture: A Reader.* Harlow: Prentice-Hall.

Storey, J. (1999) *Cultural Consumption and Everyday Life.* London: Arnold.

Storey, J. (2001) *Cultural Theory and Popular Culture: An Introduction.* (3rd edition). London: Prentice-Hall.

Storey, J. (2003) *Inventing Popular Culture.* Oxford: Blackwell.

Stout, D. and Buddenbaum, J. (eds.) (2001) *Religion and Popular Culture: Studies on the Interaction of Worldviews.* Ames, Iowa: Iowa State University Press.

Stout, J. (2004) *Democracy and Tradition.* Princeton, NJ: Princeton University Press.

Strauss, A. and Corbin, J. (1990) *Basics of Qualitative Research.* London: Sage.

Strinati, D. (1995) *An Introduction to Theories of Popular Culture.* London: Routledge.

Sugirtharajah, R.S. (ed.) (1993) *Asian Faces of Jesus.* Maryknoll, NY: Orbis.

Sugirtharajah, R.S. (2002) *Postcolonial Criticism and Biblical Interpretation.* Oxford: Oxford University Press.

Sylvan, R. (2001) "Rap music, hip-hop culture, and the 'future religion of the world'," in (eds.) E. Mazur K. McCarthy, *God in the Details: American Religion in Popular Culture,* New York: Routledge, pp.281–98.

Tanner, K. (1997) *Theories of Culture: A New Agenda for Theology.* Minneapolis: Fortress Press.

Tasker, Y. (ed.) (2002) *Fifty Contemporary Filmmakers.* London: Routledge.

Tatum, W. (1997) *Jesus at the Movies: A Guide to the First Hundred Years*. Santa Rosa, CA: Polebridge.

Taylor, F. (1911) *The Principles of Scientific Management*. New York: Harper and Brothers.

Tester, K. (2001) *Compassion, Morality and the Media*. Buckingham: Open University Press.

Thomas, G. (2002) *This is Ecstasy*. London: Sanctuary.

Thompson, J. (1999) "The media and modernity," in (eds.) H. Mackay and T. O'Sullivan, *The Media Reader: Continuity and Transformation*, London: Sage, pp.13–27.

Thornton, S. (1995) *Club Cultures: Music, Media and Subcultural Capital*. Cambridge: Polity.

Thwaites, T., Davis, L., and Mules, W. (2000) *Introducing Cultural and Media Studies: A Semiotic Approach*. Basingstoke: Palgrave.

Tilley, C. (1990) *Reading Material Culture: Structuralism, Hermeneutics and Post-Structuralism*. Oxford: Blackwell.

Tillich, P. (1952) *The Courage to Be*. New Haven: Yale University Press.

Tillich, P. (1953) *Systematic Theology* (Vol.1). London: James Nisbet.

Tillich, P. (1959) *Theology of Culture*. Oxford: Oxford University Press.

Tomlinson, D. (1994) *The Post-Evangelical*. London: Triangle.

Tomlinson, J. (1999) "Cultural globalization: placing and displacing the West," in (eds.) H. Mackay and T. O'Sullivan, *The Media Reader: Continuity and Transformation*, London: Sage, pp.165–77.

Toynbee, J. (2000) *Making Popular Music: Musicians, Creativity and Institutions*. London: Arnold.

Toynbee, P. (2003) *Hard Work: Life in Low-Pay Britain*. London: Bloomsbury.

Tracy, D. (1981) *The Analogical Imagination*. New York: Crossroad.

Truett Anderson, W. (1996) *The Fontana Post-Modernism Reader*. London: Fontana.

Tudor, A. (1976) "Genre and critical methodology," in (ed.) B Nicholls, *Movies and Methods* (*Volume 1*). Berkeley: University of California Press, pp.118–25.

Turner, G. (2000) "Cultural studies and film," in (eds.) J. Hill and P. Church Gibson, *Film Studies: Critical Approaches*, Oxford: Oxford University Press, pp.193–200.

Turner, G. (2003) *British Cultural Studies: An Introduction*. London: Routledge.

Turner, V. (1969) *The Ritual Process: Structure and Anti-Structure*. London: Routledge and Kegan Paul.

Turnock, R. (2000) *Interpreting Diana: Television Audiences and the Death of a Princess*. London: British Film Institute.

Twitchell, J. (1999) *Lead Us Into Temptation: The Triumph of American Materialism*. New York: Columbia University Press.

Upshaw, L. (1995) *Building Brand Identity: A Strategy for Success in a Hostile Marketplace*. New York: John Wiley.

Vasari, G. (1550/1987) *The Lives of the Artists, vol.1*. Harmondsworth: Penguin.

Von Balthasar, H. (1982) *Behold the Glory of the Lord: A Theological Aesthetics. Volume 1: Seeing the Form*. Edinburgh: T&T Clark.

Wagner, R. (2002) "Bewitching the box office: Harry Potter and religious controversy," *Journal of Religion and Film*, vol.7, no.2, downloaded from www.unomaha.edu/~wwwjrf/Vol7No2/bewitching.htm on 12/8/03.

Ward, P. (1996) *Growing Up Evangelical: Youthwork and the Making of a Subculture.* London: SPCK.

Ward, P. (ed.) (1999) *Mass Culture: Eucharist and Mission in a Post-Modern World.* London: Bible Reading Fellowship.

Ward, P. (2002) *Liquid Church.* Carlisle: Paternoster Press.

Warren, M. (1997) *Seeing Through the Media.* Harrisburg: Trinity Press International.

Weiner, C. (2002) *Eminen Talking.* London: Omnibus.

Williams, D. (1993) *Sisters in the Wilderness: The Challenge of Womanist God-Talk.* New York: Orbis.

Williams, R. (1999) "The technology and the society," in (eds.) H. Mackay and T. O'Sullivan, *The Media Reader: Continuity and Transformation*, London: Sage, pp.43–57.

Williams, R. (2001) "Culture is ordinary," in (ed.) J. Higgins, *The Raymond Williams Reader*, Oxford: Blackwell, pp.10–24.

Williamson, J. (1986) *Consuming Passions: The Dynamics of Popular Culture.* London: Marion Boyars.

Witkin, R. (2003) *Adorno on Popular Culture.* London: Routledge.

Wollen, P. (1972) "The auteur theory," in (eds.) J. Hollows, P. Hutchings and M. Jancovich (1990) *The Film Studies Reader*, London: Arnold, pp.71–7.

Wolterstorff, N. (2004) "Art and the aesthetic: the religious dimension," in (ed.) P. Kivy, *The Blackwell Guide to Aesthetics*, Oxford: Blackwell, pp.325–39.

Wood, R. (1992) "Ideology, genre, auteur," in (eds) G. Mast, M. Cohen, M. and L. Braudy (1992) *Film Theory and Criticism* (4th edition). New York: Oxford University Press, pp.475–85.

Woodham, J. (1997) *Twentieth-Century Design.* Oxford: Oxford University Press.

Woodhead, L. and Heelas, P. (2000) *Religion in Modern Times.* Blackwell: Oxford.

www.ecstasy.com (2003) "A selection of your personal accounts of Ecstasy use," downloaded from http://www.ecstasy.org/experiences/index.html on 20 August, 2003.

www.hyperreal.org (2003) "The spirit of raving," downloaded from http://hyperreal.org/raves/spirit/ on 20 August, 2003.

# index